BECOMING UN-ORTHODOX

BECOMING
UN-ORTHODOX

STORIES OF EX-HASIDIC JEWS

LYNN DAVIDMAN

OXFORD
UNIVERSITY PRESS

OXFORD
UNIVERSITY PRESS

Oxford University Press is a department of the
University of Oxford. It furthers the University's objective
of excellence in research, scholarship, and education
by publishing worldwide.

Oxford   New York

Auckland   Cape Town   Dar es Salaam   Hong Kong   Karachi
Kuala Lumpur   Madrid   Melbourne   Mexico City   Nairobi
New Delhi   Shanghai   Taipei   Toronto

With offices in

Argentina   Austria   Brazil   Chile   Czech Republic   France   Greece
Guatemala   Hungary   Italy   Japan   Poland   Portugal   Singapore
South Korea   Switzerland   Thailand   Turkey   Ukraine   Vietnam

Oxford is a registered trade mark of Oxford University Press
in the UK and certain other countries.

Published in the United States of America by
Oxford University Press
198 Madison Avenue, New York, NY 10016

Library of Congress Cataloging-in-Publication Data
Davidman, Lynn, 1955–
Becoming un-orthodox : stories of ex-Hasidic Jews / Lynn Davidman.
p.   cm.
Includes bibliographical references and index.
ISBN 978-0-19-938050-3 (hardcover : alk. paper)—ISBN 978-0-19-938051-0 (ebook)—
ISBN 978-0-19-938052-7 (ebook)   1. Orthodox Judaism-Relations-Nontraditional Jews
2. Ultra Orthodox Jews-Unites States-Anecdotes.   I. Title.
BM197.6.D38   2015
296.8'32-dc23   2014007443

1 3 5 7 9 8 6 4 2
Printed in the United States of America
on acid-free paper

This book is dedicated to my late brother, Mark Davidman, whose energy and spirit rested on my left shoulder as I wrote and completed this book.

You gain strength, courage and confidence every time you stop to look fear in the face.... We must do that which we think we cannot.
—Eleanor Roosevelt

A NOTE ON TERMINOLOGY

In addition to the familiar division of contemporary Jewry into Orthodox, Conservative, and Reform groups, there are important distinctions within the Orthodox communities. The primary division is between the Modern Orthodox and the Haredim, who actually consist of two distinct groups. One group is the Hasidic communities, for whom mysticism is important; and the other is referred to as "Yeshivish," due to their emphasis on men's study of ancient texts in institutes of higher learning. The term "Haredim" refer to both Hasidim and the Yeshivish. Thirty-eight of my forty interviewees were ex-Hasidim; there were two ex-Yeshivish men in my study as well. A glossary at the back of the book defines unfamiliar terms.

CONTENTS

Acknowledgments   *xiii*

CHAPTER 1   The Life Worlds of Hasidic Jews   *3*

CHAPTER 2   Tears in the Sacred Canopy   *29*

CHAPTER 3   First Transgressions   *65*

CHAPTER 4   Passing   *103*

CHAPTER 5   Stepping Out   *141*

CHAPTER 6   You Can't Turn Off Your Past   *181*

APPENDIX I   *Theoretical Framework: Narratives,
Embodiment, Religion, and Identity*   *203*

APPENDIX II   *Interview Guide for Those Who Have
Left Orthodoxy*   *215*

Glossary   *221*

Notes   *225*

References   *229*

Index   *243*

ACKNOWLEDGMENTS

My first expression of gratitude is to all the women and men who participated in this research and bravely shared their life stories with me. This book would not exist without the generosity of the many Hasidic (Ultra-Orthodox) defectors whom I interviewed for this book. All the ex-Hasidic Jews with whom I spoke were open about sharing with me their life stories and, in response to my questions, particularly their accounts of how they came to leave their strictly religious enclaves. I know from my own experience, and I was highly aware in the interviews, that many aspects of these stories were painful to reconstruct. I appreciate that each of you was willing to go back to the past and attempt, within our discussions, to reconstruct a life story that seeks to establish coherence between the period before you left your enclaves, and your lives since.

As I worked on this book, in Providence, Rhode Island and in Lawrence, Kansas, I have been blessed with many friends, colleagues, and research assistants, all of whom contributed in significant ways to the completion of this process. It was in a conversation with Shelly Tenenbaum that we came up with the idea for this project. When I began this research, four students at Brown University—Kira Ganga Kieffer, Annie Lewis, Maxine Sharavsky, Elizabeth Sher—worked with me on the initial coding and sorting of data according to the themes I identified in my interview transcripts. In addition, without my asking, they wrote memos offering insights on some of the themes, relating them to material they had read, or to their own life experiences.

Two years later Andrea Titus began working with me in her last year at Brown, 2007–2008. Andrea deeply invested herself in all tasks related to this project. In the spring of 2008 we began to work on an article based on the interviews. In order to further develop our coauthored essay, I persuaded her to spend the summer with me in Lawrence. Andrea was an amazing research assistant. She took initiative, worked efficiently, wrote beautifully, and was an intellectually stimulating partner during our work together. She read and summarized relevant research literature, made comments on my drafts, and rewrote sections of them until by the end of the summer we had prepared a near-final version for submission. We became friends as we worked together so closely over an extended period of time, and we are still in touch.

At the University of Kansas I had the good fortune of finding several graduate students who were interested in my project and worked with me for various periods of time over the last five years. Chelsea Bailey, Ray Sin, Ben Gray, Adrianne Showalter Matlock, Michelle Glorioso, Nathan Moser, and Jon Burrow-Branine all spent time playing and thinking with me, in the intellectual playground of my developing ideas. In the last few months of my final push to completion, Jon came back to help me get to the finish line. He read drafts of three chapters and made helpful comments on each.

Two graduate students, in particular, Nathan Moser and Chelsea Bailey, stand out for their superb research, analytic and writing skills, dedication to the project, as well as their steady support and friendship. Nathan, who had come to the University of Kansas to study with me, worked hard on this project for over a year, from July 2011 through September 2012. We were already friends, but our close work together over that time cemented a lifelong friendship. We had numerous brainstorming, synergistic conversations in which we strove to weave together the analytic foci of the book: narratives and embodied practices. Eventually the light bulb flashed, and we articulated an innovative argument about the mutual construction of narratives and embodied practices: Meaningful bodily routines and rituals make sense—for individuals as well as communities—only when they are situated within the framework of a coherent, overarching metanarrative.

I got to know Chelsea, a graduate student in sociology, through the seminars she took with me. I was impressed by her ability to quickly grasp reading material, ask thoughtful questions, and write up her own research in a clear and engaging manner, always situating her work within the larger analytic frameworks of the field. In the spring of 2013, knowing I needed some extra help, I asked her to work with me on the final version of the book. Immediately she became deeply engaged with, enthusiastic, and committed to working hard on this book. Chelsea read multiple iterations of chapter sections and entire chapters, offering suggestions that helped me further clarify my ideas and how I wrote about them. During the two months we worked together, spending almost twenty hours a week in my study, we worked hard but also had fun, becoming close in the process. In November and December 2013 I needed a bit of help with all the final tasks involved in completing the book. I asked Chelsea if she could spare some time for a couple of months, and she told me it felt appropriate for her to reenter the project in its final stages and see it through to completion. Her help was invaluable in my completing the book on time.

During most of the time I worked on this book, my uncle Alan Zuckerman, a political scientist at Brown University, and his son, Ezra, a sociologist at the Massachusetts Institute of Technology, read sections of the manuscript, offered constructive criticism, discussed my emerging ideas, and helped me refine them. Alan taught me to move beyond "being in love with [my] data" to analyze its larger significance in the field of sociology. After Alan's untimely passing in 2009 I was blessed by my cousin Ezra's ongoing commitment to my work. He continued to read drafts and offer support in many ways; despite his own career and large family, he always made time to help me on this project.

Robert Wuthnow stands out for his unique contribution in helping me improve the book from its first rough version. In April 2013 I explained to him that the manuscript had been produced too quickly in order to meet a publisher's deadline, and I sensed it was not ready for publication. I asked him if he could go through the entire manuscript, find the weaker areas, and help me take the book to the next level. I wrote him on a Thursday afternoon. By Friday morning I had received five single-spaced pages of insightful comments, both on the larger issues I needed to address as well as suggestions for each chapter! Bob has been a loyal friend, sounding board, and colleague for nearly thirty years, but I had not expected such a highly detailed set of comments in one day!

No matter how many times I have thanked him, I can never thank him enough.

My friend of more than twenty-five years, sociologist Arthur Larry Greil, as well as two newer friends, Jesse Tisch and Margaret Rausch, all took time out of their own demanding schedules to read the entire manuscript, which they returned to me marked up with their comments and questions throughout. Their intense engagement pushed me to deepen my analysis, as well as to clarify and highlight the central ideas. I was fortunate that several of my colleagues at Kansas, Paul Stock, Emily Rauscher, Tracey La Pierre, and Shirley Hill, read various chapters in progress, asking me about Haredi life so they could become better readers of my work. Thank you for your valuable feedback and ongoing support. Shirley Hill was genuinely puzzled about the strictness of Orthodox Jewish observance and asked why eating shrimp was "such a big deal" for defectors. I had known that it was a big deal all of my life, but her question pushed me to clarify how the intense, comprehensive, and integrated system of Orthodox Jewish laws, embodied practices, and its overarching metanarrative rendered eating shellfish a major transgression.

At Kansas I was lucky to find many others who discussed my emerging ideas with me as I wrote: Victor Bailey, Brian Donovan, Susan Harris, Neal Schuster, David Smith, Bill Staples, and members of the Jewish studies seminar series, affectionately referred to as "our intellectual community." Off campus, sociologists Caryn Aviv and John Bartkowski generously spent hours discussing my ideas and providing me with critical readings and comments on several sections of the book. For more than twenty-seven years Steven Freedman has been a loyal friend and enthusiastic supporter of my work, offering ideas, encouragement, and practical advice.

Everyone mentioned here provided steadfast encouragement and helpful ideas and contributed to the supportive social context in which I was able to persevere over the many years it took me to complete this book. Their care and feedback pushed me to be my best—to think and write clearly and to develop an argument that pushed beyond conventional assumptions.

Although my colleagues' and readers' comments and questions pushed me to write the best book I possibly could, without the financial assistance of a few generous others, such as Felix Posen and Danny Posen of the Center for Cultural Judaism, I would not have been able to travel to interviews, have my tapes transcribed, and hire research assistants. Both of them were excited about a project on defectors from Hasidic life and generously provided support to help me complete the book they were eager to read. I am grateful for their confidence in me and their open-handed support of this project.

My chair as the Robert M. Beren Distinguished Professor of Modern Jewish Studies was funded by Mr. Beren, to whom I feel grateful for his exceeding generosity and support. My position comes with a generous annual research fund that pays for most of my research costs. I thank him, and the University of Kansas, for bringing me here to take up this endowed position.

Cynthia Read, my editor at Oxford University Press, was fascinated by the topic and the types of communities I was writing about. She encouraged me to work at my own pace, understanding that creative ideas do not always emerge on schedule. After I had finished the manuscript, but before she handed it over to the copy editor, she carefully read each word of my penultimate draft, helping me to condense and clarify where needed. The first time we met she said, "This is going to be fun," and it was! We kept the process lively by sending each other amusing articles, photos, and emails. Some of hers were so funny that I laughed out loud and sent her online photos of stick figures doing a happy dance. I look forward to working with her again on the next project.

And last, but not at all least—following the Hebrew expression that the last is always the sweetest—I thank Neal Horrell, my husband, who at times worked with me so closely on the manuscript that he came to know all 613 laws from the Hebrew Bible that organized Orthodox Jewish life and could identify quotes by the pseudonym of the interviewee. In the final year of writing, when I burrowed into a tunnel so I could complete this book, Neal sustained me emotionally, as well as physically, buying groceries, cooking, cleaning up, and bringing finger food to my study when I did not have time to sit at a table and eat. Neal, I don't know how I could have finished this book without your concrete assistance and loving presence. Thank you from the bottom of my heart.

BECOMING UN-ORTHODOX

CHAPTER ONE

THE LIFE WORLDS
OF HASIDIC JEWS

It all started about fifty years ago, with a conversation I still remember vividly. I was around seven years old and my brother Pinny was nine and a half. We were standing at the top of the second-floor stairs of our house on Thornton Place. I had been reading a novel about a "dizzy blonde" who wore a beanie. I thought that was so cool. So when I saw Pinny, I said, "When I grow up I'm going to be a dizzy blonde with a beanie." He replied, "No, you won't." "Why not?" I asked. His answer was instant: "Because Daddy will never let you." "When I am a teenager," I insisted, "I will do what I want." Who could have predicted how prescient that statement would turn out to be?

By the time I was thirteen, I knew in my gut that I had left Orthodox Judaism. For me that meant no longer believing in God and no longer following his commandments, the system of myriad laws governing everything followers do, from morning to night. My mother had been sick with a rapidly progressing cancer. During the six months that preceded her death, my parents, in addition to pursuing the best medical care possible, also sought spiritual blessings from internationally known Hasidic *rebbes* (in the Hasidic world, the rebbe is at the head of the community; the word is Yiddish for master, teacher, or mentor and derives from the Hebrew word for rabbi). Each time they returned home, they assured my brothers and me that the rebbe had given a special blessing, and everything would be okay.

Well, it wasn't. On Sunday evening, March 3, 1968, my father, in a heart-stopping moment, came barreling down the stairs, yelling in shock and fright, "Pinny! Call Dr. Korman [my mother's oncologist]! Quick! Mommy's dead!" I distinctly remember my two immediate

3

reactions. The first was to scream, a wordless grief and rage for my loss, like a wounded animal. An instant later I felt great anger, anger at my mother for abandoning me and at the failure of the rebbe's blessings. As a thirteen-year-old, I thought the rebbes must be phonies, pretenders. They told lies, had no power to effect events in the world, and offered me nothing. From then on, I no longer believed in God, or in the religion in which I was raised. Over the next few years, I questioned everything about the Orthodox way of life: its beliefs, its practices, the special authority it gave men over women.

Two and a half years later, when I was fifteen, I ever so subtly came out at my younger brother Mark's *bar mitzvah*. I think the full implications of what I said were clearly understood only by my non-Orthodox relatives. Despite my mother's death, my father had invited a couple hundred guests to a hotel in the Catskill Mountains in New York to celebrate, as my parents had done for my older brother's bar mitzvah. The weekend was filled with festive meals, singing, dancing, and—of course—religious study, what sociologist Samuel Heilman had called *lernen*, studying the *Torah* (Hebrew Scriptures). Here, studying the ancient, sacred texts took the form of listening to rabbis expound the meanings of the Torah portion chanted aloud by my brother at services that morning and elaborating on the God-given commandments we should take joy in following. These activities, especially important for men, were a key way of enacting and displaying Orthodox identities. Through these practices they performed, reinforced, and maintained their Orthodox identities.

I had asked my father for a chance to give a talk myself. That I was smart was recognized by my family, and respected. Although I was not a rabbi, or practiced in lernen, I had been the one who had helped Mark prepare his bar mitzvah speech. I was surprised and delighted when I was permitted to talk at this event, on Shabbos (Sabbath) afternoon, around 4 p.m.

The topic of my talk had little in common with the other talks, but it reflected my interests at the time: "Why Are Young Adults Leaving Orthodoxy?" I sat, I remember, on a short stone wall that held up the massive roots of an old tree. I was comfortable and knew from

experience that I could present an engaging talk to the mostly Orthodox audience. Now, when I think about how, in 1971, before feminism had entered this community, "the Davidmans"—a predominantly
male, upper-middle-class, well-known, and respected family—empowered me, the first girl born in the family in two generations, to speak to
the guests, I am amazed.

So what did I tell the assembled group about why "young people"
(making the personal general) were leaving Orthodoxy? I remember
talking about the hypocrisy we (read: I) observed in the Orthodox
community. Members claimed the high moral ground resulting from
their pious observance of God's commandments, but when it came to
their finances, they often cut corners, engaging in duplicitous business
practices such as failing to pay income taxes, lying about their children's ages so they could purchase cheaper airline tickets, and hiring
undocumented immigrants to work in their homes. Although these
practices might have been common among other groups of people, it
belied Orthodox adults' claims to living God-fearing lives. In my talk,
I also invoked the differences between "us"—the generation that had
grown up in the open, liberal 1960s—and the more conformist postwar
generation our parents belonged to. We grew up in a decade in which
many young people were challenging the conservative fundamental
social institutions and values of the times. The attention devoted to
these youth movements exposed young Orthodox Jews to alternative
ways of living. We, like many others, were shaped deeply by the coun-
terculture and social revolutions of our times.

The audience was clearly engaged with my speech, which became
more of a conversation, with questions and answers. My father, who at
the beginning of the talk stood near me, eventually perched quite close.
I remember feeling uncomfortable that he inserted his presence into what
was supposed to be my moment, and I feared he might take over if I said
anything he did not want people to hear. As I felt him move closer to me,
I must have glared at him, because he backed off slightly. This silent communication was a precursor to the many other occasions when he and
I communicated and struggled for power over my life not with words—
he was not particularly articulate—but with body language.

After my talk, some cousins from my mom's side of the family asked me if I was talking about myself. I demurred with a smile; it was obvious that I knew a fair amount about, and was invested in, this topic. How had I learned about it? Clearly, from my own experiences. Interestingly, none of my Davidman relatives, including my father, said a word to me about my talk, although many other guests, including his secular Jewish business associates, complimented me afterward. I never knew whether my dad had fully understood the subtext of my speech.

These two events—my mother's death and my speech about the hypocrisies of Orthodoxy—marked the early stages of my eventual defection[1] from Orthodox Judaism. My mother's death created a tear in the sacred canopy[2] that had sheltered and protected me, my family, and all members of our synagogue community, binding us together through shared beliefs and rituals. I had many questions about why my mother died, and what a world in which mothers are taken from their young children meant, questions that my religion could not answer. With the sealing and lowering of my mother's coffin, and the thud of the earth shoveled onto her casket, I knew that my life as a God-fearing, religiously observant girl had ended.

My mother's death at age thirty-six when I was thirteen can be seen as a major biographical disruption that predisposed me to leaving Orthodoxy.[3] Being left with my father—who had never planned to raise children himself, and clearly did not know how—and my two brothers, in a religiously legitimated patriarchy, deepened my conviction that I would not, and could not, remain Orthodox. I decided that I would leave the moment I had the means to and live a life of my choosing. My father hastened that moment when I was an undergraduate student at Barnard College. Convinced that my secular education was driving me away from Orthodoxy, and unsuccessful in his efforts to counteract this "damage" by instituting increasingly stringent measures of control—which I did not follow—he demanded I leave his house. At that moment he disowned and disinherited me, never reinstating contact before he died.

Like my mother's early death, my father's decision to disown me constituted a major biographical disruption. Both events divided my life story into periods of "before" and "after" these tragedies, and shaped my sociological writing. My books *Tradition in a Rootless World* (1991) and *Motherloss* (2000) investigated how people reconstruct their life stories in order to make sense of these profound interruptions and integrate them into their narratives of self. *Tradition* was my attempt to make sense of my choice to leave Orthodoxy, by studying women who were making the opposite choice: joining Modern Orthodox and Hasidic communities. *Motherloss* was directly related to my experience of losing my mother. For that book I interviewed people like me, whose mothers had died when they were between the ages of ten and fifteen. This book also grew out of my attempts to understand how people like me, who experience major, unexpected breaks in the expected patterns of their lives, are able to create coherent narratives that integrate the disruptive event into their life stories.

Becoming Un-Orthodox is a narrative based on my analysis of the stories that emerged from my conversations with forty UltraOrthodox defectors in the United States who, like me, had abandoned the strictly Orthodox Jewish communities in which they were raised. The larger project included interviews with forty defectors in Israel as well. In analyzing social institutions and culture, context is critical. I therefore left the Israeli interviews out of the book and will pick them up at another time. My interviewees were between twenty and fifty years of age, and all had been away from their enclave communities for at least two years. Most told me they had been gone for at least ten years, and many had been "frei" (free) for over five years. I located my respondents through several means: I put a request for interviewees in H-Judaic, an Internet site for those interested in Jewish studies; I also placed ads in the *Providence Daily Journal*, the *Village Voice*, and the *Boston Globe*. The other interviewees were selected by a snowball sample, asking those I interviewed if they could refer me to others like them. The narrative approach I use in the conversations with my respondents and in my analysis of their transcripts is described in Appendix I.

Since the publication of *Motherloss*, there has been an outpouring of writings—in all fields—on the nature of narratives. This literature fascinated me, and I immersed myself in it. In *Motherloss*, I acknowledged the methodological insight that, despite important differences between my role and that of the respondents. In the end, as the author, I chose what excerpts to include as well as the interpretations I presented. All narratives are co-constructed in the course of conversations we call interviews. In this book, I have worked with narrative methodology (as distinct from using interviews as a research tool). One manifestation of this approach is self-reflexivity about the researcher/author's involvement in all stages of the research project, from developing the original question through the completion of the writing. In this book, for example, I often showed my role in the process of narrative construction by highlighting particular interactions between informants and me. These interactions reveal that respondents did not simply "have" a narrative that I, as a researcher, could "get." Rather, by calling attention to the dynamics of the interview we can see the specific ways my informants interacted with me as a woman, and as a co-defector, albeit from Modern Orthodoxy rather than a Hasidic community.[4] The narratives emerged from informants' conversations with a particular person (i.e., me); they would have been different had someone else interviewed them. I was personally interested in learning how other Orthodox defectors negotiated the difficult passage away from their families and communities and began to reconstruct their identities in new social contexts.

I analyzed the data by transcribing the recordings of the interviews and reading each transcript multiple times, looking for key topics and connections, over a period of several years. Each time I read them, I found new themes and emphases. In the chapters that follow, the narratives of eight or so people are presented in long, vivid extracts. I have also included various related quotations from others I met during the course of this study.

HASIDIC LIFE: THE METANARRATIVE AND RELIGIOUS BODILY PRACTICES

OVERVIEW OF ORTHODOXY

In the nineteenth century, in response to the forces of modernization various new, innovative forms of Judaism developed—such as Reform and Conservative—in order to maintain a Judaism suited for the new era of rationality and industry. In contrast to these liberalizing trends, numerous varieties of Orthodox Judaism developed during the same period as a way to stem the encroachment of modernity and maintain the strictest adherence to traditional Jewish practices and beliefs. The overall worldview of Orthodox Jews—their metanarrative—regards the ancient texts and their rabbinical interpretations over the millennia as authoritative, representing God's divine revelation to Moses on Sinai, which was both supernatural and eternal. The Orthodox believe all Jews are divinely obligated to maintain the sanctity of this body of law, which contains precise prescriptions for every detail of their conduct in daily life, on the Sabbath, and in the annual cycle of holidays, as well as throughout every stage of their lives. Orthodox Judaism's religious observances include strictly practicing the laws for Sabbath, reciting daily traditional prayers and studying Torah (the Pentateuch), following kosher dietary laws, and maintaining gender segregation in all realms of life. For example, the rules of daily worship and the obligation to study ancient texts are the provinces of men, whereas women's sacred duty is to rear children. Women's responsibilities include supporting the obligation of boys and men to study holy texts and observing non-time-bound daily practices.

Despite the shared commitment to strict ritual practices and doctrinal adherence at the heart of Orthodox Judaism, many diverse approaches to these obligations have arisen within Orthodoxy itself. The primary division is that between the Modern Orthodox, and the Haredim (plural of Haredi), who represent the most conservative forms of Orthodox beliefs and practices.

The larger Haredi subgroup of Orthodox Jews is split into two major divisions: the *Yeshivish*[5] (Yiddish for those groups who emphasize the study of ancient texts in *yeshivot*, institutes for advanced study of these sacred texts) and the Hasidic. The latter communities are committed not only to study but also to the emotional, spiritual, and mystical elements of Jewish observance.

Both Modern Orthodox and Haredi Jews live lives dedicated to intensive religious commitment and spiritual growth. But the groups differ significantly in their orientation to the modern world. The goal of the Modern Orthodox is to integrate "*Torah im* [with] *Derech Eretz* [Hebrew for the "ways of the land," that is, secular culture]." Adherents seek to live by the commandments, even as they engage with the secular world, attend universities, and participate in the broader culture. In contrast, Haredim follow a path of strict and unbending commitment to *Halacha* (the evolving body of interpretations of ancient texts); they seek to avoid the influence of larger society and erect numerous ideological, social, and physical boundaries to protect themselves from the ubiquitous encroachment of the secular world. A vivid example of this insularity can be seen in the Satmar Hasidic community of Kiryas Yoel, northwest of New York City. The town has one road leading into and out of the community. On the Sabbath, the gates at the entry (and exit) of this street are locked.

Members of these groups are commanded to avoid all the potentially polluting aspects of the larger, mostly secular society and to avoid situations (such as entering public or university libraries) in which they might be introduced to new, competing worldviews.

The history of Hasidism dates back to eighteenth-century Eastern Europe, a dark time in Jewish history when anti-Semites conducted pogroms against local Jews. In that era the mystical rabbi Baal Shem Tov (Hebrew for "master of the good name") started a movement— Hasidism—that appealed to and attracted the large majority of Jews who were illiterate and could not derive the meaning of Judaism through studying texts. His approach challenged the dominance and authority of the rabbis and their followers, who believed that the only form of Torah-true (meaning precise adherence to dictates of the Hebrew scriptures) Judaism was based on a dedication of one's life— more accurately, men's lives—to the study of ancient texts. The Ba'al Shem Tov promoted spiritual fulfillment among the common folk by popularizing the idea that the Divine is immanent within all Jews and is accessible through prayer, kindness, daily fervor, and exhilaration.

As he traveled throughout the *shtetlach* (Yiddish for small towns and villages in which local governments allowed Jews to live) of Eastern Europe, he gained disciples who spread Hasidism as an alternative, legitimate, and populist approach to Judaism. His followers started new Hasidic communities named after the towns in which they lived. For example, the Lubavitcher Hasidic movement, founded by Rabbi Schneur Zalman of Liadi in the late eighteenth century in the Byelorussian town of Lyuvavichi, and the Bratslaver group, founded by the great-grandson of the Baal Shem Tov in the same period, in the Ukrainian town of Bratslav. Many other Hasidic communities were founded and named in similar ways. Each group had its own rebbe. After World War II, many of these "dynasties" were re-created in the United States and other parts of the world.

Both types of Haredi Jews, the Yeshivish and the Hasidic, are committed to living strictly according to the 613 commandments found in the Torah, as they have been explicated and interpreted by rabbis throughout the generations. This body of law includes stringent commandments about diet, fast days, and proper Sabbath observance, as well as norms for physical comportment, nearly all of which are carried out through distinctive bodily rituals that shape everyday behaviors, from morning to night, throughout their lives.

Ritualized bodily practices are important for all Orthodox Jews, Modern and Haredi. Hasidim comport themselves and dress in ways that clearly indicate their separation from the larger society. Their visible set of bodily techniques emphasizes, in high relief, the centrality of bodily rituals in their lives. One can recognize a Hasidic man or woman from down the street: Hasidic women are expected to cover their bodies entirely—they are required to wear long skirts, blouses that cover their collarbones and entire arms, and high socks or stockings at all times. Their clothing must reveal no parts of their bodies that might be seen as sexually tempting. Married women are expected to shave their heads the night after their wedding, and thus they covered their entire head with hoods, wigs, wigs and hats, or wigs and kerchiefs. Particular details of their garb, however, differentiate the various Hasidic groups and establish boundaries from the others. For example, the particular type of head covering married women wear is an outward symbol of membership in a particular Hasidic community. Men may have curly sidelocks (*peyos*) and beards, wear white shirts and black slacks, and, depending on which group they belong to, perhaps a long black coat or a fur hat, or both.

During my research, an ex-Hasid took me on a tour of a neighborhood in Monroe, New York, that is a center for Hasidic life. We went to a large shopping center that contained a variety of stores where Hasidim could find appropriate clothing, religious objects, and kosher food. The supermarket was one of the largest I have seen, and every item it sold catered to Hasidic standards of *kashrut* (kosher laws that outline in great detail what foods are permitted and forbidden). Although to me the women looked similar to each other, my tour guide taught me to notice the differences in women's hair coverings and stockings, and the group membership they signified. He similarly showed me how to differentiate male Hasidism by noticing the type of coat they wore, the color of their socks, the presence or absence of peyos, and whether their beards were trimmed or not. Although each Hasidic group distinguishes itself from the others by adopting slightly modified versions of dress and hair covering, all Hasidic Jews nevertheless live in a world where the cosmic and ethical worldview seeps through the most banal of daily activities and where every activity is dictated by God and is thus outside of the realm of personal choice (Fader 2006).

Upon arising, Hasidic Jews[6] may walk only three steps from their beds before they ritually rinse their hands in the prepared two-handled bowl of *nagel vasser* (a Yiddish word meaning "nail water"), an embodied ritual intended to sanctify each person in God's holiness. The foundation of this text is the biblical commandment that all Jews "should therefore sanctify ourselves in His holiness, taking our hands with a vessel, to carry out his duty and service." As they wash their hands, they say a blessing to God, thanking him for returning their souls to them after sleep.[7]

After this ablution, and going to the bathroom, Hasidim recite a blessing thanking God for keeping their bodily organs functioning smoothly. Blessings accompany most actions throughout the day; for example, there are specific blessings for each type of food and rules about the order of blessings if one is eating a mixture of different foods. Bodily practices—performances—are essential in the creation, maintenance, and external display of Hasidic identity. These repeated, daily bodily rituals continually work to establish and maintain their relationship with the Divine.[8] By the time Haredi—Yeshivish and Hasidic—children reach adolescence, they are expected to observe all applicable traditional precepts practiced by adult members of their religious communities, according to gender.

Hasidic groups require women and men to dress and comport themselves modestly and humbly. There are fewer rules for men than for women. Men are not allowed to shave their faces, and they are taught to avert their gaze from all they might perceive as lascivious. The laws regarding women's *tzniyus* (modesty) are much more complex, detailed, and specific. They grew out of rabbinical interpretations of the meaning of Psalm 45:14, as translated into English: "The whole glory of the daughter of the king is within." Over the centuries rabbis have developed various interpretations of that phrase, all of which agree God meant women to be modest in all aspects of their lives. What does it mean to "be modest"? Haredi women must be humble and discreet; they speak quietly, and avoid presenting themselves in a way that could be construed as loud, including the clothes and ornaments they wear. The women are instructed to avoid all contact with men prior to marriage. Breaking that norm could have serious consequences for a woman's ability to find a desirable marriage partner.

Most of the people I spoke with described growing up with no knowledge of their body parts and having no language with which to discuss them. Information is distributed solely on an "as-needed" basis. Women told me they were not taught the word vagina, and so, when they suddenly found themselves bleeding "down there," thought something horrible was happening to them. The night before their wedding, Hasidic women are taught how to maintain the laws of family purity, which are based on women's menstrual cycles. No one told them sex could be fun and pleasurable or how to recognize sexual feelings. Many of the women told me they were terrified on their wedding night.

The rules concerning separation of the sexes before marriage are essential to the Hasidic organization of gender, sexuality, and families. Young adults marry young; ideally, women should marry between the ages of eighteen and twenty and boys should be between twenty and twenty-three. Getting married early and having short engagements— three months or so—are strategies to minimize the time between the onset of puberty and allowable sexual behavior within a marriage. When parents believe their children are of marriageable age, they look around their community and talk to trusted friends and rabbis to see who might make a good *shidduch* (match) for their children. The greater the parents' social and religious capital (*yichus*), combined with the length of time the families have been in that particular Hasidic community,[9] the more likely their children will be matched with those of equally prestigious families. Young adults know they always have to be on their best behavior. Their actions and choices would affect not only their own options for potential mates, but also those of their siblings.

In their emphasis on the minute details of embodied rituals, Haredi and other Orthodox Jews practice a very different type of religion than those whose central doctrine concerns faith; what clearly distinguishes Orthodox Judaism from Christianity, for example, is the Jewish emphasis on the proper and exacting performance of ritualized techniques of the body. In contrast, statements of doctrinal acceptance mark the "good Christian." Jewish religious practices are intended to sanctify everyday activities as part of a comprehensive regime of constructing religious identities.

HASIDIC FAMILIES

Hasidim identify themselves to others as continuing to live according to the model God set out for the ancient Israelites at Sinai. They believe this model is the foundation of a pious, happy life. They convey to all that by shaping their lives to the yoke—and joys—of God's laws, they will have an ideal structure and set of practices for close, moral family lives. They continually contrast their type of family, which is based on Divine moral codes, with those prevalent in the dominant society, which they see as abject, debased, fragmented, and lacking the guidance of moral principles. Hasidism base their family life on the principles of self-control, restraint, modesty, clear gender distinctions, and keeping God and the community at the center of their lives. They perform their beliefs, all day, every day, through embodied practices that display and reinforce their constant devotion to God and create clear boundaries between themselves and other Jews, non-Jews, and even other varieties of Hasidic and Haredi communities.

The model Hasidic family has a patriarchal father as the center of authority. The patriarchal father represents the continuing line of tradition from Sinai; he sets down the rules that the mother and children are expected to follow unquestioningly. His authority is grounded in the rebbe's interpretation of the ancient texts, and in the patriarchal nature of Orthodox Judaism, where men are allowed many privileges denied to women, such as public ritual roles in the synagogue. As a counterpart to this patriarchal father, the woman is expected to be a dutiful wife and mother, caring for as many children as God blesses the couple with. Often these families are quite large; there is nothing unusual or surprising about a family with ten children. Hasidim forbid the use of birth control—unless a woman's life would be at stake if she were to become pregnant.

This model of family life is believed to produce stability for the children and for their families and serves as the basis for the continuity and stability of Haredi community life. Hasidim teach their children, through language and modeling, that they must be obedient to all forms of authority: the rebbe is, like Moses, God's representative in this generation, and all members of the community look to him for the final word on all matters in their lives. The presentation of these laws is situated within the threat of punishment if the children fail to adhere to them.

Nevertheless, the various forms of Haredi families, like all others, raise children who may question or even go against the families' values and behavioral rules. In liberal communities, where families are generally more lenient, it is possible for parents and children to negotiate the realm of acceptable behaviors. In Hasidic families, however, there is no room for doubt: Even the slightest deviations in Orthodox practice can deepen into a desire to leave the community, an act that constitutes a major biographical disruption and that bifurcates the lives of the defectors into the period when they were Orthodox and that which followed.

Children within Hasidic communities are brought up in an environment that discourages questioning the authority of Divine precepts enacted in all details of members' a daily lives. They are taught all the minutae of how to follow the rules and regulations and their significance for religious actions. Socialization practices create a solid sense of identity that is rooted in the fulfillment of God's laws; remaining true to these commandments, and observing them within the gaze of the community, ensures a stable, unquestioned sense of identity for members. Haredi culture, especially the Hasidic, rejects the postmodern idea of the fluidity of identity and discourages the development of an individualistic sense of self, which is viewed as reflective of the selfish tendencies of the outside culture. Only God can legitimate an authentic Hasidic identity. In order to encourage proper fulfillment of all religious commandments and to ensure that children grow into their appropriate roles within the Hasidic worlds, individualism is shunned. Children are socialized to fulfill God's commandments and play their proper roles in the community. The denigration of egoism is particularly significant for this study, as exiting the community thrusts defectors into a larger society that encourages and values individuality. Inside the enclave, identities are highly scripted and their proper performance is continually monitored. The process of leaving reflects defectors' growing independence and their acceptance of the wider culture's orientation to free choice.

NARRATIVES AND EMBODIMENT

In the defection narratives that emerged from conversations between me and my informants, two central types of embodied practices, essential aspects of living a Haredi life, emerged: appearance, which is manifested through demeanor and comportment; dress; hair, leg, and head coverings; and the dietary laws about kashrut. The majority of commandments concerning ritual observance are gendered. Distinct gender roles are foundational to the performance and maintenance of the Haredi world.

Thus, in defection, there are distinctly gendered ways to disinscribe[10] the markers of community membership: Men may shave off their beards in the process of exiting, whereas women cease shaving or covering their hair. Formerly Hasidic Jews who change their diet, hair, shaving practices, and clothing as they exit the community perform a sort of identity negotiation by beginning to play out personal, religious, social, and political questions of self on the bodily canvas. By doing so, these defectors reject the gendered Hasidic ethical framework surrounding bodily action and adopt the somatic society's multifarious frameworks for understanding bodily practice. They reject the Divine origins of the rules and regulations of their homogeneous enclave rituals and instead adopt the notion that fluidity in appearance is acceptable.

For Hasidic Jews defecting from enclave communities, this transformation involves a negotiation between the corporeal performances that sustained and reflected their religious identities and the extensive range of bodily practices available in the wider society. Just as I found in *Tradition in a Rootless World* that the women and men who become Orthodox as adults must learn new ways to eat, dress, and engage in other bodily practices, those who leave must disinscribe and shed the embodied practices of their former lives, simultaneously taking on new bodily routines.

To comprehend the significance of changing long-held bodily practices, it is important to understand that a person's bodily behavior is deeply tied to her/his ontological security (Giddens 1991; Turner 1984, 1992). Drawing on the work of Erving Goffman (1959, 1963, 1967, 2005) and Anthony Giddens (1991), Bryan Turner argued that as the individual "performs" identity within various theaters of life, the appearance of "normalcy" in bodily comportment and interaction upholds a fundamental feeling of a secure identity. This security can fall apart, however, if a young Hasid begins to feel a significant distance between bodily routine and self-identity, such as when defectors continue to perform daily religious practices when they no longer believe in the doctrine associated with them. This situation creates anxiety and anomie, as described by Giddens: "When this dissociation happens as an unwanted feature of personality, it expresses existential anxieties impinging directly upon self-identity" (1991, 59). These existential anxieties are a key feature of the narratives of Hasidic defectors. Respondents described how they resolved these feelings of dissociation by changing their bodily practices. Respondents described these physical transformations as a crucial means of both disinscribing their Hasidic bodily markers and negotiating a new, ontologically secure, non-Hasidic identity.

Respondents' personal crises concerning the role of religion in their lives were thoroughly intertwined with bodily, cognitive, emotional, familial, social, cultural, and political doubts. In learning to create, re-create, and represent themselves as non-Haredim, changes in bodily practices were essential to their transition into the wider society. With what they perceived as newfound freedom, these defectors performed new selves through the "medium of the socially-interpreted body" (Turner 1984, 40). Framing the analysis of religiously embodied practices in terms of gendered identity construction and reconstruction illuminates the role of the body as a key means of enacting and transforming identities.

In our conversations, the respondents described how, when they first disrupted their familiar everyday routines, they were highly aware that their very identities were at stake, a profound realization that led many to make gradual changes in bodily rituals. A common pattern emerged in the way exiters approached transformations of bodily practices and self: Defection was a process that began in private explorations of new bodily practices in which they temporarily stepped out of their prescribed roles and identities and into new ones. Here the concepts of *defection* and *exiting* are used in a relatively broad sense, encompassing not only a singular moment in which one publicly communicates a break from Hasidic identity, but also the hidden process that led to such a moment. Exiters typically began their exit with a period of private deviations from many Orthodox laws, including prescribed bodily routines.

Erving Goffman's discussion of public and private acts and identities provides insights into the ways people shape their behavior by differentiating between what they do in public, the "frontstage," where their activities conform to the values, norms, and expectations of their reference group, and their conduct in the "backstage" areas they consider private, where they are unlikely to be seen by community members who are invested in maintaining their group's integrity (Goffman 1959).

By changing a particular bodily practice in the backstage, in private—in a way that is not visible to fellow Hasidim—but even more so in the frontstage, in public, the defector establishes violation of the laws as a moment with substantial emotional weight. Informants reflected their understanding that this transgressive behavior signaled a concrete resistance to Hasidic life. Backstage experiments with bodily practices reveal that defection is under way well before it is made publicly manifest through bodily signals to the community. That my respondents felt a backstage was even possible is significant because it presupposes a significant departure from the Hasidic worldview—a tear in the sacred canopy. Even those transgressive bodily acts they performed in private reflected a growing loss of commitment and belief. An omniscient God is either not part of the audience (thus his existence is challenged by denying his omniscience) or "he" is unconcerned with obedience to the laws regarding the bodily practices defectors changed.

As Emile Durkheim (1915) has illustrated, religious practices and myths are interwoven and mutually reinforcing. Through performing the prescribed physical routines, members create, perform, and reinforce the group's narrative in an ongoing, systematic way. Conversely, repeating these rituals is a way for the individual to internalize the group's worldview and accept its practices as "common sense." Durkheim defined religion as "a unified system of *beliefs and practices* relative to sacred things, that is to say, things set apart and forbidden, which unite into one single moral community called a *Church*, all those who adhere to them" (p. 44, emphasis added). The beliefs of each religious community provide a rationale that explains and supports their system of precisely defined ritual practices. For all Haredim, their way of life is just right. Its beliefs and rituals bound members together in the past, as they do in the present, and will do in the future. Just as beliefs shape embodied rituals, these rites form group membership, create bonds among members, and simultaneously establish boundaries between themselves and other groups.

In *Becoming Un-Orthodox* I develop an argument that builds upon and extends Durkheim's insight that religious myths, the stories groups tell about themselves, cannot be understood or sustained if they are not embedded in a system of bodily ritual practices and techniques. This study highlights how leaving a religion is more than a matter of "losing faith." For defectors from Orthodox Judaism, the primary transformations involve their embodied practices. As they leave, defectors must disinscribe their internalized routines of the body. Narratives of those who leave the Hasidic community demonstrate how such exiting is accomplished through the medium of the body. Respondents spoke of the serious difficulties of disinscribing habitual, routinized practices. Although I did not ask questions about bodily rituals, in my conversations with respondents they spoke a great deal about the difficulties they experienced in disinscribing Hasidic bodily routines. In analyzing the transcripts of these interviews, I was struck by the centrality of bodily techniques in their accounts. Over time, I saw embodiment as a central theme of this study; Hasidism provided an exemplary case study for understanding the important role the body plays in shaping, maintaining, and shedding religious— and other cultural—formations. When individuals experience irresolvable contradictions between their activities and thoughts and those of the group, they move away and eventually seek other paths to creating harmony between themselves and their new reference group.

For this study I had long conversations with thirty-eight adult women and men in the United States between the ages of twenty-five and forty-five who defined themselves as being an ex-Hasid, and two men who had formerly been Yeshivish. In addition, I interviewed forty Israeli "exes" but they are not included here due to the enormous cultural differences between the two countries. Respondent's accounts of defection highlight the great fear, angst, and sense of anomie that accompanied leaving their highly bounded enclave communities.

Many spoke of feeling marginal in their own communities, the result of having grown up in families that differed in obvious ways from the majority. In some cases, one parent had been lost to death or divorce; in others, the mother and father had profound religious differences; or, most distressingly, within these families the defectors experienced sexual, physical, or verbal abuse, or a combination. Hasidic teachings emphasize that if one observes all the commandments, families will be joyous, warm, and close. It was painfully obvious to my informants that the emotional dynamics of their families fell far short of this ideal. Other significant predisposing factors to exiting included: an acute awareness of gender inequality; exposure to secular relatives; and exploring forbidden media, such as televison, movies, Internet sites, and books (including philosophical treatises on relativism).

The obvious differences between respondents' actual families and the idealized, normative family, revealed to my respondents holes in this seemingly integrated system of beliefs and practices. As they became aware of these inconsistencies, they began to question fundamental Orthodox assumptions and rituals and, ultimately, the Hasidic metanarrative. They had been taught that God had created the world, "chosen" the Jewish people, and instructed them to become and remain holy, as he himself is holy. God had commanded the Jews to sanctify their lives by stringently following all 613 laws in the Hebrew Bible, as they have been interpreted by scholars and rabbis throughout the generations. This basic premise is set out in Deuteronomy 30:16: "For I command you today to love the Lord your God, to walk in obedience to him, and to keep his commands, decrees and laws; then you will live and increase, and the Lord your God will bless you in the land you are entering to possess."

Both my respondents and I began to feel at a young age that following the prescribed religious practices of Orthodox Judaism did not yield the promised experience of wholeness, morality, and sanctity. The ex-Hasidism whom I interviewed described how their community's metanarrative and the physical rituals through which it was enacted began to lose sense and meaning for them, as they (like me) became increasingly aware of the contradictions in their lives. As we questioned the disjunctions we felt and found ourselves unable to assuage our doubts, our commitments to Orthodoxy and the bodily ritual practices that are at its core began to waver. We sought to test the truth claims of Orthodoxy by violating one of the hundreds of commandments that guide all aspects of Orthodox Jewish daily life.

I vividly remember the first time I defied an essential commandment and broke the laws of kashrut. I was in my junior year at an Orthodox high school when two rebellious senior boys led me around the corner to Leo's, a casual restaurant where I ate my first nonkosher burger, which tasted even more delicious because of the cheese melted on top (Jewish dietary rules forbid the mixing of meat and dairy). Although Leo's was a nonkosher public restaurant around the corner from my religious high school, for me it functioned as a "private space" in which I felt free to transgress. I knew my lapse would not be seen by anyone I knew; after all, my family and community would not have entered a nonkosher restaurant.

My respondents told me their first experiments with breaking religious commandments took place in settings that were, from their perspective, in the "backstage" area where they would not be seen by community members who would report their violations to their rabbis and their parents. Dina, a formerly Bobover Hasidic woman (Bobover is a Hasidic sect, as is Satmar, to which Shlomo belonged), recounted eating *treyf* (nonkosher food), her first violation of God's commandments. To ensure that her transgression would be hidden, she drove miles away from her home, to what she described as a "lower-class" shopping plaza, where she enjoyed her first bacon, lettuce, and tomato sandwich. The expression "you are what you eat," underscores why following the kosher laws is essential to the ongoing performance of Hasidic embodied practices. Shlomo, an ex-Satmar young man, regaled me with tales of the times he and his friends visited what he called "dancing clubs." As he watched the dancers, Shlomo felt uncomfortable that his peyos announced his "otherness" to all who saw him. Eventually, he started to tuck his peyos behind his ears when he and his buddies went to these clubs.

When my conversation partners (and I) found that God did not immediately strike us down for breaking "his" laws and, further, that we enjoyed these forbidden activities, we continued to violate these and, over time, other sacred commandments. After these rebellious excursions, however, we returned home and resumed our lives on the frontstage, with our families and communities. Hasidim changed their entire demeanor, comportment, dress, and diet as they moved back and forth between two radically different worlds and tried to behave appropriately in each, a strategy I call "passing." They were crossing boundaries; the more they did so the bolder they became in seeking knowledge about the world beyond their insular religious communities.

At this stage, they had to closely monitor their behavior at home, making sure not to repeat the new physical practices they had learned in the secular spaces outside of their communities. Switching back and forth between these two worlds, repeatedly crossing boundaries, grew increasingly challenging over time. The contradictions in their lives, and the implicit lies they told at home, led to feelings of cognitive dissonance, the psychologically uncomfortable state in which people hold two contradictory beliefs or find themselves acting in ways contrary to their beliefs. Eventually, the distress produced by these incongruities created sufficient pressure to compel them to make a decisive choice.

Becoming Un-Orthodox focuses on those who chose to resolve their cognitive dissonance by leaving their communities. In our conversations, those who had left Hasidic enclaves spoke with great emotion of the fear and turmoil that arose as they contemplated leaving their familiar worlds. If they stepped out, they would lose the security and certitude of living with a comprehensive script that accounted for their group's way of life and provided a comprehensive and detailed system for conducting themselves in all activities of their daily lives. They had no scripts for how to conduct themselves outside of the enclave, no means of support, and no place to go. They knew that by exiting they would risk losing everything they had ever known, including their families and communities.

As they contemplated leaving, my respondents' lack of knowledge about how to act, speak, and comport themselves in the larger society produced great anxiety. Their strong reservations and fears about defecting illustrated just how deeply they had internalized the repertoire of language, rules, stories, values, and roles that constituted the cultural tool kit of their enclave communities (Swidler 1986).[11] Although Swidler's focus was on culture, I argue that the bodily practices they were socialized to take for granted were equally central. They could not imagine where they might live next, let alone how they would reconstruct their identities by learning new social and cultural norms that would guide their actions, creating new performances of self and identity. As one respondent poignantly recalled, she did not even know "what regular people talk about."

For these defectors, constructing a new self, outside the boundaries of their religious enclaves, required their conscious disinscription of the automatic, taken-for-granted routines and practices inscribed on their bodies from the moment they were born. Although they could not yet envision even the basic requirements of finding work and a place to live, their accounts showed how they eventually learned new norms, metanarratives, and practices in the context of their chosen social and cultural settings. The large majority of exiters eventually resettled their lives by adopting their new community's bodily routines, which eventually became instinctive, embodied, and taken for granted.

The great challenge facing my informants was made more difficult by their parents' and fellow Hasidim's oft-repeated warnings about the dangers lurking in the world outside the enclave, where they would inevitably meet immoral and animalistic *goyim* (non-Jews; also used by Hasidim for secular Jews). In order to step out, they had to establish a sense of themselves as individuals, a self-concept abhorred in Hasidic communities. In secular society, "The self has to be reflexively made" (Giddens 1991, 3). For those who grow up in a strictly controlled enclave community, defectors have to create a self amid a puzzling diversity of options and possibilities. The secular world does not offer ready-made scripts for the conduct of everyday life. By leaving, defectors asserted their right to the pursuit of individual happiness and control over their own lives. Exiting their communities was the culmination of years of asking questions, not finding answers, and transgressive, rebellious behavior. Defection was an act of defiance, but it was also a process requiring great courage and self-confidence.

Although the other defectors and I intended to leave our Orthodox lives completely behind, we did not realize that deeply internalized remnants of our old habits and practices would inevitably stay with us and make their appearance in unexpected ways, at unexpected times. Many respondents described incidents, or periods of time, in which they became aware of the metaphorical "return of the repressed"[12]—the lingering influence of their original socialization. One man described a day, about a decade after his defection, when he was walking down the hall of the hospital where he worked and suddenly realized he was not wearing his *yarmulke*, the skullcap that Orthodox men never remove except to bathe and sleep. Strong feelings of guilt and shame washed over him, revealing that the bodily practices he had abandoned had never been completely erased. For some of my respondents, becoming parents triggered ambivalence: How would they raise their children? Did they want their kids to learn about and identify with the Jewish religious beliefs and practices they themselves had left, with such great difficulty, years ago?

The argument of this book linking self-transformation with bodily behaviors extends beyond this case study of Hasidim to all groups in which members' sense of self can become out of sync with the cultural metanarrative and its prescribed bodily routines. Significantly, several of my conversation partners actually used the trope "coming out." Members of the lesbian, gay, bisexual, transsexual/transgendered, and queer/questioning (LGBTQ) community, like Hasidic defectors, are born into a cultural landscape with taken-for-granted assumptions about society, especially gender and sexuality. Gender is widely presumed to be binary (masculine-feminine) and commensurate with biological sexual categories.[13] Furthermore, the cultural dominance of "heteronormativity" leads people to assume that heterosexuality is normal, whereas all other types of sexuality are deviant. All cultures, such as the religious culture of the Hasidim, prescribe specific bodily practices and comportment. Bodies are expected to conform to the sexual norms of their culture; the body can be a site of conformity as well as resistance.

"Coming out of the closet," which refers to the process of leaving one's former way of life and becoming openly gay or otherwise genderqueer,[14] is an identity transformation produced through the medium of the body, comparable to the stages of Hasidic defection described by my conversation partners. According to LGBTQ writers, "coming out" entails a process of identity transformation: "We are reinventing ourselves in the very process of coming out," a process that is "continuous, not instantaneous" (Kaufman and Raphael 1996, 105). This gradual process is deeply embodied; the bodily changes involved in the stages of coming out mirror many of the steps my participants described.

The first break in their acceptance of heteronormative assumptions occurs when an LGBTQ person experiences feelings of gender or sexual differentness. These may manifest as fleeting glimpses of same-sex desire and can appear at any point in a person's life, but begins, according to Kaufman and Raphael (1996), as occasional feelings of erotic desire for members of the same sex. Experiencing same-sex desire or feeling that one has a transgendered identity can be confusing, shame-inducing, and alienating for those who grow up in a heteronormative culture (Downs 2012; Kaufman and Raphael 1996; Seidman 2002). Although these feelings can arise at any time, many people first become aware of these in adolescence, when they might experience involuntarily corporeal betrayals. For example, adolescent boys may find themselves physically (and visibly) aroused in the shower after gym class, an experience that makes them feel ashamed. Such experiences may lead to gay-shaming and, ultimately, self-contempt as the body "gives away" their secret differentness. Each instance of shame inseparably entwines the body with shameful experiences of nonnormative sexuality.

It is, however, risky to challenge the dominant social and cultural assumption that all people are heterosexual. For those coming out, their first "transgressions" are experimental and often take place in "private" spaces beyond the gaze of everyone they know. The men Schrock and Boyd (2005) interviewed who were transgendered began learning to embody womanhood through observing and experimenting with women's bodily practices. They studied mass media and women they knew personally and practiced imitating their gestures, voices, mannerisms, and general styles of comportment. As they altered their bodily comportment, their bodies came to feel as they did internally. Wearing women's clothes and makeup actually "shaped their bodies into gendered conformity." High heels reinforced feminine hip movements while walking, and lipstick changed the way one held a cigarette or sipped from a glass (Schrock and Boyd 2005, 324).

When same-sex or transgender interactions become more frequent, closeted LGBTQ folks develop distinctive identities that either conform to or resist normative gendered behaviors. They begin passing between two worlds, a challenging and risky process. In their home world, they present a "pseudo-self" that is acceptable and enact the bodily rituals of heteronormativity, such as reading pornographic magazines and going to the prom with an opposite-sex date. LGBTQ individuals feel shame as they pass between the frontstage of heterosexuality and the backstage of their same-sex desires or transgendered identity (Downs 2012; Kaufman and Raphael 1996; Seidman 2002). The passing stage, in which individuals perform a heterosexual identity in public but act like their true selves in private, as Seidman's participants reported, is one of great physical and emotional discomfort. One of Seidman's interviewees expressed it thus: "You can't hide, you'll have a nervous breakdown" (Seidman 2002, 65).

Eventually, the tension arising from constant border crossing pushes LGBTQ people, like Hasidim, to make a decision. Those who come out often seek a community of people like themselves, who challenge heterosexual norms and accept a wide range of sexual practices. Up to this point, coming-out narratives mirror those of Hasidic defectors—personal and social predispositions exist, initial transgressions are made, and patterns of transgressive behavior lead individuals to pass between two worlds or identities. A major difference between the narratives of people in the two groups becomes apparent as soon as individuals "step out." LGBTQ people are able to find others like themselves, who teach them new norms and bodily routines. They have guides who help them create a script for their new lives. In essence, some LGBTQ folks exit the closet to find another community in which to find a sense of self, belonging, and meaning. Hasidic defectors, in contrast, have no established script to adopt when they step out; instead, they have to search for a community wherein they might feel comfortable and safe creating their new identities.

The major themes of this book are readily applicable to people in similar kinds of transitional situations, such as those who leave their homes (be it country, religion, or sense of accepted sexual orientation) and establish themselves in a new "world." This is common in the United States, particularly when we think of the major waves of immigrants who peopled this country. Immigrants arrived in a new land in which most aspects of daily life—talking, eating, dressing, working—were dramatically different from those they had taken for granted in their "old countries" and that no longer applied. In order to fit into their new situation, they had to learn different ways of being, including a new language as well as new habits of eating, dressing, and comportment. The following chapters describe how Hasidic defectors accomplish identity transformation through disinscribing and reinscribing gendered bodily practices.

CHAPTER TWO

TEARS IN THE SACRED CANOPY

The sacred canopy, a metaphor developed by sociologist Peter Berger, refers to the overarching shelter enclosing and securing a religious community's way of life and shielding its boundaries from outside intrusions. Respondents described how the Ultra-Orthodox enclaves in which they were raised were based on an exacting system of laws, beliefs, and practices, which, when followed stringently, would result in a holy, moral, and satisfying life. Those who defected told me of a moment in their childhoods in which they became aware of serious contradictions between their own experiences and the idealized views of Haredi life they had been taught. In our conversations, they described how their growing awareness of these disjunctures led them to doubt and question the seemingly complete, integrated, and solid way of life of their enclave community.

Within the narratives that my respondents and I co-constructed, I discerned three types of significant childhood experiences outside the realm of normative Hasidic behavior that predisposed these youngsters to doubt and question their religious beliefs and practices. The first was exposure to the world outside their enclave, either through secular relatives and friends or various secular media (books, television, and movies), all of which taught them about alternative ways of living and of understanding the world. Through extensive and intensive reading—something the young men in particular had been trained to do—they learned theories of relativism. They described how their vision was widened by interactions with relatives who were not religious but who were not being punished by God, which was contrary to what my respondents had been taught.

The second childhood experience that led young Haredim—both Hasidic and Yeshivish—to question their lives and their community's way of life was growing up in a family that deviated from the ideal Haredi norms; their family life was out of line with community expectations. Sometimes both parents were not similarly committed to ritual observance and/or there was conflict between them, or, in the saddest cases, the parents abused their children physically, emotionally, or sexually. If the rules governing the Haredi world truly came from God through Moses on Mount Sinai—the metanarrative by which the Ultra-Orthodox defined themselves—their families' lack of conformity raised questions in the children's minds. Defectors described experiences and situations that clearly showed that their family did not meet the community's expectations for family life. In a community where closeness—cohesion—rested on conformity, my informants knew they and their families were shunned. Their narratives all described a moment when their families' failure to live up to the group's norms made the children unsure of whom they could trust: their parents, or the laws and norms of the larger enclave community. Either the parents failed to reproduce the ideal model, or perhaps there was some flaw in their leaders' interpretation of the ancient texts and thus their teachings about the ideal type of Haredi family was flawed. Perhaps the Haredi paradigm is not feasible; and many members inevitably failed to live up to the normative standards.

The third circumstance leading respondents to question their community's norms was described by almost half of the women but very few men. When they were young, generally under the age of six, Hasidic girls were allowed to go with their fathers to synagogue on Shabbes and hang out in the men's section, where all the ritual action took place. But when they turned seven or eight, they had to stay home on Shabbes and help their mothers. As they began to attend school, it became obvious to them that their brothers' education was more important in their families than their own. They could see that growing into women would seriously limit the choices and activities available to them. They could not see their mothers as models for the life they wanted for themselves, but they had no alternative vision of what a woman's life could be. This inequality, which they knew would define their place in the community for the rest of their lives, enraged them and produced doubt about their ability to remain in the Hasidic world. These three types of early experiences revealed holes in the seemingly solid sacred canopy that bound together group members and shielded them from dangerous outside influences.

My conversation partners spoke of the deep and lasting impact of these childhood experiences. Their early experiences led them to question their religious norms and practices, after which a series of events ultimately led to their leaving their communities. My own life narrative generally followed the same chronology—from my mother's premature death to when I left my family home and went to live at Barnard College. The connections here, the correlations, are vivid. But defectors remain a minority; most Haredi young adults who experience the same or similar circumstances do not choose to leave. I do not try to explain why one sibling left while others stayed, because my interest is not in comparing these two groups. Rather, I chose to analyze the nature and process of defection. I have met many Hasidim who find their religious lives rewarding, meaningful, and sometimes joyous. Thousands of Hasidim around the world are spiritually uplifted through their religious lives.

In all types of enclave communities—including the Amish, strict fundamentalists, and Ultra-Orthodox Jews, fitting in with norms is essential to feelings of belonging. As Emile Durkheim demonstrated, societies hold together when there are shared values, commitments, and feelings of closeness among their members (1915). These factors act as social "glue," maintaining the solidarity of the group. But when these common bonds are disrupted and individuals are at odds with their families and communities, the powerful attachments necessary to the continuation of religious and communal life begin to fray. This is the metaphorical tear in the sacred canopy that shelters community members from all possible threats to their way of life.

EXPOSURE TO THE SECULAR WORLD

Respondents described how exposure to the world outside of the enclave, either through secular media or non-Orthodox relatives, widened their sense of the possibilities of life outside their enclaves. Many of the male respondents (who were trained in intensive study) and some of the women (for whom intellectualism was generally discouraged) described going to public or university libraries, where they began to learn about alternative ways of understanding the world, particularly the idea of relativism, a concept that shook up the internalized absolutist religion in which they had been raised. The first two respondents we hear from in this section were distinctive because they had been brought up in Yeshivish and not Hasidic communities. where being a brilliant Talmud scholar was the most important accomplishment a boy could achieve. (The Talmud is a central text of Rabbinic Judaism, considered second to the Torah.)

Eнud

She taught me to ask some big questions, to develop a much broader perspective, rather than just contenting myself with the answers that have been handed down over generations.

Ehud was the intellectual star of his family. He was raised to be a *talmid chacham* (an unusually gifted and wise student of ancient texts). As the first son (after two daughters) of Holocaust survivors, born into a community in which girls were not taught to study the ancient texts in depth, Ehud was the one on whom his parents put their expectations for the family pride that comes from having an *ilui* (a brilliant, enlightened scholar) as a child. He felt that he carried a heavy burden to fulfill his parents' expectations for carrying on the Orthodox tradition and its standard of male intellectual achievement. Ehud's father had lost nearly all his family in the Holocaust. Ehud later learned that upon his son's birth in 1952, his father had said, "Only now do I feel avenged for what the Nazis did to my family." Although Ehud had two sisters, his family lineage is carried in the male name. Ehud's birth symbolized Hitler's failure to eradicate all the Jews.

Ehud's first glimpse of tears within the sacred canopy of his religious community came when he was exposed to ideas radically different from those dominant in his Haredi world. His sister was the agent provocateur in his narrative; she provided the context for conversations about alternative belief systems.

> EHUD: I guess it really started with some form of critical inquiry, thinking, reflection. It was, to the best of my recollection, largely the result of my Friday evening [*Shabbes,* the Jewish day of rest] chats with my sister. This was my second sister, who was four years older than I and was rebelling herself by studying alternative idea systems. She became quite interested in Marxist philosophy and wanted to share these exciting new perspectives with me. I said Friday evening because I remember fondly those times when we were doing the dishes after, you know, the Shabbes meal, and that would be one of the times when she would open my eyes to philosophy and the beauty of this completely unknown territory to me, where you use your mind to order things. She taught me to ask some big questions, to develop a much broader perspective, rather than just contenting myself with the answers that have been handed down over generations. And I'm sure she did it very artfully without hurting my religiosity too much, at least in the beginning, but I think this really planted the seeds of some deep questions I had.

Perhaps Ehud was attracted to the Marxism his sister taught him because this set of ideas, like the Haredi worldview, offered fundamental explanations of the state of the universe and how it got that way. These ideas had the appeal of "reason" to Ehud; they were logical and made sense. His sister showed him that Marxism offered a robust, historically based alternative metanarrative to the Haredi premise that the world was created by, and is continually under the watch of, a God who demands complete and utter devotion. Like Orthodox Jews, Marxists base their dogma on their interpretations of texts, about which they could argue, chapter and verse, just as the ancient Rabbis did when they worked to comprehend and codify ancient sacred texts.

Ehud worked hard to bracket his deep convictions about religious practice from any threat or intrusion of secular realities. He knew the questions he discussed with his sister were "big" and challenging. These conversations started him on an experiential, existential quest to understand the order of the universe. Nevertheless, he continued to be precise and exacting in fulfilling all the religious commandments.

> EHUD: I was so committed to observing every single law I was actually going a little over and beyond what was expected from me; my parents did not observe the ritual of washing when they awoke in the morning. I wanted to please my parents. I was happy when my parents were proud of me, and I was responding to their encouragement and fulfilling their expectations. My perfectionism about how I fulfilled every commandment was also in my temperament; it was my inclination. So I even observed commandments that were not important in our community, such as doing *nagel vasser* [ritual hand washing] first thing in the morning.

Ehud described the precise way he began his day with this ritual performance. Like those of other respondents, Ehud's narrative revealed his sense that the ritual commandments were hierarchically arranged, such that in his community observing the practice of nagel vasser was not as essential as following other commandments, such as observing *Shabbes* and eating only kosher food. By being even more stringently observant than the demands of his Haredi community and practicing this particular ritual and the numerous other embodied practices that constitute Haredi daily life, Ehud established, maintained, and performed his identity as a strictly observant Jew. He separated the new perspectives his sister was teaching him and the questions they raised from his convictions about obedience to God's commandments.

As an intellectual, Ehud was drawn to a rational, empirical view of history and the creation of the world, a view that completely contrasted with the dominant ideology and worldview of his community. But he was not ready to leave the Haredi world. So he redoubled his efforts to meticulously observe all the rules of the community.

34

SAM

I had never seen a television in my whole life.

Sam, like Ehud, was brought up to be a brilliant Talmudic scholar. After high school, his parents sent him to Baltimore, Maryland, home of one of the best Haredi *yeshivot* in the United States.

> SAM: At the age of seventeen I moved to a yeshiva in Baltimore. This is a very important detail because if I had stayed in the seminary in Lakewood, New Jersey, where I had studied earlier, I would have had to take the bus to the center of the town. In Baltimore I walked everywhere.

Sam told me that when he was walking around, he entered stores that sold secular media and discovered a public library full of secular books. He lingered in the library; he regularly sat down and read newspapers, literature, and philosophy:

> SAM: All of a sudden everything was accessible to me. What was accessible? Newspapers, for example, television—I had never seen a television in my whole life.
>
> LD: Where did you find television?
>
> SAM: In hotels. There were lots of hotels in town and I used to go and sit in the lobby and watch television. I was amazed by the diversity of programming, and I asked why the people I grew up with don't watch television. What is this thing? You can watch about China, about India, about Africa. You see people arguing. What is this thing? It's amazing! And movies too. Back then I didn't know what movies were, but I also watched movies. I saw blue movies, pornography. I saw a lot of action movies; in fact, I am an expert on action movies, even though I haven't seen one in a while, since then.

Among various other taboo media, none of which is mentioned in the Hebrew Scriptures, television is forbidden because it exposes watchers to a vast array of banned and immoral activities. Television is a powerful medium that can convey a great deal of useful knowledge about other cultures, science, history, among other topics. Haredi parents do not want their children exposed to wider society. Television reveals a variety of worlds that stand in stark contrast to Ultra-Orthodox values and practices. Sam's ability to watch television helped him fulfill a desire mentioned by all my respondents: learning about the larger world.

In town, Sam also discovered the public library, which was only a five-minute walk from the *yeshiva*. He told me that on his days off from studying he went to the library where he discovered new worlds through the books and other media he consumed there. The more he learned the greater his intellectual curiosity about a wide and varied range of interests grew.

The relative anonymity Sam experienced living outside his enclave in a vastly different, more diverse, and larger society provided him with the opportunity to explore the secular world. But its very unfamiliarity made certain aspects of it confusing, as several respondents also described. Some noted seeing things outside of their enclave but not knowing what they were. For example, when Sam first discovered newspapers, he found their format particularly confusing.

SAM: And I remember secular newspapers like the *New York Times* and the *Washington Post*, but I did not know how to make sense of them. On the same page they had, for example, an advertisement, a picture of a half-naked girl; and on the other side of that page was news about United Nations' statements about Israel. And I remember all sorts of pictures. So I couldn't understand which parts actually reported the news and what all the other stuff was.

The pages of secular newspapers were nothing like the Talmud, where every word on every page was critical. Instead, Sam found that newspapers published serious ideas next to frivolous advertisements, mixed reports of global concerns with those of local interest, and used words with which Sam was unfamiliar. He told me his head was spinning after his first day-long visits to the library. At the same time, however, his curiosity compelled him to investigate further.

When Sam went to the library, he felt the entire world was open to him—even if he did not understand it all at first. He said, "And I read everything that there was; lots of garbage because I didn't know, I didn't know anything. I read anything that I got my hands on, anything they had." Of course he had not wanted to waste his time reading nonsense, but at first his lack of secular knowledge made it hard for him to single out the books most important to his newly developing knowledge. His readings broadened his world immensely. Abby, whom we meet next, similarly rebelled by pursuing forbidden books in the library.

ABBY

A period is something you put at the end of a sentence
and you don't need a bra.

Abby grew up in a Hasidic community in which all secular media were banned. When I first met Abby, a former Satmar, she was in her mid-thirties. She was separated from her husband and involved in a relationship with another woman. She told me that the Satmar banned all secular media. Her curiosity, however, led her to break that norm and enter the public library outside her immediate neighborhood.

ABBY: My mother didn't allow us to go to the library and get books out on our own. She would have to read every book we took out, and she's Israeli, so her command of the English language was not very great. It was difficult because there was a lot she didn't understand, and yet she was censoring everything that was coming into the house.

One day I brought home a book from the school library called *Are You There God? It's Me, Margaret*, by Judy Blume. It was a very well-known coming-of-age book. Everyone in school was reading it, and on the back cover, there was a summary of the book. And it said, "Some of the girls in the class have gotten their period, and I don't even have anything to put into my bra." So I went to my mother, and I asked her, "What's a bra, and what's a period?" And my mother said, "A period is something you put at the end of a sentence, and you

37

don't need a bra." And actually, I really did at that point, but that's a whole other story. And she took the book away, and she said, "You may not read this book." Basically, I think that's when I was about ten, and when I was about twelve, I started menstruating. It was horrible. The worst experience ever; my mother put me through hell.

LD: Did you first know what was happening to you when you started bleeding? Were you freaked?

ABBY: Yeah, and I didn't know what it was. And I went to my mother, and she said, "OK, you wanted to know what your period is; that's what it is. Now go and wash your panties out with bleach." [Laughs.] And this is gonna happen once a month, and you'll use these, and she handed me a pad. You know, it's like, "Hello?" But I didn't know to question anything. I figured, OK, this is what I'm gonna do and that's it.

Her mother's matter-of fact manner, and her immediately sending Abby to wash her panties, affirmed Abby's comments elsewhere in this chapter that her mother was emotionally distant from her. I heard from many of the women I interviewed how shocked and scared they became when they had their first menstrual period. None of their mothers had prepared them, nor did they react to the news with any information about what was happening in their daughters' bodies. Luckily, Abby had already discovered a place where she could seek information about what was happening to her body: the library. Abby, Sam, Ehud, and others were excited by the new knowledge and perspectives they were learning through reading taboo books. Reading gave access to material that offered doubters tools and a language for questioning the Hasidic world. Haredi families knew the potential dangers of secular knowledge, so they forbade their children from even entering public or university libraries.

Not only was reading material tightly controlled, but so were the people with whom young Haredim could interact. Hasidim who lived in tightly encapsulated communities rarely encountered anyone—Jew or non-Jew—who was not like them. They had been raised to consider all non-Orthodox Jews as the equivalent of goyim, and interactions with goyim were completely forbidden. Nevertheless, some parents who had married into Hasidism wanted to maintain their family connections, and so brought their children to meet their nonreligious relatives.

SECULAR RELATIVES

LEAH

Everything about our cousins made us doubt our brainwashing.

Leah, who had grown up in a Hasidic family, described meeting her Jewish, albeit secular, cousins, who seemed to lead fabulous, exciting lives.

> LEAH: On my mother's side we had these cousins who lived in the big world, and that was really interesting to us. Their whole sensibility was different, and it helped me to see they were living with sin but without dying or being punished. They seemed to be doing all this stuff, and there was no sign of illness or death. We were trying to understand how their lack of punishment fit in with what we had been taught, and all we could come up with was the idea that maybe it doesn't happen immediately.... But here were these fabulous cousins who were living this life and I don't know... they're just living these dream little lives and seem to have more interesting toys and more interesting candy than we did. And so everything about them made us doubt our brainwashing.

As we talked, I could hear in her tone how much she had envied these cousins when she met them and had gotten a glimpse of their lives. Her occasional get-togethers with them led her to question the veracity of all she had been taught. As a Hasidic girl, she was supposed to shun all goyim. But Leah was attracted to these cousins and their lives. Their families had more money than Leah's; they went skiing, took vacations in exotic places without kosher restaurants, experimented with drugs, and had boyfriends or girlfriends. Her visits with these cousins made Leah aware of the deep contradictions between what she had been taught and what she observed of her cousins' lives. Here were these relatives who did not follow any of the laws, yet there was no evidence that God was punishing them. Seeing these cousins

39

exposed Leah and her siblings to a vision of other ways of being in the world. Her relatives' freedom from the constraints of following the commandments and the exciting, enviable lives they led opened another tear in the sacred canopy sheltering Hasidim and protecting their way of life.

RUTIE

My non-frum (not Orthodox) cousins really made an impression on me.

Rutie, a tenured professor of literature and culture at a small college in the Northeast, grew up in a large Hasidic community in Los Angeles. Like Leah, Rutie spoke of secular cousins who had an influence on her.

> LD: Tell me about the first time you thought, "I want out." Under what circumstances did that happen? How old were you? And what was the process?
>
> RUTIE: Right. We had cousins that came to my house, non-frum cousins.... My non-frum cousins really made an impression on me. I distinctly, and I must have been six, maybe seven, I distinctly remember looking at them, and longing, longing to be like them. And I wasn't—I couldn't imagine feeling any other way. And I think I remember my brother talking about them with some contempt. And boy, did I not feel that contempt. I mean, I realize that in the Hasidic world the way you talk about people who are not Orthodox is with contempt—period. And I don't remember feeling anything like contempt, ever. I just remember feeling envy. There were not a lot of opportunities to meet these kinds of people. I just loved the way they looked. I just loved the aesthetic. As I expressed these feelings to my mother, she was afraid I would never find a husband with these ideas.

Growing up in a family that stands out from others in the community helped the children learn to question their Hasidic lives. Several types of non-normative families were reported in my interviews.

NON-NORMATIVE FAMILIES

Leah's narrative described several experiences and situations that exposed her to the outside world, or revealed flaws in the sensibility and coherence of her Hasidic world. Not only was she exposed to secular cousins, whose free way of life she envied, but her parents differed in their levels of commitment to and attitudes toward the Hasidic way of life. The socialization of Hasidic children is more powerful when both parents share beliefs and have the same commitment to observance of all the commandments. Children prefer clear answers and are uncomfortable with ambiguity; the religious differences between their parents made them wonder if one parent was more right than the other.

LEAH

We grew up in this sort of weird kind of household.

Leah was the eldest of five children. Her father, a Hasidic World War II veteran, was intrigued with American culture. Leah sensed that he had dual loyalties: He was a thoroughly observant Hasid who was also a patriotic American. These competing dogmas created a tension in his life; Haredi enclave communities demand the full devotion of all members. They sought to exclude competing allegiances by erecting high and strong physical, ideological, and emotional boundaries between themselves and all outsiders, even other Hasidic groups. Hasidic groups are jealous guardians of their members; their first loyalty must be to God, then to the rebbe, and then to their enclave community.

Leah's mother had grown up as a secular Jew; she "married into" Hasidism. Leah said that her father's choice of a wife outside the Hasidic community was due to his fascination with the "other." True to the internalized gender norms of Leah's community, her father expected his wife to manage the children and create a Jewish atmosphere in their home. Her mother, however, knew little about creating a normative, let alone spiritually inspiring, Hasidic home life. So, he

41

thought, whatever their mom left out about *Yiddishkeit* (Jewishness), they would get at schools. Leah's description of the challenges she faced growing up in her household was vivid and powerful.

> LEAH: I think my parents didn't...my parents were the kind of people who didn't want to have children, in that they weren't really interested in children. They had us because that's what was expected, but they didn't want to talk to us. They thought we were boring. They'd say things like, "Look, you're dribbling. Could you go in the other room and..." So they always would treat us like little children who did not know what we were doing.
>
> They were overwhelmed with their own lives, so they weren't really interested in us. So we were pretty much able to sort of raise ourselves in terms of the books we'd read and the kind of philosophies we were studying because they had no interest in asking about what we were thinking. After a while my brothers and I started buying the *Village Voice*, and I mean, you know, it just expanded our universe. Some of us in that house were very different little human beings than anyone would have guessed. Our family was just so different from those of my friends: They failed at the brainwashing, introduced us to secular cousins, and allowed us to read whatever we chose. Otherwise it might have worked. I think the Hasidim normally do a good job of socializing children to fit into the community.

Continuing the theme of failed brainwashing, Leah explained that her parents, who, according to Hasidic traditions, were supposed to teach their children *Hasidus* (the Hasidic way of life) and model the ideal type of family, did not know how to do this. One way Hasidim created loving families was by celebrating *Shabbes* together, and singing all the songs. But Leah's parents did not do any of this very often, if at all, because they were always tired from fighting with one another. Leah contrasted her own nuclear family with the caring atmosphere in the home her sister has made, which made it even clearer to her what she had missed out on:

LEAH: Shabbes was kind of a wash. We didn't do a lot of *zmirot* [cele-bratory songs in honor of Shabbes]. My father was always tired and so was my mother. They were fighting. We were fighting. And so there was not that kind of love and joy that makes the brainwashing really stick.

I see the contrast between my growing up and my sister's house now. It's going to stick for her kids. The parents are going to make it work, because they do the singing and loving and the singing and the loving and the singing with the loving [Leah repeated these words several times in a singsong fashion] and the *braches* [blessings] with the loving, and you know, if you don't keep the commandments God's going to punish you [Laughing]. You know what I mean, and all the kids are worried and fearful. And it's all associated with the love of their parents...you know, it's a very good system.

Leah insightfully observed how, in the context of a loving and joyous religiously observant family, the parents would be successful in raising children who will remain in the Hasidic world. In contrast, Leah felt her parents' inability to create a family consistent with their Hasidic community's norms for family life adversely affected her own ability and desire to conform to Hasidic norms. She began to question the rebbe's and her teachers' claims that the Haredi world and its strin-gent rules led to wonderful families. Leah's family demonstrated the contradiction between the ideal and the real, which, along with other factors, led to her eventual defection from her Hasidic enclave. At the same time, she was introduced to other options through contact with her cousins.

Sarah, a woman who had grown up in the strict enclave of the Satmar Hasidim, told a tragic story of how her family was broken apart by an uncle, the husband of her mother's sister.

SARAH

From then on, I have to say, it became misery for me. Not only misery, but the questions that I've had ever since I was little grew deeper, and I became outraged—I just couldn't understand my way of life!

43

Sarah, a forty-year-old psychotherapist when we met, told me of her early biographical disruption. When she was growing up, her father had a high reputation as a scholar and teacher, and people outside the community came to study with him. His growing influence, however, became troubling to the Satmar community. Sarah told me her father had taught his children, and those who came to study with him, to question interpretations of the Scriptures. Such deep questioning was seen as dangerous in Hasidic communities.

Sarah had an uncle who was a lawyer within the *Beis Din* (Rabbinical Court). As a member of this elite group, he intervened in families' lives by removing children from parents who did not meet his standards. Sarah described him as "a very wild, wild person."

SARAH: This uncle was very jealous of my father's amazing abilities in Talmudic studies. My father was a very spiritual person and my uncle wasn't; my father was a very learned person and he wasn't. So this uncle started to be nasty and rude to my dad.

My father had a reputation as a brilliant teacher, and many young students came to study with him. He had taught his children and all who came to study with him to question interpretations of the Scriptures. His growing influence became worrisome to the Satmar community, who felt his teachings were substantially different from those of their community and that he was threatening to the rebbe's authority. My uncle from the Beis Din became involved with this issue, and he started spreading outrageous rumors about my father being a heretic. He convinced many parents to stop sending their sons to study with my dad.

And I would kind of hear little bits and pieces and I would hear my mom crying on the phone and yelling at her sister saying, "Your husband can't do that," and things like that. At one point I was standing with my dad, we were talking, and then a lot of boys came down from a bus and they started throwing like, little rocks, whatever they could find, at my dad. So, suddenly I found out more and more that my father's really not liked in this community. My uncle and his friends sought to make my father's life so miserable he would leave the community.

Although Sarah's mother tried to resist her brother-in-law's efforts to ostracize her husband, she was a passive individual (as is expected of women in Hasidic enclaves) and ultimately surrendered.

> They threatened my mother by telling her that if she chose to go with my father, she would lose her children, her community, her family, including the sister she was very close to. Further, your children won't be able to return to the Satmar school. And my mom, being who she was, didn't want to lose all that. And she chose to stay in the community. But the person who actually kicked my dad out of the house was my sister. She started screaming and yelling at him, "You're not coming back here embarrassing us." My sister's very tough and very into the community, still is. So she just didn't let him come in. And that was the end of it. We were told not to talk to him. My uncle was so involved in our lives, he was the one making the decisions. From then on I have to say it became misery for me. Not only misery, but the questions that I've had ever since I was little, became even more, and I became outraged—I just couldn't understand my way of life! But in Satmar, you don't ask, you're not supposed to know. So I basically live in a, in a world of questions, unanswered questions.

This extended quotation from Sarah's narrative reveals her strong feeling that her father's excommunication constituted a major biographical disruption in her life. The lack of answers, and the "misery" she felt as a child in a community that prides itself on its model families, ultimately led her to question whether the Satmar world was as ideal as leaders claimed. This early fissure in her world made Sarah prone, throughout the next twelve years of her life, to question the routine of embodied rituals and the community's metanarrative linking their way of life to the God who spoke to Moses, gave him the Torah, and chose the Jews to follow his commandments. The community served as the social context, the base, in which their religious practices and beliefs were routinely upheld and made to make sense. When Sarah's uncle excommunicated her father, he took away the sense of stability she had in her community. She and her immediate family were marginalized, as she was in the school she attended, where she was shunned and disregarded by her peers and teachers. Her life began to lose its sense of meaning and stability, and she began to question the Satmar way of life. Sarah's description of her family reveals how far they were from the normative model of large, happy families in the Hasidic community.

Sarah's life changed significantly when her father left the community. When Sarah's father was with the family, her life was settled and secure. She described the period when her father was at home as "unbelievable" in the positive sense of the word. When Sarah's uncle persecuted her father, it exposed a negative side of the community. I think Sarah responded to this trauma by attributing positive qualities to her father—the ability to think critically, intelligence, kindness, and a loving disposition. At the same time she associated her father with positive qualities, she described her mother as sweet but weak and indecisive and her uncle as a "wild" man who was not well educated. It is significant that Sarah depicted her father with glowing terms; she had turned him into an idealized man.

Like Leah, Sarah's experience with parents who had different commitments to the Hasidic way of life led to her confusion about the "right" way to live. She was no longer sure of her identity and religiosity. Sarah's father's open and questioning approach to interpreting the Scriptures inadvertently shaped her response to this incident. Her dad's influence on Sarah eventually led her to be unwilling or unable to conform to the community's expectations. For Sarah, as well as almost all others who spoke with me for this study, the destabilization of identity experienced by growing up in a non-normative family continued to gnaw at them for a long time.

Sarah's father's early influence in her life, and the way in which he left the family, may have "ruined" her for a life in Satmar Hasidism. From then on she lived in a world of "unanswered questions." Her father's excommunication was, for Sarah, a devastating emotional loss that the Hasidic world would be unable to heal. Sarah's sacred canopy had begun to tear, and its tangible effects were experienced on her body as stress, anxiety, depression,[1] and anorexia, physical marks that would remain with her throughout her process of defection.

SHLOMO

The hardest part was I had to say kaddish for my father as
a five-year-old. I just stood out in the crowd.

Like Sarah, Shlomo grew up without a father. When he was five, his father died, and his mother struggled to take care of all eleven children on her own. His father's death was a major biographical disruption that led to him feeling different from others and isolated. He was one of very few young boys saying *Kaddish* (the prayer for the dead) in synagogue, and he disliked the public nature of this religious obligation (the prayer can only be said in a public prayer service). His family kept silent about his late dad, and they never discussed the impact of his loss on his mother or his siblings.

> SHLOMO: When I was about five or five and a half years old, my father passed away. And I can't say it was hard on me because I was only five years old. So when you're five, and one of your parents dies, it's not a big deal.... You know, you're not thinking that much. For some reason, somehow I did not like going to *heder* [school], because— I mean I loved the company, I loved everything, but I didn't grow up liking learning. I didn't like the whole part of the studying too much. I didn't think it was important.

Although Shlomo stated that his father's death did not have a significant emotional impact on him, he and his ten siblings comprised a non-normative family afterward. Shlomo felt responsible for supporting his family and did not want to go to school. As he said, "For me it was different because I didn't have my father, so I had to make money on my own."

47

With his father gone, Shlomo did not have a role model or a close mentor to help him develop his skills as a scholar, the most highly valued role for men in his community. He found himself unable and unwilling to conform to the age-appropriate role—student—assigned to him by his community. He clearly told me that: "I didn't like the whole part of the studying too much." He was marginalized for being a weak student. The other students ostracized him. Shlomo told me how painful it was to be the recipient of his peers' taunts. As a doubly marginalized child—his father's death creating a single-parent family, and his own lack of scholarly interest—Shlomo began to question the Satmar way of life at a young age.

Shlomo was the only respondent who spoke of a desire to earn money as a child. His father's death isolated him from his peers: He was more concerned about helping to support his mom than with studying at school. He made it clear that his mother was so busy trying to raise eleven children with meager funds that she could not offer Shlomo the kind of positive feedback that might have helped him develop a strong and secure sense of self. He felt unsure of his place in the community and his life aspirations. He spoke of the difficulty of his circumstances as he grew up:

> SHLOMO: The hardest part of all of it was I had to say Kaddish for my father. As a five-year-old, I stood out in the crowd every time I stood up to say this prayer for the dead. I'm a shy guy, so for the first year immediately after his death, I said Kaddish three times a day and then, even though I didn't like the idea of doing this, I decided I would observe *yahrtzeit* (the anniversary of a person's death) by going to shul and saying kaddish every year. I didn't like the idea of doing this, but I decided for my father, I gotta do it once a year, so I did it.

Shlomo felt uncomfortable when he said Kaddish. He felt all eyes upon him. Since the prayer is said after the death of a parent, adults primarily partook in this commemorative ritual. When the rite is performed by a child, however, it evokes sympathy among all others in the congregation, attention Shlomo did not want.

Leah, Abby, and Shlomo all grew up in families that were marginalized by others in the community, and their childhoods were tainted by the stigma of difference. Leah's parents did not match each other religiously, and Shlomo was raised in a single-parent family, a difficult situation. Other respondents told equally unhappy stories of growing up in households where community norms for family were not met: homes in which abuse took place.

ABUSE

The hardest stories to hear were those of adults who had grown up in families that were abusive—physically, sexually, or emotionally. Of all the stories about non-normative families, these accounts reflected the most serious damage that can be inflicted on children, especially in a tightly enclosed community where members bond together to avoid outside threats. A recent *New York Times* article described how, when sexual abuse was reported in a Hasidic community, nearly all members condemned the family reporting the abuse.[2] The abuse revealed the hypocrisy of Hasidic parents' claims to be living pious and moral lives.[3]

Adina

I have a loss of memory, I think, from the abuse.

Adina was in her forties when we met. A lesbian, she struggled growing up with an identity no one could embrace—not even her. She sensed that her mother "resented her," which was confirmed when her mother "admitted to hating [her] several times." She was deeply depressed, which is not surprising. Adina carries remnants of this trauma in her body and her mind. During heated arguments, her mother agreed with Adina's sentiment that she should kill herself. Thus Adina grew up feeling she "did not have a place anywhere," at home or in school. I myself felt deep pain as I spoke with Adina; her depression was palpable. Adina described feeling "very isolated and closed off" as a child. Her parents' relationship was troubled, and there was no peace at home.

ADINA: I never knew that parents hugged. I never knew that parents touched each other. I never knew from anything. My mother never even passed anything to my father in our [the kids'] presence.

Adina, like so many of my respondents, knew very little about her body, because Haredim never discuss sexuality until the last possible moment—for instance, before a young woman or man gets married. One woman told me that instead of teaching her to say vagina, her mother simply said, "down there." This is not unusual in the Hasidic world, given how most adults understand the laws guiding modesty. When a woman is menstruating, and for seven days thereafter, she and her husband are forbidden to touch each other; the Ultra-Orthodox follow this law so stringently that a woman will not, for instance, hand her husband a salt shaker, lest they accidentally brush hands. It would be considered immodest for children to know when their mother had her period, which they would eventually figure out if they saw their mother showing affection to their father for two weeks of the month, and then not touching him at all for the other two. Adina's parents, like most Ultra-Orthodox, avoided this problem by never touching in public.

Although Adina lacked knowledge about her body and sexuality, her innocence was destroyed by a shattering instance of sexual abuse by her uncle:

ADINA: When I was young I had several experiences of sexual abuse on the part of an uncle. It was really weird. I have a lot of loss of memory; I think because of the abuse. My parents were also very much believers in the spare-the-rod-spoil-the-child mentality. And they did not hesitate to beat the crap out of us. I was the one that got the brunt of it because I was the eldest, and I was expected to be the example for my brothers and sisters. So I suffered quite a bit. The fact that I am not crazy at this point in my life is a complete surprise to me. I don't know how I turned out the way I did. I can only praise and thank myself.

LD: Was this uncle Hasidic?

ADINA: Yes. But not only Hasidic—this is someone who is supposed to be
100 percent *Yorei Shamayim* [pious], observant of everything, because
he's a sofer—a scribe. He writes *Sifrei Torah* [the Torah scrolls]. So he's
supposed to be a holy man. He was a holy man and here he was abus-
ing young children.

Adina was particularly incensed by the hypocrisy of her uncle's actions.
He was a "holy man" with a reputation for being pious and trustworthy,
but he treated his young niece in a way that contradicted his stature in
the community. When she was in her late teens and early twenties, she
went through a period during which she felt "majorly suicidal," on account of her unrelentingly difficult childhood in which she experienced
physical and sexual abuse.

She told me that after she moved out of her family's home, she called
her mother and told her about her uncle's actions. Her mother shocked
Adina when she made it clear that she had known about the abuse.

ADINA: I called my mother and said, "You know what, I'm twenty-one
now, and I'm just realizing that I never told you about this, but when
I was very young, so and so molested me." And she said, "Oh, your
sister told me he did that to her too." I was like shocked, and my
mouth fell open, and I was like, "Well, if you knew this happened,
why didn't you tell me to be careful of him. Why didn't you tell me to
stay away from him? Why did you not keep me away from him? You
let me go to his house. You let me be abused time and time and time
again." And her only response was, "Well, I figured you'd get over it."

Her mother's failure to intervene is not uncommon in situations of
child abuse, but Adina's knowledge that her mother did not protect
her was devastating. This abuse was a major biographical disruption
for her, and she, like other interviewees who had been abused, was left
with a damaged, if not shattered, sense of self. She felt dirty, guilty, and
ashamed and could find no place for herself in her community. The
abuse left permanent scars. That her uncle was so religious—outwardly
so pious, so trustworthy—only added to the trauma. Adina ran away

from home in her late teenage years to try to sort things out. She lived with a female acquaintance for a while but was eventually summoned home by her parents—who needed her presence to maintain appearances—and, also, by the very uncle who had abused her.

Being raped as a child made Adina acutely and horribly aware of her extreme vulnerability as a girl. Sexual abuse is one of the most underreported crimes. In a community where girls are not taught anything about their bodies, and are not even given a name for their vaginas, sexual abuse was not only utterly devastating but mystifying and confusing as well. Adina had no understanding of affection, let alone sexuality.

Adina told me she has never gotten over the abuse, hypocrisy, and lack of love in her childhood. It opened the door wide for her to question whether Hasidism was actually a moral approach to religion because she felt that people who are pious would never abuse their children. As a child she felt terribly confused, but over time the confusion waned. She came to see Hasidic life as deeply flawed and intensely hypocritical. She was brought up to believe her group was special and had been chosen by God to follow his commandments. The Satmar, who are known to be one of the most stringent of the Hasidic groups, protected members' religious identities by building protective boundaries—ideological, social, and physical—around their communities. What Adina had not known until she was raped was that the community's shelter sometimes failed to safeguard those inside from each other. She began to consider leaving the enclave; she could not remain in a group that tolerated acts of impiety and immorality by adults against children.

ABBY

There is no type of treatment to help you. No one in the community wants to hear whether you were neglected or beaten. And therapy is a stigma which will automatically scar you for life.

Abby's family was different from others in her community in several ways. Her parents were not equally committed to the strict Ultra-Orthodoxy of others in their enclave. Her mother was somewhat less exacting in her ritual performance than the other women in her community. Abby felt her mother's self-presentation was different from the other women—she did not wear the appropriate garb, such as the requisite heavy black stockings—led other mothers to keep their daughters away from Abby.

Even worse, I imagine, than her social isolation was the abuse she endured at home. She never mentioned the source of the abuse or provided much detail about it, but she spoke of it several times in our conversation.

> ABBY: In addition to everything, I have to also say that I come from an abusive background. My family, the way I grew up was quite abusive. And when I—
>
> LD: Could you elaborate what you mean by that?
>
> ABBY: It was severely abusive emotionally, physically, verbally. You know, a lot, a lot.

Abby told me she would try to run away from home, to get away from the constant abuse, but where could a young Hasidic girl go? She became the prankster in her class and eventually was dismissed from school. Her parents sent her to Israel to study and made clear they did not want her home during breaks, making her feel isolated at home and abroad. Her parents' refusal to let her come home during breaks made her feel even more alone.

> ABBY: We had break three times a year, and a lot of the girls would go home, but my parents didn't want me to come home. And there was one particular break, when I really wanted to go home, I don't know if I was missing home, or all the girls were going home, or I felt like I wanted to be normal. It was heartbreaking to know that I didn't have a home, but on the other hand, I kind of understood it. I never had a place in my home because of the abuse that was going on there.

When you come from a broken, dysfunctional, and unhealthy family, you always question yourself as a child because you trust your parents and you trust other people around you, so you are always doubting yourself. Am I the crazy one, or are my parents crazy? You don't even know what normal is because you haven't been exposed to other families.

Abby's abuse as a child negatively impacted her and had a lasting effect on her sense of self and her perceptions of the world around her. When I asked her whether therapy was an option, she told me it was stigmatized in her Hasidic community: "Therapy's a stigma. Just to tell anybody what's happening, whether you're neglected or beaten or whatever the case is. It's automatically going to scar you for life."

The defectors who spoke of abusive families told me they still struggle with a lack of self-confidence. That their parents showed them anger and contempt instead of love left them with long-lasting insecurities. The few who sought support from other adults in the community were turned away, their concerns trivialized. For example, Abby told me when she sought support from some of her teachers at school, they refused to listen. Abby's teachers explicitly told her they did not want to hear about her abuse. They denied her depiction of what went on in her household and claimed such behavior never happened in their community. Sadly, they conveyed to Abby they did not believe her, shattering any hopes she had for finding support and understanding. Her teachers and rabbi denied that abuse happens in their Hasidic community. But—God forbid—if it ever did, Abby should keep her mouth shut and not tell anyone. If she spoke out, she would be defamed, making it difficult for her to find an appropriate marriage partner.

HADAS

I used to read books in the dark because I wasn't allowed to sit in the living room. I wasn't even allowed to sit anywhere in my house.

Hadas was young, twenty-three years of age, when we met. Like Adina, she, too, described an abusive family, although the abuse was verbal and physical but not sexual. In response to my customary first question, "How did you come to leave Orthodoxy?," she immediately spoke of her mother's disdain for her. She described her mother as cold, angry, and abusive.

Her mother's poor treatment of her set her family apart from the Hasidic ideal. Her father was warm and loving toward her, but he deferred to his wife. Hadas vividly illustrated that abuse is not only devastating for a child, but it also creates a non-normative family that is shunned by the community. Hadas tearfully told me there was nowhere she could go and feel accepted and welcomed.

> HADAS: So my mother—she has lots of inferior feelings. She feels bad about herself. She doesn't like herself. She doesn't like anything that has to do with herself. She doesn't say that, but she broadcasts it very strongly. That's the feeling you get from her without her even saying anything. She's an irritable woman. She has complaints about everything. My father, like a great man, stood through it; he suffered through it. Ten months after my parents married, their first son was born, and she was ecstatic that she had a son. And then, afterward, she had a daughter, me, although she had been sure that she'd have another son, and so she was furious.

Hadas told me that her mother had preferred her own father over her mother. Since her father disliked girls, his daughter, Hadas's mother, came to identify with her oppressor.

> HADAS: She really liked her father. Even today, she still loves him and, for some reason, feels very connected to him. And her father didn't like girls; he thought girls were a bad thing. So I can imagine her thinking, "If my father doesn't like girls, and he knows what he's talking about, then girls are not a good thing, and if I have a daughter..."
>
> I have an aunt who is in very close contact with us, and she too remembers that my mother didn't ever touch me affectionately, that she wouldn't change my diapers, that she really was cold to me. Today I understand where it came from, although I cannot forgive her. It's something that had to do with her past. She didn't understand that

there was any other way to be around girls. It seemed to her that was how you had to behave.

My father, on the other hand, was really affectionate toward me; he hugged me, loved and protected me. His fondness for me annoyed my mother even more. She would throw me at him coldly and say, "She's your daughter, take her, and take care of her." Over time her anger grew, and she would say to him: "She's your mistress; she's your second wife." It was so obvious she was jealous that my father showered affection on me.

I tried to understand what was going on, and I thought, perhaps she feels my father's attention to me meant less for her, and she worried if his great affection signaled he was engaging with me in an inappropriate way. At least, that is how I understood it when she said to him: "A father should regard his daughter, not love her like that, not hug her and love her. You're doing something improper."

My father told me this story about when I was very young, I think under age five. My parents had taken me to the family doctor for a checkup. And the doctor said to my mother, "You don't like this girl." And she got really angry and said, "You're talking nonsense." When we left she remarked that she was an idiot doctor who didn't know what she's talking about. And my father was smiling because his perceptions had been affirmed; it was obvious to people from the outside how she really didn't like me. Because of this I had a terrible childhood, all in all. At home, I was always hidden in a corner and not moving all day. It's like the most typical description of abused children.

Although there were six children in her family, three boys and three girls, only Hadas was singled out for abuse by her mother. I asked why, if her mother did not like girls, her sisters did not receive the same treatment. She replied that it was because she was the eldest daughter, and so all her mother's hang-ups about girls were directed at her. Everyone else could see it, but her mother would never acknowledge it. She abused Hadas brutally, although she never gave any of Hadas's siblings more than an occasional slap.

When we spoke, Hadas was a young adult and was able to clearly define her mother's behavior as abusive and pathological. When she was a child, however, she simply blamed herself and turned her anger inward, eventually becoming seriously depressed, a common reaction among abused respondents.

The lack of love Hadas described was reminiscent of Leah's narrative about the absence of love in her childhood household. A critical difference, however, was that Hadas's mother was abusive and brutal; whereas Leah grew up with healthy self-confidence, Hadas had none. Her despair led her to question her community's way of life. If her neighbors and the rabbis could shut their eyes to abuse of vulnerable children, they were not as moral and pious as they claimed. These insights made her question the value of subordinating her individual will to the community's collective demands. Before she was even twelve years old, these experiences led her to develop a critical way of thinking about the world, and she began violating the commandments.

FEMINIST CRITIQUE

ADINA

I wanted to sing, but men are not allowed to hear a woman singing, lest they become sexually aroused.

Adina's abuse, and her awareness that her parents valued her brother's education more than hers, confirmed her sense of the "second-class" status of girls and women in the Hasidic world. She expressed deep anger about the gender inequalities she experienced in her own life. Her early abuse opened her eyes to women's vulnerability. Further, the lesser respect for of her education in contrast to her brothers' made it painfully obvious that there were other major disadvantages to being a girl in the Haredi world. For example, although she believed she was talented musically, her artistic interests and talents were never cultivated at home, or at school:

ADINA: I had to beg to take piano lessons. And then I realized what I really wanted to do is sing, but I was not allowed to sing—men are not allowed to hear a woman singing lest they become sexually aroused. So I kind of stuck with the piano, and I couldn't even express to my parents how unhappy I was. It was pretty horrible when I look back at it, because I know I had so much potential. And they never, ever, encouraged me.

Adina's anger was directed at both parents. They had failed to offer her any encouragement and, even worse, failed to prevent her abuse. As Adina told me, the community was not interested in supporting girls with education or arts training, because it was seen as a waste. Girls were supposed to spend their youth preparing to raise the children that God would bless them with when they were older.

RUTIE

I am still missing part of my education.

Rutie's account of her growing unhappiness as she discovered gender inequality resembled other women's. For example, both Adina and Rutie sensed at a young age that, despite their considerable intellectual abilities, their learning and scholarly development was not encouraged, as their brothers' had been. Rutie became further aware of women's second-class status when she reached the age of seven or eight and was told she could no longer sit in the men's section of the synagogue. Instead, she was banished to the women's section, which was entirely curtained off from the men's, which is where the singing, chanting, and other interesting activities took place.

RUTIE: Our Satmar shul [synagogue] had two separate rooms with heavy curtains between them; there was a small hole within them so the women could hear. If you weren't quite close to it, you wouldn't see what was going on. Davening [praying] was not a big deal for women

or girls. I mean they weren't even expected to come, which was somewhat of a relief. Although as a young girl I sat on my father's knee in
the men's section, he didn't try to teach me anything. So I still don't
know how to daven because I just had no exposure to it. I am missing
part of my Jewish education. At that level of Ultra-Orthodoxy there
wasn't even any attempt to educate the women about what's going on
in the *siddur* [prayer book]. And there was also this kind of weird
alienation—the rabbi would actually preach hellfire and damnation
and would just shriek at us. So my Jewish education got drastically
cut off at that age, at least from the synagogue perspective. It still gets
me so mad; Jews claim to believe in education, but it is really only the
boys they care about.

Rutie sensed her mother was depressed while she was raising her children, something others, including Leah, described as well. These women
developed a feminist critique of the Haredi world by observing and dis-
tancing themselves from their mothers' roles. At a young age they saw
clearly that Hasidic women were much less valued in their communities,
and they decided they wanted no part of that life. Both Rutie and Leah
clearly felt that their mother's lives were not satisfying, which led them
to question their place in the Hasidic world where they saw no satisfying options for what they might become as adult women.

That Rutie's mother's depression eased after she left the home to
work reminds me of Betty Friedan's "problem that had no name," the
unhappiness of educated women who were constrained by homebound
roles (1963). It sounded as if her mother, a bright woman, felt trapped,
like the women Friedan interviewed.

Depression was frequently mentioned by respondents even though
I had not thought to include a question about it in my original guide.
Informants' spontaneous allusions to and stories about depression—
either in their mothers' lives or in their own—made it clear that it played
an important role in their desire to exit the community. If their mothers were depressed, respondents often internalized those feelings and
began to wonder if Haredi strictures for family life left women feeling

powerless and without agency, important features of clinical depression. Women were not the only ones who talked about depression. Certainly abuse contributed to depression, but so did the psychological impact of growing up in a marginal, non-normative family. Many of the men spoke of feeling intensely depressed during their stage of intense questioning. Some spoke of feeling trapped within the confines of their religious worlds, and perhaps some felt guilty about feeling trapped. Their frustration and anger were turned inward; by not externalizing the sources of these feelings, they developed an internal, painful response: depression.

Leah believed her mother was unaware of her depression, just as she was oblivious to women's second-place status in Orthodoxy. Leah was outspoken and lucid in her devastating criticism of patriarchal domination in Hasidic life, the topic with which she began our conversation.

LEAH

The way they treat women is wrong, sinful.

LEAH: I need to let you know I have not told you my actual name because I come from a pretty prominent family, and they're still in the community, and as outspoken and bold as I have been [laughing], I never want to burn bridges, nor do I want to hurt them in any way, but I know that they are wrong. I guess it will become obvious, so I might as well start with my story from a very female feminist point of view, and I think that the way they treat women is wrong, is sinful, and at some point they will wake up and realize it, and I hope women flee from their midst. You know, clearly nobody's listening. I have a sister who doesn't listen to me, so...who has five children and is twenty-whatever...

Note that Leah used the word sinful to describe the immorality of Haredi patriarchy. Although Leah had been gone from her Hasidic enclave for more than twenty years, the language of the community in which she was raised—an important element of her cultural tool kit—sometimes emerged in our conversations. Language is learned in a social and cultural context; even years after they had defected, Leah and other respondents continued to sprinkle their vocabulary with language reflecting the moral views of their former Haredi community. The continuing influence of their early socialization came out not only in their speech but also in their description of other behaviors such as suddenly feeling momentarily guilty about not making a *bracha* (blessing) or not wearing a yarmulke.

LD: Can you give some concrete examples of what it was that made you aware of the unequal treatment of girls and women in your Hasidic community?

LEAH: The inequality between me and my brothers. What happened was that as a girl I was really into going to the little *shtieblach* [small intimate synagogues] with my father, and I really loved it there. It was fun. Not that I prayed or anything. I didn't. It was just about running around, and the men would give the kids candy. I don't remember any moment of my standing still, but the women were sort of behind some heavy curtain, like in another room and whatever. I would never want to be in there with them. I went with the men. But at some point when I was seven or eight my parents made clear I could not go to the *shtiebls* with my dad anymore. From that time it became clearer and more obvious that I had no place within the Orthodox religious world; I was unable to publicly express my religion. I understood that all public religious rituals and honors were exclusively the province of men and there would never be any participatory religion for me. It was over, basically.

So from then on, I had to stay in the house with my mother, who would make me set the table or something or just do kind of stuff in the house, and it was boring and stupid. They were mindless chores. I was at a loss as to who I could be. Well, let's see. I'm a girl, but I don't want to be in a woman's role; I did not want to be like my mother. So I was sort of lost at the time, and I couldn't figure out who I could be. There was nobody else like me so by that time I knew that I wasn't going to remain in their world.

Leah's depiction of her synagogue experience was nearly identical to Rutie's. Her choice of the words *boring* and *stupid* to describe being home with her mother on *Shabbes* revealed her disdain for the limited roles of Hasidic women, who, in her view, did mindless chores in the house all day. I identified with Leah's comments that she did not want to be like her mother. My mother, like hers, worked in the home, and by the time I was six years old I understood my mother's role was clearly secondary to my father's, at which point I announced my desire to become a medical doctor, a highly valued profession in my family.

> LD: As you began to become so critical of the life you were rejecting, were you afraid God might punish you?
>
> LEAH: Yeah, at the time I was very much filled with fear. If I sinned before I was twelve—the age at which Jewish girls are defined as adults, meaning, they become responsible for their own deeds and sins, according to Jewish tradition—my parents would be punished.
>
> LD: So what sorts of sins did you feel you were committing?
>
> LEAH: Well, everything to do with my mother, because we didn't get along because I knew she felt that the boys [her brothers] were more important, and she was more proud of them. I don't blame her personally, I mean, she just doesn't know how screwed she's been by society, and it's not a reality that she will ever be able to understand. Gender inequality in her world is so deeply embedded that she can't even see it.

Since her mother was unable to teach her and her siblings at home, I asked whether schools played a part in their Haredi education. She told me that they all went to gender-segregated schools. Her brothers had been sent to Hasidic schools, where they were required to attend every day, including Sundays; the only exception was for *Shabbes*. On Fridays they were let out early for *Shabbes*, but every other day they were at school from 6 a.m. till 10 p.m. Leah laughingly said that on the surface it appeared girls were treated better because they had Sundays off and did not have to wake up to start prayer services at 6 a.m. She described the girls' education as "Judaism light." They were taught to study the Bible but were not allowed to study the Talmud, the text boys and men at *Yeshives* pored over day and night. The difference in the rigor of boys' and girls' education was rooted, in part, from the section in the Talmud in which "Rabbi Eliezer" formulated his position as follows: "Anyone who teaches his daughter Torah [it is as if] he is teaching her *tiflut*."[4] No one today knows the precise meaning of this word. The rabbis in the Talmud similarly were not sure. One suggested it referred to immorality, and another translated it as triviality, implying that women's minds were not sharp enough for deep study.

Hasidic schools had quite different goals for girls and boys: Boys were educated to become learned scholars, whereas the girls' teachers emphasized stories from the Hebrew Bible as well as laws and other information they would need when they became wives and mothers in charge of the religiosity of their households. Leah told me she resented that her school offered girls less rigorous training in textual study than her brothers had.

I made it clear to Leah that I understood and completely empathized with her feminist anger against Orthodoxy. We both had been about eight years of age when we realized we would eventually leave the religious communities in which we were raised. I, too, knew I would be a rebel. I asked her whether any of her other siblings had rebelled.

LEAH: When I look at my brothers, they rebelled in their own way and blamed it on their wives, and continue to remain in the community. The pattern for them was similar to that of my mother and father, with the wife being the more secular one. My brothers who kept their indiscretions hidden thought I was bad because I was sort of "out" and let my parents know how much I hated being a Hasidic woman. I was always out, and my brothers were always closeted about it. I was always the person who just sort of said it or did it and got punished or something. And they were always protecting my father and protecting the family and protecting everything. Whereas I figured, you know, I'm already an outsider being female, so [laughing]... anything I was going to do would be wrong anyway.

Leah's choice of the words *out* and *closeted* suggests she might have been aware of the similarities between leaving Orthodoxy and the processes through which gays, lesbians, and bisexual and transgendered people emerge from their closets and construct new identities. Both exiting processes involve shedding the bodily practices and comportment that created and signified their membership in their former worlds and learning new physical routines as they find communities in which they begin to establish new identities. It was not only the non-normative nature of her family that raised questions for Leah; she, like my other informants, described a variety of experiences in her childhood that exposed her to alternative views, leading her to question the absolutist norms with which she had been raised.

CHAPTER THREE

FIRST TRANSGRESSIONS

I thought I had committed bloody murder.

Nearly all the respondents described the first time they deliberately broke a religious commandment as a moment of great drama and significance. When young Hasidim first saw a tear through what they had previously experienced as a whole and interwoven system of commandments from God, many were tempted to break one of these laws, just to see what would happen. In their accounts, respondents linked their urge to rebel to the same circumstances that had revealed a tear in the sacred canopy of their Hasidic community. They had sought answers to their weighty questions, hoping they would be able to reconcile their feelings and new ideas with the metanarrative and practices of their enclaves. Not finding satisfactory answers, they became curious to see what would result if they broke a commandment.

These initial rebellious acts were experimental; my conversation partners tested the system of laws and ritual practices through various forms of embodied resistance. They wondered whether and how God might punish them, which they had been taught would be the inevitable consequence of violating commandments. When they first began questioning, they were not yet old enough, nor did they have the resources, to leave their communities. By starting with just one transgression, they were able to maintain their place in their community even as they were testing its validity. All the sins respondents cited as their first were acts of bodily resistance to one or more commandments.

In Orthodox Jewish life, offenses against the commandments are typically those that violate prescribed bodily practices. Belief in God is not explicitly commanded in the Hebrew Scriptures. The first of the Ten Commandments, "I am the Lord your God, who brought you out of the land of Egypt, from the house of slavery" (Exodus 20:2), does not require belief. Instead, according to the ancient Near Eastern scholar Theodore Gaster, it introduces YHWY, the giver of the commandments, and provides a basis for why the Israelites should follow his laws. Similarly, King Hammurabi, who ruled in Babylon during approximately the same time period—the second millennium BCE—began his code of law with a very similar introductory statement: "Hammurabi, the prince, called of *Bel* am I...enriching Nippur and Dur-ilu beyond compare,...who conquered the four quarters of the world."

Rabbi Buchwald, whom I quoted in *Tradition in a Rootless World*, made a similar argument concerning the role of faith and ritual practice: "It's really a meaningful religion irrespective of whether you believe in God or not. The *mitzvahs* [commandments] make sense even if you could prove black and white there is no God. This is just a meaningful way of life" (1991, 142). A Lubavitcher Hasidic rabbi quoted in this same book similarly told the women he was teaching: "Just do it!!! Don't worry about belief; just do what you are supposed to and belief will follow."

As my respondents thought about violating a commandment, they sought to do so in a "private" place, meaning outside the boundaries of their enclave, where no one in their community could see them and report their transgressive behavior. Many of the places in which these acts of resistance were first committed are actually "public," such as restaurants, dance clubs, and city streets. From the point of view of the speaker, however, they were considered "private" because they were definitely not places where they would be observed by anyone else in their religious group. In order to explicate this notion of private and public, I draw on Erving Goffman's terminology of *backstage* and *frontstage* performances: "A back region or backstage may be defined as a place, *relative to a given performance*, where the impression fostered by the [frontstage] performance is knowingly contradicted" (1959, 112; emphasis mine). First transgressions take place backstage, beyond the community's gaze, so that the transgressors can maintain their frontstage performances without being accused of deviance or risking their reputation. For my respondents, violating the commandments and finding that they were not immediately punished by God empowered them to repeat the transgression, or perhaps try a new one.

In our conversations, many of the respondents sounded almost proud when they recalled these first rebellious acts, such as eating treyf, desecrating the Sabbath by smoking or turning lights on or off (use of electricity is forbidden on the Sabbath), or entering taboo spaces where they might be exposed to licentious acts or forbidden knowledge. Some sounded amused by their particular choice of rules to break, such as those young women who spoke of violating the proscriptions against premarital contact between young women and men by deliberately touching, generally more than once, someone of the opposite gender. Other stories detailed how, when, and where they disobeyed Hasidic laws regarding demeanor, comportment, modesty, and dress, by privately experimenting with altering their appearance.

In describing their first transgression, many respondents described acts of bodily resistance to one particular type of law, such as forbidden interaction between the sexes prior to marriage, whereas others broke several commandments at once, such as when a man entered a dance hall (a forbidden place) and, in order to fit in, violated the law that he must display his peyos by moving them behind his ears. These laws ensuring members' conformity can be organized into several types: Those that govern gendered and sexual behaviors, diet, dress, and other aspects of physical comportment, as well as those limiting members' exposure to places, ideas, and knowledge that might contradict Hasidic ideals. In analyzing defectors' first transgressions I have organized the sections of this chapter according to this typology of taboo behaviors.

BREAKING GENDER TABOOS

Some Haredi bodily regulations are distinctly gendered; they shape the social meaning of differences between male and female bodies, their physical and sexual functions, as well as their social roles. For example, the obligation to pray daily and study pertains only to men. Both men and women are commanded to follow dietary laws, stay away from ideas and people outside the physical, ideological, and social boundaries of the enclave, and follow the regulations forbidding interaction between women and men prior to marriage. Men as well as women are commanded to obey their respective rules for dress, comportment, and demeanor. Although the obligation to follow the laws of tzniyus in its most general form—such as being humble—pertains to both women and men, there are many more specific and detailed rabbinical rules concerning the precise ways a woman should embody modesty. If a woman, "God forbid" (this is the language of the community), became pregnant, the stigma on her family would be devastating.

ABBY

My rebellious thing was talking to boys.... For me, it was an escape.

Abby's very first transgression planted the seeds of her continuous resistance to the norms of her community.

> LD: Can you remember the first time you broke the rules? Tell me what you did.
>
> ABBY: I talked to boys, and of course, you're not supposed to talk to GUYS! That's like a big no-no—did you know that? That was like a very big thing. You know, *I'm talking to guys.*

In this exchange, as in many others with my respondents, Abby was testing my knowledge of Hasidic practices, which are stricter than those of the Modern Orthodox community in which, as she knew, I had grown up. She was uncertain whether I knew how serious a breach talking to boys was, so Abby carefully explained the community's norms, although they were already familiar to me. Abby emphasized her last phrase, especially the word *GUYS*, to make sure I understood the seriousness of her transgression.

LD: At what age did you start talking to boys?

ABBY: I was nine, ten.

LD: So were you afraid when you did that? Did you feel guilty?

ABBY: I didn't feel guilty because I enjoyed talking to boys. But I was not supposed to enjoy doing anything that was forbidden. And of course, I was very afraid that my parents would find out.

LD: Right, so where would you talk to guys? Where could you have gone in the Satmar community in Williamsburg, where no one would see you engaging in these rebellious activities?

ABBY: For example, I'd go to a neighbor's house, and I would strike up a conversation with their kids. And I would start playing chess with the boys on the block and make sure that nobody else could see me. Like, we'd play chess in their rooms. For me, it was an escape. I wanted as much as I could to get out of the yelling and screaming in my parents' house. But I also liked talking with boys, and at one point I had a sort of boyfriend; we fooled around, you know.

Abby explained to me that *fooling around* meant sexual play. She, like other young Haredi women, had been socialized to instinctively and habitually avoid all transactions with boys. I asked whether at the time she was aware she was acting in forbidden ways. She concurred, saying of course she knew it was wrong, having grown up in a Satmar Hasidic community. I wondered aloud whether these taboo behaviors symbolized a more generalized resistance to being a *frum* girl. She emphatically denied it and told me those thoughts never crossed her mind at the time.

I asked whether she felt guilty about her physical contact with men, but she did not directly answer the question. Instead, in keeping with the importance of the therapeutic in U.S. culture, she offered me a retrospective and psychological rationale for her actions:

ABBY: Well, some of this I did for the wrong reasons. I was seeking attention in the wrong places. And if guys would tell me, "Oh, you're so cute," and give me attention, I thought they meant it seriously. But a lot of times I was taken advantage of sexually. I was taught all my life that my place in the community was to be a wife and mother. That is how we were brought up—that we'd get married at eighteen, and have kids and build our own homes. And before that, you protect your reputation by strictly following all the laws related to tzniyus.

When Abby was telling me she was seeking affection wherever she could find it, she connected her transgressive behavior to her parents' cruelty toward her when she was young. This abuse led to low self-esteem and a belief she was unlovable. As a teenager, she sought intimacy and closeness wherever she could find them. She knew her behavior was wrong, but her urge to commit these violations stemmed from her desperate need for all she missed as a child: attention, acceptance, and affection. I asked her whether these transgressive acts were symbolic of her desire to leave Hasidic life, to which she replied, "No, I didn't think about it. That was not even close to my mind. But if I had broken Shabbes laws, that would be much more serious. If you break Shabbes, you are no longer a Jew."

Abby's ideas about distinct levels of transgression are evident here. Although she clearly knew that she was not allowed to mingle with boys, she did not recall those violations with a deep sense of regret. Had she violated the commandments pertaining to *Shabbes*, instead, she would see it as a significantly more serious sin, representing a complete breakdown of her identity as a Jew. Abby was not alone in describing a perceived hierarchy of serious violations. Others also had an idea of which transgressions were the most serious. Although Some seemed minor to the narrator, other transgressions seemed so egregious they could shake the foundations of their identities as Jews. Nevertheless, the emphasis on praxis in Orthodox life made it surprisingly easy to violate commandments without affecting their conception of God.

> LD: And when you were rebelling, were you questioning God? What was going on in your head while you were rebelling? I understand you were growing up in a really tough situation, and you needed to escape it, but were you starting to think, question...
>
> ABBY: I did not think to question God, because I was always very afraid of him; I was scared God would punish me if I did something wrong.

I always had this fear which I hated. But despite that I would dare to do certain things. It was strange because I still wanted to obey the rules, I didn't want to burn in Hell; for me it was just a way of escaping the pain at home. I felt very stifled all the time. And my nature was to explore, to learn, to find out. It's not in me to just sit there and just, "OK, I'll do this, I'll do that," and not be able to do anything else. Anything that was a little more excitement, I was searching for that. Anything that would give me a little bit of stimulation, I was there.

But the attention from guys was negative attention. It wasn't— I mean they took advantage of me sexually, and I was very naive at that time, thinking that they really cared about me. I wasn't thinking about God at that point. I was pretty young. I was only ten years old when I started doing all these things and I was sexually taken advantage of.

I understood from Abby's adult reflections on these acts of resistance that, with the help of a therapist, she had come to see her interactions with boys as self-destructive behavior, it was behavior that suited her needs at that moment. Her choice of this particular act of resistance as her first sin was the first stage in the growing disconnect between community expectations for girls and Abby's pursuit of sexualized experiences. Although she followed Hasidic norms by getting married at eighteen, her ongoing resistance became even more obvious when she realized she was attracted to women. The strict emphasis on women's modesty made it even more tempting to break these particular gendered regulations.

Adina

And one of my games was to touch the boys.
I'd be like, ha-ha, I touched you,
I touched you! I awoke your urges.

Like Abby, Adina grew up in an abusive Satmar home; their narratives linked their transgressive behaviors with their unhappy childhood situations. They differed, however, in their approach to breaking rules about strict segregation of the sexes. Abby tried to have her interactions with boys in "private spaces," within the walls of her friends' family homes; although, she did face some degree of exposure there. In contrast, Adina blatantly violated these taboos in public, within full view of her peers. Adina and Abby did not perceive themselves as rebelling against their Haredi lives; they were not seeking to leave the community. Abby minimized the importance of these transgressions by referring to them as her little "games." Nevertheless, both chose to touch boys as their first acts of resistance, despite their knowledge of the importance of proper gendered bodily performances in maintaining the stability of the community. As Adina and I continued to talk, however, she revealed that her underlying motives were more serious than simple child's play.

> ADINA: When I began to touch boys, I was not internally debating whether to stay religious. I could not even imagine my life without Orthodoxy. But there were some rules I just did not think were right, such as the one forbidding girls and boys from touching each other. By the time I was turning five, I was required to strictly follow the rules of tzniyus, in my clothing and actions. God had decreed that part of these laws included avoiding all physical contact with men.
>
> But no one taught us why we could not touch, or what touching really meant. No one had explained to me or my friends that touch has a sexual definition. Our parents and teachers did not even let us know words such as *hugging* and *kissing*, and *sex*. We were never told precisely what was forbidden. It was just you never touch boys before you married; they did not have to explain anything else as long as we obeyed that law.
>
> As we became teenagers, they explained to us that touching boys could wake up all the evil urges that boys have. That really annoyed me because I also have evil urges, so why isn't it, like, when he touches me, it might arouse my evil urges. Why is the prohibition on me? Why do I have to guard myself not to touch him? So that irritated me.

Adina, even as a girl, could see the gender biases of her Hasidic enclave and was angered by them. She was never taught that women had sexual urges. In contrast, when boys entered puberty, their bodies betrayed them, showing obvious external signs of sexual arousal (such as nocturnal emissions), so the rabbis had to explain what was happening to them. Girls' sexuality was more inward, so their teachers and mothers did not have to teach them about their body parts and their functions, such as menstruation and sexuality. In fact, most of my female and a few male conversation partners made angry comments about the ignorance in which they were kept, such as: "How can our parents and teachers keep knowledge of our bodies away from us?"

The community regulation against the mingling of boys and girls served as a fence to prevent an even deeper violation: having sex outside of marriage. Adina highlighted the double standard regarding male and female sexuality that feminists have criticized for decades. There is an assumption that only young men, not women, have intense sexual urges. Male sexuality is like a steam engine: Once turned on, it cannot be stopped. Therefore, it was incumbent on young women to stop the train before it can even get rolling. In addition, women potentially bear visible signs and extreme physical consequences of sexual behavior; therefore women have a greater stake in reigning in men's powerful sexuality.

ADINA: Despite this absurd notion, I had always had friends that were boys. I had one friend; I grew up with him since the third grade. So, so what is the big deal? So, until I was twelve I could have this friend and no one worried about arousing his urges, and then all of the sudden in the sixth grade or you know, whatever, twelve years old, then suddenly these instincts woke up? All of this really seemed nonsensical to me. And one of my games was to touch the boys. I'd be like, ha-ha, I touched you, I touched you! I awoke your urges. And these games were not accepted as games or with a sense of humor. Instead, people asked, what's wrong with this girl? It was like, why is she trying to break the most fundamental rules? These are the community's rules; this is the way we Hasidim do things. Why can't she accept it as it is? Why does she have to ask these questions?

LD: Did you rebel intentionally? Like when you were playing these games, I'm touching you, I'm touching you, were you consciously rebelling?

ADINA: No. No. Other people from the outside, they saw it as rebellion, but I didn't see it that way really. I had a different goal. I wanted
to like, expose society. Like you know the story where the kid is crying
out that the emperor is naked. I wanted to be this kid. But it wasn't
like, with the intention of rebellion. Like that same child, he didn't
see it as a rebellion, he saw it as truth. And that's how I felt about it
then. And that's how I often still see it now. It just simply didn't seem
true to me, it didn't make sense, it didn't seem right. And this feeling
increased over the years.

Adina was trying to hide her anger, but it remains palpable in these
quotations. Adina had two interpretations of her violations. On the
one hand, she claimed her transgressions were not rebellious actions;
she did not intend to be defiant. Yet, in the same breath, she told me she
wanted to expose the Hasidic community, a bold and defiant statement.
Her analogy to the child who saw clearly and spoke the truth about
the emperor being naked highlights her desire to uncover the hypocrisies and indignities of Hasidic life: the horror of abusive parents who
were supposed to be pious and moral, or parents closing their eyes to
abuse. Her analogy suggested that she felt that these deceptions were
so obvious that no one could miss them, but, like the emperor's subjects,
members of her Hasidic enclave would not see or comment on them.
Adina thought that just as she could see the hollowness at the core of
her community, if she pointed it out, all others would see it too. But
they could not see the emptiness of their lives. The Hasidic emperor is
naked, but if members of the community could see that, their lifeworlds
would shatter, something they could not allow to happen.

Adina's desire to touch boys may also have been an expression of
her desire for physical contact that was not brutal, the only kind of
contact she was familiar with at the time. It was as if she were asking:
"If the rabbis all say that if our Satmar community follows the commandments we would produce good, moral, and happy families, then
why was I so abused and lacking in affection?" Adina wanted her community to *see*, to become aware of and take seriously the physical,
sexual, and emotional brutality within families like hers.

Both Abby and Adina spoke of willfully breaking the laws concerning the separation of the sexes by touching boys. They did so within the boundaries of their community, blurring private/public distinctions. In contrast, since men were given more degrees of freedom, it was easier for them to wander out of the enclave and reach a place that was, in terms of the eyes of the community, more private. Their greater mobility allowed them easier access to forbidden spaces. Shlomo broke the norms of gender separation by entering a taboo space—a dance club— an experience that, as he told me the story, revealed several transgressions: He entered a prohibited place, where he saw, danced with, and touched scantily dressed women.

FORBIDDEN PLACES

SHLOMO

I was never really into dancing clubs because my friends and I still had the curls and people were like starin' at us, instead of starin' at the girls dancing.

In the previous chapter we met Shlomo and learned of his difficult childhood—his father died when he was five, leaving him with his mother and ten siblings. He was a poor student and was beaten by the rabbi at the yeshiva for his poor attendance, lack of skills, and lackadaisical attitude. He was also marginalized by the other kids, who did not like or respect him. The basic biographical disruption in his life, his father's death, revealed holes in the canopy encapsulating his Satmar community in Monroe, New York, and set the stage for his later rebellion.

SHLOMO: Now I think when I was fifteen years old, I, and two or
three other guys, first went to a club, a dancing club. I was sort of uncomfortable at these clubs because we still had the curls [peyos]. And
I always hung out with a lot of my friends, but they had their curls

75

down. So I didn't like the idea of goin' to a club and people like starin' at us. Instead of starin' at the girls dancing, they were starin' at us. So whenever I went outside the village, I just put my curls over my ears. I tried to hide it. And a lot of my friends started to make fun of me like, "Oh, now you're not Jewish. I don't even see that you're Jewish because I don't see your curls." I'm like, "Listen, I'm going to try to hide it because I don't want people starin' at me instead of looking at the girls." Why, when five or six Hasidic Jews come into the bar, is everybody is starin' at us? I don't like the whole idea.

Just as Abby told me that breaking *Shabbes* was equivalent to no longer being Jewish, Shlomo's friends saw one of his transgressive behaviors—putting his peyos behind his ears so they would not be visible—as rendering him not Jewish. The physical transformation of the male body through circumcision marks a boy's entry into Judaism. Then, as he grew up he was taught the Satmars rules concerning bodily practices, which are essential to the maintenance and display of an ongoing gendered Jewish identity. From birth, Satmar children are socialized to believe that the Satmar interpretation of all the commandments is the only proper way of being a Jew. Wearing peyos is so foundational to the bodily appearance and comportment of Hasidic men that Shlomo's friends automatically assumed he could not be Jewish without his peyos.

Shlomo and his friends developed an ongoing routine of visiting clubs. What had been a first transgression developed into a habit, one that Shlomo knew was forbidden. The clubs' licentiousness was a major part of their appeal; there, these young Hasidic men saw sexually inviting women, something they would never see otherwise. Over time, as they became more comfortable in the clubs, the power of the Haredi metanarrative and its strictly controlled system of bodily routines weakened, which encouraged them to try other private experiments, even as they maintained their membership in the Satmar community.

SHLOMO: One night we went bar hoppin', and we just bumped into one bar. We were like five of us. And I think it was like Saturday night. All of a sudden this DJ, this short, blonde Polish girl, looked at us; she stared at us and she was like, "Where you guys from?" She was very friendly. So we started talking with her. She was like, "Wow, you guys are really cool, and I want to hang out with you." She was like maybe twenty-nine years old. For us, she was a little old. But she was cool; she was very cool. We got to meet the owner, and she took us around, introducing us to the bartender and showing us what was at the bar. She told us everything; she was so different from the girls in our community. So we thought, "Wow, this is really cool. This is our place. We're going to hang out here." So that Saturday night—

Oh and I think back then this song, the Macarena dance. You know the song. I think that's when it came out. It was very popular then. So we showed up at this bar, and this girl was like, "Listen, all you guys come together, and we're going to dance." And for us, their doing this Macarena dance was so strange. There were people in the bar, and all of them got up, and we all started dancing. It was just the funniest thing I've ever seen.

Shlomo's comment about the Macarena dance being "funny" signaled he thought it was odd. It certainly was radically different from the kind of dancing he knew and had grown up with. Hasidim, like many other Orthodox Jews, had their own exuberant style of circle dancing at weddings and bar mitzvah parties. Men formed one circle in which they held each other's shoulders and, it seemed, ran around in a circle—or shuffled if the group was large and there was limited space. Often the close family and friends of the celebrant(s) formed a small group that danced in the center of the circle. It was a rare treat when a young man, or an older man with stamina, entered the circle's center and performed challenging renditions of Eastern European dances such as the *tzatzkeh*, a Russian dance in which the performer squats down with arms folded and, in time with the music, kicks each leg out to the side, one after the other, until he was too exhausted to continue.

In Hasidic communities, men are not allowed to see women dance, so men and women dine and dance in separate rooms. Women form their own circle and sometimes dance highly choreographed routines they all readily follow, from the moment they hear the first bars of the song.

When I told the story of Shlomo's first coed dance to a group of colleagues, they could not fathom why doing a line dance, the Macarena, was such a big deal for Shlomo and his friends. It was such an ordinary, well-known dance. I described to them as well as I could the commandments governing all details of Haredi daily life and the absolute sacrality the community attributed to them. The separation of the sexes is fundamental to Hasidic life. The dance was not "just" a dance for my respondents. It was a transgression of a commandment that was meaningful only in the context of a tightly integrated system of embodied ritual practices that substantiates the group's metanarrative. As Mary Douglas wrote in her essay "The Abominations of Leviticus," the ancient Israelites gave holiness "a physical expression" by organizing their laws in a way that reinforced the total structure of their thought (1966). If the fundamental order of Hasidic life rested on the segregation of women and men, violating that rule was taboo; it was a profane act, taking Shlomo and his friends outside the realm of holiness and the group's sense of order.

The rituals and beliefs resembled a tightly woven garment; if you pulled one of the threads, the rest unraveled, indicating the interconnectedness of all the commandments. Each one made sense and had meaning only when it was understood as part of an integrated whole, in which all bodily rituals were equally important, despite the various hierarchies of observance described by some of my respondents. The enclave religious community and its ritual performance protected members from any experience that could lead them to question their system. Dancing with women could lead men to licentious behavior. To avoid this risk, the community thought it was wise to forbid all contact between the sexes before marriage.

Shlomo knew his dancing broke not only one law, but several. He entered a taboo place where sexually suggestive dances lured men in, including him and his friends. Shlomo was well aware he was strictly forbidden to see scantily clad women. Many Haredi men walk down the streets of their neighborhoods with their gaze averted, a hand covering the eye and side of the face that was closer to the street, in an effort to keep all temptations squarely out of sight. In all Hasidic communities, including this Satmar one, the commandment forbidding all contact between unmarried boys and girls was taken very seriously. Violation of this norm had serious repercussions for the family's standing in the community. And here was fifteen-year-old Shlomo, holding hands with a woman he had never met before, doing this strange new dance with women and men.

I asked him if he felt awkward dancing at this club, and he nodded.

SHLOMO: It was because we're not used to this. Especially like when we have female dancers and males, we were mixed, and for us it was like "Whoa, this is great!"

LD: That didn't happen when you were growing up.

SHLOMO: No, no. All of our teachers were male, and we were always wishing we had a female teacher. But that night we hung out till like one o'clock. And it was really good. This girl I met invited me to come back next weekend or even during the week. So that became our place. It was like our home away from home. And a few of my friends, we used to go there on Shabbes.

Shlomo spoke of the dance club he and his friends frequented as their special "place," which reminded me of Leah, another respondent, referring to Henrik Ibsen's *A Doll's House* as "her" book (see her narrative later in this chapter). The dance club, like the book, provided an opportunity for teenage Haredim to see and explore alternative worlds they liked better than their own. Leah's reading helped her envision another life for herself. Other defectors also described the excitement they felt when their questions and doubts were validated by reading taboo literature. Many men and some women spoke of entering forbidden spaces, such as libraries, and discovering new ideas that challenged the absolutism of their way of life.

THE PURSUIT OF FORBIDDEN KNOWLEDGE

BINYAMIN

I know that in many Hasidic communities certain
philosophy books, such as those by Kant, Hegel,
or Marx, would be taboo and forbidden, but I had this
entire treasure trove right at my fingertips!

Binyamin, an American in his late twenties when we met, had grown up as an extremely bright boy in a Lubavitcher community in upstate New York. He was raised in an uncommon type of non-normative family. His father, who was not Jewish, had left Binyamin's mother shortly after they married. It was the 1970s, and his mother went to live in a commune, where she met her second husband. After they had been living in the commune for several years, the group's leaders became followers of the Lubavitcher rebbe, bringing the group's willing community members into Lubavitcher Hasidim.

I arranged to meet Binyamin in a coffee shop next to the university where he was pursuing a master's degree in mathematics.

LD: You seem so enthusiastic about your program at school. Were you always such a great student?

BINYAMIN: I always enjoyed learning. It is just being inquisitive. Maybe part of inquisitiveness comes from not being satisfied with where you are, so you're searching and looking. And if your community is holding you back so you cannot pursue your questions on the outside, you may eventually find, somewhere within the community's confines, the data that exposes you to other ways of thinking. Let me give you an example: When I was younger, I studied at the Lubavitch men's yeshiva in Morristown, New Jersey, where I also had a part-time job in the library.

Now, in Morristown, every couple of years they had a committee of rabbis who came up from Washington to give religious legitimation and certification to the yeshiva seminary. These were not the only accreditors who inspected the school, however. A group of people from the secular high school board also showed up to judge whether the school should be accredited by their system. When I was there, it was one of those times. Now, to impress the rabbinical inspectors and to be up to par with the standards that they were looking for, they stored, out of sight, the boxes and boxes of books in English. Then, the night before the secular accreditation committee came they took out all those cartons of books that were kept out of the sight of the inspecting rabbis. They took them out of storage and filled up the bookcases, which they would again take down right after the inspectors left. As part of the library staff, I had the keys to the library.

Binyamin recalled, somewhat humorously, the hugely hypocritical and duplicitous acts of the rabbis who ran his yeshiva. Although the school needed a library of English books in order to receive its secular accreditation, its religious certification was based on the exclusive presence of religious texts. To solve this quandary, the rabbis at the Lubavitch yeshiva created, in each instance, a visible sign of compliance by rapidly switching the books, displaying either secular or religious titles, depending on who was watching. Binyamin recalled this rotation of cartons of books with some bemusement. But he also understood the implications of seeing rabbis, who were supposed to be role models, acting in a way that was hypocritical and duplicitous.

For Binyamin, viewing the rabbis' hypocrisy had two important effects. First, he continued to question, even more deeply, the legitimacy of the Lubavitcher metanarrative about the position of the Lubavitchers in God's world. Second, he turned his part-time student job at the library into an exciting opportunity to read as widely and deeply as he wanted.

BINYAMIN: So I had access to the library and suddenly I saw all these fascinating and forbidden books. I knew that in Hasidic communities certain philosophy books, such as those by Kant, would be taboo and forbidden. But since I had a key, I could access these special books even when they were in storage. So I pulled out one book, and it was a Yiddish translation of Tractatus Theologico-Politicus. I also discovered Spinoza in that library; he was as compelling to me as Kant and

Hegel. So I continued to struggle and ask the rabbis questions and they just told me I was young and would understand more when I was older.

LD: And did you find their answers satisfying?

BINYAMIN: Well, I thought I should give myself some more time to see if they were correct. When I finished the yeshiva in New Jersey, I was sent to study and teach the younger students at the Lubavitcher yeshiva in London. I thought that some of the rabbis I debated with throughout the trip would distract me from my questions and doubts. But even as I continued within the system and lived with these internal questions, I was also getting stronger and stronger in my abilities to think for myself. I found some close friends who were also beginning to express questions.

In the Lubavitch Hasidic community, even more taboo than questioning the existence of God is questioning the infallibility of the rebbe. So when I would speak about things like the existence of God or omniscience of God and all this stuff, or whether the rebbe was a mere mortal man—in the context of the development of messianic fervor centered on the rebbe—people would entertain my questions because...well, it's two things. First of all, I was thinking in an abstract, philosophical way, and secondly, whether I believed in the Hasidic teachings or not, at the bottom line, the only thing that mattered was following the commandments.

At one point, when I was sort of debating, I was speaking with my stepfather about God and why it doesn't make sense and this and that, and he said: "Binyamin. You don't get it. Judaism doesn't have to do with believing in God or not! Nowhere in the *Shulchan Aruch* [the most authoritative Jewish legal code, authored by Rabbi Joseph Karo in 1563] does it say to believe in God. It's all about doing. Judaism doesn't have to do with believing in God or not. It's a lifestyle, a way of living. And just like every lifestyle, in everything you do there's a manual. So Judaism has a manual, the Shulchan Aruch, and it tells you what to do from the moment you wake up until the moment when you sleep. And you follow this manual. Whether you believe in God or not, that isn't as important."

Binyamin had a hard time separating religious practices, which he knew he had to perform, from beliefs. He told me that the beliefs seemed to be more basic, despite his stepfather's explanation of the code of laws, which does not include any requirements for belief. He felt that if the group's metanarrative, tracing its way of life back to God and the commandments at Sinai, was not true, as he had been taught, then there was no reason to engage in any of the ritual practices. As he said, if you don't believe in God and all that, why get involved with this way of life anyway?

He told me that he was not exactly an atheist, but by the time he was seventeen, he began to become an agnostic. But his position pained him. He did not want to leave the community and was not yet fully confident in his new ideas or in his ability to actually leave the enclave. He redoubled his efforts to believe, because, as he said, he was young, and maybe he would understand it all better when he was older.

Binyamin was still struggling with these questions of belief and practice in his mid-twenties and decided to follow his own gut sensibilities. He left the advanced yeshiva where he was a student and started quietly—privately—breaking laws, such as eating nonkosher food or listening to the radio on *Shabbes*.

Although the gendered nature of education in Haredi communities made it more likely that a man would share a story of reading taboo literature in a forbidden space, many of the women were equally interested in new ideas and found them in whatever ways they could.

Leah

None of the friends I grew up with escaped like me.
They are all married and wearing wigs
in some little place somewhere.

Leah, whose feminist criticism of Orthodoxy raised her consciousness at a young age, desired to learn more about other ways of life. Luckily for her, the library was not a forbidden place; her parents allowed her to go there. Her love of books and thirst for secular knowledge brought her into a larger world than the encapsulated Hasidic one in which she lived.

> LEAH: Well, one thing that allowed us to think about the general world out there was the library. Our access to the library was the key to escape, because I was a great reader and read everything in the children's section and then everything in the adult section, which meant there was a lot of stuff that is pretty unbelievable. I mean, they had sex books.
>
> LD: And your mother didn't think to censor your reading?
>
> LEAH: No, she didn't. Remember, she was brought up more secular. My parents encouraged us to go to the library, and I simply didn't bring home those books I knew I was not allowed to read; instead, I consumed them at the library. When I was growing up, Hasidim did not see how the library could threaten their children's sheltered way of life. Now the rules are different: Haredi children are allowed to enter libraries or bookstores, except for those specializing in Judaica.[1]
>
> LD: So the library was a key point of access for you.
>
> LEAH: Right. But the funny thing is, even at my school we read Henrik Ibsen's *A Doll's House*. I remember reading it then, and I just loved that book. I was like oh my God, this is so unbelievable. And the teachers taught it simply from a literary perspective. But I would be just crazed, like oh my God. This is my book. I can't believe they assigned it! It was amazing that they just couldn't get how deeply profound the sense of women's liberation in that book was for people like me who felt so lost and alone, who saw the same things going on. Nobody took it personally there. Nobody. It was sort of *la di da*. You know, it was just a book.

Leah's unlimited access to books in the library stimulated her imagination and taught her about worlds and lives outside of the Hasidic enclave. She sought literature, like Ibsen's *A Doll's House*, that spoke of women's liberation. Reading these works gave her a language and set of ideas that deepened her criticism of the patriarchal nature of the Hasidic world. In contrast to what she had been taught, it was not God who commanded men to rule. Hasidic patriarchy was constructed by men and upheld through their social structures, institutions, culture, and daily practices. She identified with Nora, the heroine of *A Doll's House*: "It became my book." Nora's story showed her a liberating alternative to the limited women's roles in her community.

> LD: You said that your parents did not censor your reading carefully. Did your parents engage with you about what you were reading at the library?
>
> LEAH: No, they were not particularly interested. After a while, my brothers and I became bolder and started buying the *Village Voice*, and I mean, you know, it just expanded our universe. Some of us in that house were very different little human beings than anyone would have guessed. Our family was just so different from those of my friends: They failed at the brainwashing, introduced us to secular cousins, and allowed us to read whatever we chose. Otherwise it might have worked. I think the Hasidim normally do a good job of socializing children to fit into the community.

Leah's parents' relative disinterest in their children's socialization was quite unusual in the Hasidic world. Perhaps her mother's secular upbringing made her unaware of the dangerous ideas that could be found in library books, and so she encouraged all her children to go to the public library, unintentionally giving them freedom to pursue knowledge of the world outside their enclave.

BODILY VIOLATIONS: DRESS, COMPORTMENT, AND APPEARANCE

The gendered separation of women and men in Hasidic life was visible in members' clothing, demeanor, and comportment. Men were expected to wear the "uniform" of black pants with a white shirt and to maintain their beards and/or peyos as dictated by their particular community. Among the numerous religious commandments concerning dress and comportment, a major proscription for women was wearing pants. In the Hebrew Scriptures there is a commandment that men should not wear women's clothes, or vice-versa. Although pants made for women are shaped differently than men's pants, Haredi rabbis often employ a stricter prohibition than is actually in the Scriptures, so that members do not come close to violating the actual commandment.

My respondents spoke of changing their habitual modes of comportment and their public representations of "self" as a great, dramatic act of bodily resistance. Hasidic dress and demeanor were internalized from a very young age; they represented members' identities within their religious enclaves and their separation from all others. By disinscribing these ways of performing their gendered identities, and trying out secular alternatives, the exes were experimenting with a different presentation of themselves, which would ultimately lead to new identities. Another act of public embodied resistance was wearing one's hair in a style that violated community rules. Manipulating hair, such as Shlomo did by putting his peyos behind his ears at the dance club, was a way of changing public presentation of identity in different spheres. Yossi similarly changed his representation of self by wearing his hair longer than the community's standards permitted.

Yossi

Well, I felt I couldn't control anything, so at least
I could let my hair grow....In retrospect, it seems that
I put a lot of rebellion into the way I looked,
because that was about all I could do.

Yossi was a thirty-year-old medical student when we met. His story of beginning to question his frum life differed from those of my other conversation partners. Unlike them, Yossi represented himself as *always* certain that he felt no attachment to the religion of his Hasidic community. Similarly, when he began to transgress, he did not fear punishment from God or exclusion from his community. He told me that as early as the first grade he knew that he was uninterested in the Hasidic way of life, and it angered him to be forced to comply with it.

> YOSSI: I felt angry. I felt like, you know, this whole thing is being imposed on me. I don't want it. It's your [his parents' and community's] way of life, and you're really forcing me to follow it. I'm sorry that you have to live it, but don't make me live it. I had no interest in, like, not watching television on Shabbes. I wanted to do as I pleased and not with those rules that says you can't. Well, that's your problem. And you have some rule that says you've got to be up at 8:30 in the morning on Saturdays, well, that's your problem, because I don't want to be anywhere and listen...participate in this two-hour davening thing on Shabbes in the morning, because well, I simply don't like it.

Not only does this excerpt show Yossi's early desire to break out of the enclave, but it also illustrates his remarkable ability, at a young age, to experience himself as an individual apart from the community. Hasidim deemphasized individuality and instead stressed conformity to community roles and structures. Yossi managed to not fully internalize the group identity that is a goal of Hasidic socialization and recognized that he as an individual had no desire to take part in the wide variety of rituals required of him. He similarly made individual choices by rejecting the gendered socialization of boys to be Talmudic scholars. Yossi had no interest in attending a yeshiva and being compelled to study Talmud all morning, every day.

Until the eleventh grade, Yossi kept his rebellious thoughts private; he did not act out on them in public displays of embodied resistance. Despite his misgivings, Yossi continued to participate in Haredi rituals (with the exception of "small" transgressions, such as not always wearing his *kipa* [the skullcap worn by observant Jewish men, also known as a yarmulke] when he was supposed to). However, the experience of being expelled from school in the eleventh grade pushed Yossi to violate the Sabbath, a transgression many respondents—in their descriptions of hierarchies of transgressions—spoke of as particularly egregious.

LD: At what point did you start breaking the rules?

YOSSI: Well, I think early on, like when I went to St. Louis at the end of eleventh grade, I started smoking. I remember smoking on Shabbes a lot, and I remember thinking like, "Oh, big deal." And that sticks out in my mind as the early things I did. And then I remember eating in like these not kosher restaurants around that time also. Probably late eleventh grade, twelfth grade; I felt, "Hey, why not?" And those were like the big things, and then there were all the girl things that one does with girls when you are an adolescent and older.

Yossi did not perceive his not wearing his kipa all the time as a serious transgression. Once he broke the Sabbath, however, other violations, such as eating nonkosher food, rapidly followed. His story exemplifies the fluidity of the stages of defection traced in this book. On the one hand, he recalls an incident with a particular time and place where his first transgression occurred. On the other hand, his breaking numerous rules while still living in the enclave indicates the stage of "passing." After he was kicked out of school, he felt even more comfortable openly transgressing the embodied rituals of Hasidic life. He began regularly smoking on *Shabbat*, eating treyf food, and dating women casually. He dressed and wore his hair in a style that was out of keeping with the norms of his community, leading to tension between him and his parents.

YOSSI: It was deliberate. You know, I'm going to wear my hair the way I want to. Hair was always a big thing for some reason. It was always like I just want to do it this way, and every day my parents would say, "Why didn't you get a haircut?" And I said, "I like it this way." Their response was always the same: "Just go get one, will you?" In retrospect, I see I felt like one of those women with eating disorders who, unable to control their lives, asserted full control over what they ate. Well, I felt I couldn't control anything else, so I let my hair grow long. I'm not sure if that's really why it was, but in retrospect, it kind of seems that I put a lot of rebellion into the way I looked, because it was the only act of rebellion I could do within my family's home.

Yossi's disregard for Hasidic bodily norms marked him as distinct from the other members of his community. The public display of his long hair made it obvious that he no longer cared about being an acceptable member of his group. His failure to observe Hasidic norms for dress and hairstyle signified his resistance and his developing individuality. His insight that the only thing he could control in his life was the length of his hair highlighted the intense social control in his community, something all the other respondents spoke of as well.

Many respondents described breaking commandments concerning observing *Shabbes*, eating nonkosher food, violating norms of appearance, and ignoring the rules governing the strict separation of the sexes. They made clear that they had come to feel that the community's rules were too restrictive for their bold and independent spirits. Violating God's commandments signaled the beginning of these interviewees' taking charge of their own lives and choosing to act on their own desires and choices, instead of following the laws and roles designated by the community.

Just as growing his hair long represented an act of defiance to Yossi, his parents, and other members of the community, for women, putting on pants had the same dramatic effect.

SIMA

I felt as if I was naked…exposed.

Sima was in her early thirties when we met. She had grown up in a Hasidic community whose religious regulations, dating back to the Hebrew Bible, forbade women from wearing pants. In the course of her teenage years she rebelled in small, private ways, such as turning lights on when she was at home alone on *Shabbes*. In response to my question, she told me her first transgression—as she saw it—was buying and wearing a pair of pants, although at first she wore them only in a backstage, private place. She would wear them publicly only when she was ready to leave the community. Sima's example underscores the embodied nature of becoming an "ex"; it is through the act of changing her garments by dressing in pants that her identity transformation is accomplished and broadcast. Wearing pants publicly happens only when the defector has begun to separate from the community. For Sima, her first experience breaking the rules concerning gendered embodiment was a decisive moment in her life.

> SIMA: For me, putting on pants was the equivalent of taking off your kipa or stopping to put on *tefillin* [leather boxes containing Torah passages that Orthodox males strap to themselves] for boys. It was like the, the most. And really when I wore pants for a few hours at a friend's house, I felt lots of things. First, I felt like I was sort of naked, like I was really exposed. But on the other hand I was very, very happy.

Linking her process with male disinscription of significant Haredi markers, such as kipa and tefillin, underscored Sima's perception of the gravity of her actions. She could have related her transgression to women's ways of enacting bodily resistance. Her choice to equate her transgressive bodily behavior with that of men, however, reveals her awareness that men's deeds were considered more important in her community. Sima's choice of the words *exposure* and *nakedness* indicates how deeply she had internalized the tenets of modesty required of women in all spheres of life. Her language showed how Haredi norms are deeply inscribed as appropriate habitual behavior. Her language of vulnerability and exposure suggests she experienced a sense of shame along with happiness and liberation. The intense pleasure Sima found in experimenting with wearing pants signaled her resistance to remaining in the Haredi world forever. Her combined expression of vulnerability—*exposure*—and happiness is understandable. She had grown accustomed to hiding her individual thoughts and desires by conforming to the norms of the group. Transgressing the norms thus produced an unnerving combination of feelings, embarrassment along with liberation.

Aliza

You were making it clear to everyone who might
see you what you were doing.

Aliza, who was working within a Jewish community agency as a fundraiser when I met her, grew up among the highly strict and segregated Satmar Hasidim in Kiryas Yoel. Her exit from Haredi life was aided by her open-minded grandmother, with whom she lived when she moved away from her parents' home. In that way, she delayed coming out as a defector and maintained good relations with her family.

Her story about beginning to wear pants complicates our understanding of the stages of defection, making it clear that the stages are not always so neatly divided. Aliza described the first time she wore pants in private as a moment of great internal and external transformation. As we have seen in other narratives, for Aliza, her first transgression—breaking the clothing norms of the community—was an emotional moment during which she started to proclaim her individuation from the Haredi enclave. As she described her first experience of buying pants, a garment she had been taught since birth was forbidden for women, she expressed anxiety about the public nature of the purchase, even though at first she wore the pants backstage.

> ALIZA: The first time I put on a pair of pants...that was one thing
> I didn't do right away, I waited...it was this store that was right near
> the subway station, so I walked in and picked up the first pair of pants
> I saw; black velvet, very simple. Held it against me, it looked like it fit.
> I wasn't going to try it on; I was too scared to. So, I just bought them
> and took them home.

Aliza described how much she enjoyed wearing slacks outside of her community; she found them more comfortable than a skirt and pantyhose. She told me that she understood that if she continued wearing trousers enjoyably, and started wearing them more frequently, eventually she would wear them in a public space where she might be seen by members of her community, which would be a definitive statement of movement away from Haredi norms and practices. Aliza was ambivalent about her purchase. Changing her mode of dress translated Aliza's cognitive objections into concrete, public symbols of rebellion. The Haredi clothing norms were so deeply entwined with religious and community significance that breaking them in public could result in the loss of her place in the group and the accompanying feelings of abandonment, guilt, and isolation. Conversely, wearing pants would let others know she was beginning to consolidate her individualized, personal identity. She felt liberated but daunted by the prospect.

Breaking clothing norms could also transmit other messages, according to Esther, our next respondent, who saw wearing different socks as a way to express the anger she felt toward members of her community because they had shunned her, although she had been "sincerely religious."

ESTHER

I wanted to wear different socks because I was very angry
at being ostracized from the community, especially
when I felt I was being sincerely religious.

Esther's violation of the Hasidic dress code took place when she was a teenager. She tells of a narrative progression similar to that told by Abby. She began our conversation with a detailed description of her unhappy childhood, the physical and verbal abuse she suffered at home, and her perception of the deep flaws in the Hasidic community in which she was raised. Esther told me she was eager to leave the familiar, depressing community in order to seek the larger world outside her enclave. She began transgressing at a young age.

ESTHER: I must have been fourteen, fifteen, and I went out of the house
for the first time with different socks. Socks that were considered very
modern that only people in Flatbush wore. You know Flatbush?[2]
LD: Of course I do.

ESTHER: Flatbush is very religious, but they are Modern Orthodox, which is much less strict than the Satmar Hasidim are. They wore bobby socks, you know, those short cute white socks.

LD: So what occurred to you that led you to wear forbidden, short socks? Because so far in the story you have shared with me, despite your unhappiness, you desired to be pious.

ESTHER: I wanted to wear different socks because I was very angry at my family for my abuse and at the community for refusing to come to my aid, even though I felt I was being sincerely religious. I was very hurt, and I wanted to show people that they couldn't win over me or break me. I could have revenge on them. I had more power over them because I had the courage to do what I wanted to do. And I remember feeling this powerful feeling putting on these socks and walking out.

As I did this, I felt my neighbors were looking at me as if I was carrying a pig through the street, or a ham, or being naked—as if I did the most daring and craziest thing. I remember these looks of shock in their eyes, and I just loved it. It was like I was saying, "You hurt me for fifteen years or whatever it was. You made my life miserable and I'll give it back to you!"

LD: And for how long did you keep doing this?

ESTHER: No, I only did it while my parents were gone. God forbid, my mother wasn't allowed to know. I had to do this in a way where it wouldn't get back to harm me or haunt me...

I always thought of—I always wanted to get the attention of the people in the community who were so mean to me. And the only way I could do it was by showing them that I was different from them, that I didn't care. And I was free from their total control over me. I was above it all, a feeling I could create whenever I wanted.

In her account, Esther presented herself as a strong teenager who refused to be treated poorly, as she had been earlier in her life. She was clear she would not take any more nonsense from anyone, and she actively and visibly rebelled by violating the dress code in her own neighborhood. I was surprised to hear her say her mother could not know of her violation of the dress code because she knew if the neighbors saw her they would tell her mom. I wondered why she did not seem to realize any neighbor could tell her mother. Unlike others, whose first transgressions happened in private spaces away from the eyes of the community, this was not a private transgression where no one would see her; rather, she was blatantly challenging the rules. By publicly breaking the commandments ensuring women's tzniyus, Esther was practically shouting about her anger and rebellion against the system that had repressed her spirit when she was a child. Esther wanted it to be public when she violated a community norm; it provided her with a way to stand out and show she was different from other members of the community. Looking back carefully over Esther's interview transcript, I noticed that she repeats the pronoun *I* quite frequently, occasionally three times in one sentence. By defiantly exposing her legs in her community, she was making progress in becoming an *I*, an individual who could, and would likely, continue to oppose the rules and restrictions of Haredi life.

In our conversations, most respondents described their first transgressions as experiences they enjoyed and were likely to repeat. Several also showed how their first transgression loosened the community's hold over them, making it easier to slide into other—still private—violations of the commandments. As we have seen in this chapter, some acts of rebellion were isolated and involved breaking only one rule, such as Esther's wearing bobby socks and Yossi wearing his hair long. In contrast, Leah's first transgression, like Shlomo's, involved multiple transgressions at once: She broke gendered norms of appropriate dress, entered a forbidden space, and carried money on *Shabbes*.

LEAH

I just had to get out of my home. I don't know.
I had to have a cigarette. I had to watch TV.
I had to be in the world.

Although respondents often spoke of wearing different clothing as a major act of resistance, in Leah's story, that transgression was combined with several others. She had known since she was at least eight years old that she did not want to remain in the Hasidic world. Perhaps those years of inward, cognitive resistance emboldened her to use her first transgression to defy several rules at once.

> LEAH: At some point, Shabbes became claustrophobic, and I couldn't stand it anymore. I just hated it. I *hated*, you know, the way we frenetically raced around to get everything done by Friday afternoon, so it would all be ready for Shabbes, which started on Friday at sundown until it became dark on Saturday. I couldn't stand just being locked up like that for twenty-five hours. I just would go nuts. At the edge of the Brooklyn neighborhood where I lived there was a bar, and I would just sit at home on Shabbes, and have this fantasy I should go to a bar, like I'm an international adventuress or something. I have no idea where I got this, but I thought I should be able to walk into a bar, have a drink, you know, like the women in the movies [that she watched when she snuck out to Greenwich Village], Bette Davis or something. That's who I was. Lauren Bacall. Yeah, that was me. You know, Katharine Hepburn. And they would walk into a bar and say, "Give me a drink."
>
> So I started to sneak out of my house, wearing my pants under my skirt, and I would hide the skirt outside of the bar. When I walked in, there were all these men I didn't know, and I was so afraid one of them would talk to me because I had no idea what I would say. So I would do this, you know, on a Friday night sometimes. I would do this on a Saturday afternoon. I was trying to be a woman of assertion, and I'd smoke cigarettes...
>
> LD: How did you know what to order?
>
> LEAH: Oh, a martini of course, just like the women in the movies. I just had to get out of my home. I don't know. I had to have a cigarette. I had to watch TV. I had to be in the world. It just was too restrictive. There were more activities that were forbidden on Shabbes than were allowed, and those few were so limiting and boring to me at some point.

Leah's account included several types of "first transgressions," each of which reinforced the others. She read taboo material in libraries, which taught her more about the world outside the enclave, deepened her doubts, and made her feel freer to continue breaking her community's laws. From her description, I could tell that Leah took great pleasure in breaking the rules that restricted her behavior as a woman and in the sense of danger arising from the risk of getting caught when she snuck out of her parents' house on *Shabbes*. Leah delighted in narrating this adventure, replete with mystery and hints of danger.

These secret visits to the bar became a regular weekly event. Leah's breaking the laws of "modesty" demanded of women by wearing what was considered men's clothing was a critical step in her exiting process, as was her breaking the laws of Sabbath by carrying money and going to bars. Leah never mentioned eating at the bar; if she had done so, she would have transgressed yet again by eating treyf. Ehud's story focuses on that particular form of religious defilement.

EHUD

And then the chicken happened.

In chapter 2, Ehud's narrative emphasized his own and his family's pride in his scholarly talents and prowess, and his dedication to strict standards of observance. But as he grew older, and his ideas were influenced by his conversations with his sister about Marxism—a different lens through which he began to see the world—he wondered about the truth claims of the Haredi yeshivish system of beliefs and practices. Ehud's close relationship with his sister exposed him to secular ideas, which created doubts and questions in his mind.

Due to these conversations, Ehud felt conflicted. He wanted to follow the commandments and maintain his religious practices, as he had been taught. But intellectually, he also harbored questions about God and the Orthodox commandments. Ehud's first experience of tears in the sacred canopy did not arise out of a sense of feeling suffocated by the Haredi world, as Abby had described. Ehud did not feel constrained by the religious laws. Instead, he described a long period of intellectual turmoil in which he struggled to reconcile his emotional connection to the Haredi world and his continuing desire to follow religious laws with his weighty questions about God, the Torah, and rationality.

> EHUD: But you know, even though my rebelling was intellectual at first, it was perhaps precipitated by all the things that happened on an emotional level. After my talks with my sister I still kept kosher and went to shul [synagogue] to daven every morning. I mean, there was no question about my religious observance. I continued in this way for quite a few years, and at the same time, it was this sort of struggle intellectually. I tried to find some kind of way to accommodate both my questioning and my desire to stay within the framework of the Haredi world. I felt I was having what you'd now call an identity crisis. I was torn between my need and desire to conform, but at this time I was becoming increasingly uncomfortable with Judaism—not only on the intellectual level, but also on the level of daily practice. At that point, it was becoming just too painful to keep continuing, keep putting on the tefillin every day when I did just not believe. I had decided for myself I was just completely atheist, and so I kept asking, "What am I doing here? Why am I pretending?" And it's really painful to be split in this way. I knew I couldn't continue doing this, but it would be hard to change, and I was afraid I'd lose all my Haredi friends.

Ehud struggled for years to reconcile his intellectual questioning and new secular ideas with the Haredi worldview and conception of God's commandments. I remember our conversation vividly. For nearly half of the interview he looked anguished and held his head in his hands. By this point in his narration of his life story, he was describing himself as he had been at the age of twenty-two or twenty-three. He had stopped believing in God, and he was deeply conflicted, with his nascent atheism pulling him away from his earlier, devout religious observance.

For many years, although he continued to maintain his religious observance, Ehud sought to make new friends with people who did not know his past. With them he was free to speak his mind. These friends provided him with a new reference group where no one he was familiar with, or cared about, could see his violating the religious commandments. It was with these friends, who provided him with an alternative place to belong, that he broke two major Jewish laws at once: the commandment to observe the Sabbath and eat only kosher food.

> EHUD: The chicken happened...the first time the chicken happened I can tell you exactly, because I remember the day so well. I was taking some guitar lessons with this famous guy who had studied with world-renowned guitarists.
>
> He was a great guitar teacher. I was not a great student, but I was trying. And, you know, he could see that I was frazzled all the time and sort of drifting off in my mind. One day he saw me coming and asked, "Did you comb your hair today at all?" Then I had this big head of curly hair, a long beard, round glasses...

In recalling his first transgression, Ehud used passive language as if to suggest that the event happened to him. His language did not reflect deliberation or conscious agency on his part. Ehud's use of the word *drifting* is a metaphor for his feelings of rootlessness, of not having a solid ground on which to stand—not in the Haredi world and not in the secular world either. His comportment and physical presentation— his long, uncombed hair and his large beard—reflected the inner turbulence that characterized his life at the time. His unkempt appearance was unacceptable in the Haredi world. Perhaps looking a bit wild was his way of expressing his individuality.

Ehud told me that the guitar teacher was trying to resocialize him to be more of a *mensch* (a person of integrity and honor) and, at the same time, introduce him to new and interesting people. He arranged a meeting with Ehud and another student of his, a piano player, and suggested they might want to play music together. Ehud met this man and his girlfriend, who suggested they get together on Friday night at a particular restaurant. Ehud realized that he had never gone to a restaurant on *Shabbes*, nor had he carried money, and that, of course, they were going to a nonkosher restaurant.

EHUD: Since I had gotten to that point, I figured I should just jump in and do it. It was my first time, you know.

Ehud's use of "it was my first time" when confiding to me that the restaurant event was his first violation of the commandments was interesting, reminiscent of the way people often speak of their first sexual experience. Although I knew he had not yet had sex at that point in his life, he intimated that breaking all of these commandments at once symbolized his loss of purity and sense of wholeness. His body had been defiled by the treyf food he had eaten.

This linkage between treyf food and forbidden sexual behavior was made explicit by Rabbi Manis Friedman, the Lubavitcher rabbi quoted in *Tradition in a Rootless World*, who made a clear analogy between Orthodox Jews eating nonkosher food and women's loss of virginity at a young age:

> I think that innocence is a native condition and there is an intrinsic need to be innocent....Innocence means that you're created a certain way and you've never corrupted that condition. You never tampered, a virginal territory. Untouched. That's innocence. And if God says, "I created you kosher," then to have eaten nonkosher means you've been tampered with. You introduced an ingredient that doesn't belong so you are no longer virginal or innocent, and that hurts.

Friedman's goal in making this comparison was to teach the young women he was training to become Orthodox that—although in their lives until that moment, they had lacked innocence and took forbidden objects into their bodies—they had the opportunity to come to God and start anew, freshly cleared of all pollutants. Ehud's reference to eating non-kosher food as "his first time" might have been his way of describing his own loss of innocence. By absorbing treyf food into his body, he had lost his essential innocence.

EHUD: So I was sitting there with this piece of treyf chicken on my plate, and I thought to myself, "I'm going to eat this?" I felt so conflicted, and this battle was going on through my mind, and of course

99

these two people across from me, this guy and this woman, had no idea of what I was going through. None whatsoever.

LD: Were you sweating?

EHUD: I don't really remember. I just remember it was a big...the irony of it was that when I first tasted it, it tasted just the same as my family's Friday night chickens. It wasn't all that different...

LD: You sound surprised, as if kosher chickens are not only slaughtered differently, but they must taste in a way that is distinct from nonkosher chickens....Were you afraid when you took your first bite?

EHUD: Well, I wasn't afraid that God would hit me.

LD: You weren't?

EHUD: Of course not. No, I was completely, like I said, I didn't believe in anything at that point. No. It's just the act...the act of transgressing. You know, it's just there's this invisible line that you're stepping over, this is the first time in your life that you're doing it. And I had transgressed another time, maybe a few months earlier, which was when I turned on the light on Shabbes for the first time in my life. I was twenty-two or so when this happened. It is one thing to do it when you're sixteen and it's another when you're in your twenties. It's a little harder probably, because it's so charged. You know, and I wasn't fully a man at that time. I never had...didn't go with women before, so I was still pretty much like a kid.

Ehud's talk of stepping over an invisible line was a powerful metaphor for his understanding that eating treyf put him outside the boundaries of the Haredi world. The enclave's distinct borders are designed to keep nonmembers out and insiders in. His transgressive act made it clear to him that he had left the safety of the community and might not return. His account of eating treyf also vividly illustrates the embodied nature of Haredi religious practice. Although Ehud had, by this time, completely lost his belief in God, he still struggled over changing his ritualized, bodily habits.

Unlike Ehud, who sat with his head in his hands looking anguished, Rachel did not come across as a troubled soul. Nevertheless, she described the first time she ate distinctly nonkosher food (bacon) as a momentous biographical disruption in her life.

Rachel

I was like trembling the whole time, but I managed to . . .
you know, I survived it and that was like the start
of the rebellion at that point.

Like Ehud, a number of my respondents experimented with breaking Orthodox laws by eating nonkosher food. They did so in places outside the community's gaze, which is to say, in private. Even if they were in "public" places, such as a restaurant, they chose an establishment a great distance from their communities so they could avoid being caught and punished. These actions were a serious step in the process of breaking away from Haredi understandings of the body's orientation to the divine. Rachel, an American woman who was in her late fifties when we met, described in some detail her experience of breaking the laws of kashrut, which was her first transgression. Rachel described the precautions she took to commit this sin far outside the gaze of her community:

> RACHEL: I went to this shopping center that was like, I would never have gone to in a million years, and I very furtively ordered a bacon, lettuce, and tomato sandwich. As I was eating it, I was waiting to be . . . you know, the lightning to strike me or something, and of course, the lightning didn't. I mean, man, bacon, it's got to be the worst, and I mean . . . it was just a coffee shop in a very, you know, a poor neighborhood type shopping center far from where I lived. That way nobody would see me. I was like trembling the whole time, but I managed to . . . you know, I survived it and that was like the start of the rebellion at that point.

The popular American adage, "You are what you eat," is relevant here: If you eat only kosher foods, you are a "kosher" person, meaning one who is ritually pure and follows all the laws. But if you transgress and eat treyf food, you, yourself, become treyf, defiled. By eating forbidden foods, defectors opened their bodies up to any number of polluting elements from the secular world. Rachel, like Binyamin and Ehud, had been questioning her community's laws, values, and norms for a long time before actually breaking a commandment. All three stories demonstrate the greater importance of actions over beliefs in the Haredi world. Questioning was written into the ancient texts; it was not problematic. But acting out bodily resistance to Jewish laws is a momentous event that might be the first step in defecting. These respondents were deeply aware of the difference between intellectual questioning, an internal, mental process, and violating a commandment, a physical act, as evidenced by the reported intensity of the physical experience—expressed by Rachel as "trembling the whole time."

The processes of questioning and experimenting with breaking commandments by privately transgressing against Haredi laws were described by all respondents as important phases in the journey out of the enclave. The journey is one of individuating, a skill they had not been taught as children. As we spoke, I recognized the courage it took to break the boundaries that were engrained in them, marking them as different and somehow superior to those outside the enclave. Hasidim raise their children to obey the community's preferences and rules; they continually reinforce their children's desire to fulfill their proper role and duty in the group and not trouble much about themselves as separate individuals. As the respondents transgressed community boundaries of comportment more and more often, they entered a phase of passing betwixt and between dual identities: that of their life in the enclave and that of their emerging selves in the secular world.

CHAPTER FOUR

PASSING

In the last chapter, I described how my respondents spoke enthusiastically of the first time they violated a biblical commandment. In our conversations, I could sense a tone of triumph: They dared to risk God's wrath and punishment—which they had been taught would swiftly follow all *halachic* (actions and objects in accordance with Jewish law) violations—and nothing happened. Their first transgressions were against one of the hundreds of Hasidic bodily rituals that had been inscribed upon them through socialization and had shaped their repertoires of automatic, taken-for-granted behaviors. Finding that this first violation did not result in undesirable consequences, they became more daring and began to violate other commandments, in the "back stage" outside of their community boundaries. There is a Talmudic saying: that once a person breaks a commandment, that individual feels as if the transgressive behavior is now permissible. Nearly all my conversation partners told me they continued to violate rules governing bodily behavior, such as eating nonkosher food, dressing and comporting themselves inappropriately, engaging in taboo conversations, and touching a member of the opposite sex. Over time they developed a routine of passing between the mutually exclusive realms of their enclave communities, where they publicly performed the embodied routines of Hasidim daily life, and the larger, more open society, where they continued to transgress freely, ignoring religious strictures and experimenting with new ways of being in the world.[1]

In this book I use the word *passing* to designate the stage in defectors' narratives when they speak of manipulating bodily practices so they could vary their public presentation of themselves in different contexts. It is a liminal state of being betwixt and between two radically different identities and the habitual bodily practices through which they are both created and sustained. The physical rituals of Haredi life vary significantly by gender; hence, passing behavior is distinctly gendered. Shlomo manipulated his appearance by playing with the placement of his peyos as one of his passing strategies. Aryeh, another man, told me he took off his skullcap when he left his Hasidic neighborhood, only replacing it on his head when he came close to home again. He explained that over time he became bolder and took off or replaced his kipa closer and closer to his home. In order to successfully cross the boundaries between these two distinct realms, informants carefully and consciously manipulated their routines of bodily practices, making sure they comported themselves appropriately in each context. As these eventual exiters crossed boundaries between worlds, their external and internal identities were in a state of flux.

LEAH

Leaving the Hasidic world was an amazingly frightening prospect.

In the previous chapter we read Leah's lively story about passing back and forth between her Hasidic home and a paradigmatic secular space, a bar. I had asked her to detail for me her process of ceasing to follow the commandments. Her narrative was unusual, as no other Haredi woman told me of regularly going to bars as a stage in her exiting process. Leah's life story was vivid, fascinating, and dramatic; it provided such a powerful model of the stage of passing that I am reproducing our conversation here in some detail.

Leah's account provided a powerful model of the stage of passing by illustrating how what seems to be one transgressive act—going to a bar—actually involved several. She entered a taboo space, wearing forbidden clothing, and carrying money on Shabbes.

At this point Leah was no longer experimenting with a few transgressive acts; she was becoming bolder in her rebellion and was eating nonkosher food. She had entered the stage of passing, of moving back and forth between two radically different worlds and trying to maintain credibility in each. Leah and my other informants described passing as a difficult stage; they were caught between their community and the freer outside world, uncertain of why they were caught or who they might become. Flipping their behaviors and the identities they performed between the two realms led to an increasingly uncomfortable sense of cognitive dissonance that they eventually sought to resolve in one way or another. Leah knew that she really wanted to defect from her Hasidic world, but she recognized it was a fearsome and daunting move.

She spent several years in the unnerving stage of passing because she had nowhere to go, did not have a job, did not want to risk the loss of her family, and, due to her socialization, had internalized deep fears of the dangers looming in the larger, *goyische* (non-Jewish) society.

> LEAH: Leaving the Haredi world was an amazingly frightening prospect. You have no idea where to go. Like you...it was just so hard for me to make sense of the outside world. The hardest part of leaving is you can't gauge safety. As we grew up we were always told stories about the evils that befell upon those who left; there were older people who I had heard of who exited and, for example, one guy got into drugs and was eventually shot in the head. The dangers of the larger society were so daunting. I mean, New York is a pretty scary place. If you're going to depend on the kindness of the people in Manhattan, you're in big trouble. You don't know how to tell a good person from a bad person. They're all the same. They're all goyim. So you don't know what's going on. I had been told that all goyim were drunks, and I did not know if I would recognize a drunkard. I just did not know how to tell whether anyone I met was trustworthy or not.
>
> So my dilemma in thinking about leaving was the issue of how I would find responsible and kind people. I think it was very hard to locate them, because I didn't know anything about anybody. I didn't know what an Irish American was like, or an Italian, or what were the differences or what their home lives were like. It took such a long

time to find any commonality with others, because in order to make friends you have to share your life, and how could I possibly do that? My life was so crazy I thought no one would ever understand.

Part of Leah's hesitation was based on her knowledge that leaving posed a risk of losing her family, her community, and the only world she knew. She had no idea where she would live or how she would support herself, a dilemma described by all my respondents as a barrier they had to overcome in order to exit. When Leah and other respondents first thought of leaving, these overwhelming fears led them to attempt to reconcile their doubts and maintain ritual practices. Hoping for a resolution that would not lead them into this dangerous larger society, they continued to ask questions throughout high school even as they continued to transgress. Leah knew her life would be much simpler if she could find a way to quell her doubts and lower her level of anger at the gender inequality in her Hasidic world.

The challenges of leaving were exacerbated by the strong opposition to individualism that was central to the functioning of Leah's and other Hasidic enclave communities. Parents, teachers, rabbis, and neighbors were unified in teaching conformity and submission to the larger goals of the group. Through socialization children were discouraged from asking too many questions; they were taught that God requires them to fulfill their appropriate roles in the community at every stage of their lives. The group's cohesion depended on the conformity of all its members; if a child showed a rebellious streak that might lead to an independent sense of self, parents and teachers worked to squash it immediately. To keep the boundaries of their enclave strong, children were raised to subsume their own selves in the service of the enclave community.

For Leah—and all my Hasidic informants—defecting from the group required a strong sense of herself as an individual who was free to act on her own desires. Leah could not imagine where she could find a place to be herself and express her "radical" ideas among a group of like-minded people. The Satmar enclave was all she knew; beyond it there was a vast and confusing world. Leah "still felt a desire to belong," so she worked hard to find answers that would reduce the cognitive dissonance between her own feminist ideas and the patriarchal reality of Orthodoxy. Intuitively she felt it was not possible for her to remain in the enclave, but she was not yet ready to exit on her own.

It was emotionally, socially, and physically challenging for my informants to continually change their costumes, comportment, and presentation of themselves, and over time they became increasingly uncomfortable. Sociologist Ann Swidler's (1986) concept of unsettled lives provides an apt description of how my respondents' experienced themselves in this stage of passing. When they were squarely within the bounds of their Hasidic communities they lived "settled lives." They had deeply internalized all necessary knowledge of the religious worlds they relied on to guide and provide a framework for their everyday lives. Haredi culture served as a structure in which to eat, sleep, speak, work, pray, and learn. But once they started and then continued to transgress, their lives became unsettled; their usual skills and practices did not equip them to function in the world outside the enclave. They told me that during the stage of passing they struggled to learn basic cultural guidelines for how to act, speak, eat, dress, and comport themselves in the larger society. As Leah said to me so plaintively, "I did not even know what regular people talked about." Passing provided my respondents with the opportunity to spend their time learning and internalizing the habitual bodily practices and elements of a new cultural toolkit that could provide a framework for their new lives in the larger society.

As they moved back and forth between radically dissimilar universes, they did so as gendered beings. In the public world of the Haredi community, where they could be seen by family and neighbors, women and men adhered to the taken-for-granted rules for dress, social and cultural roles, and comportment. The larger society they explored, however, offered a multiplicity of alternative ways of comporting oneself in all aspects of daily life, including new ways of constructing gender and sexuality. Beyond the community's boundaries, respondents felt free to shed their community's rigid definitions of masculinity and femininity and experiment with new and more open approaches to defining and performing gender. As they crossed borders between the bounded enclave and the larger society, they sought opportunities to "try-on" various components of the new identities they would ultimately assume.

BINYAMIN

Maybe I'm just going through a phase, an episode,
and maybe at some point, as time goes on,
I'll have a change of mind and heart and I'll go back.
So I might as well be part of it anyway.

In the last chapter we met Binyamin, a bright young man who began his journey of defection by reading the books in his yeshiva's library, a rare opportunity for a Hasidic boy, whose community tightly controls what members are allowed to read or even see. Like Ehud, Binyamin was a child prodigy in the study of Jewish texts, and the community had great hopes for his scholarly achievements. Ironically, however, the same analytic skills that earned Binyamin so much respect in his Lubavitcher enclave in Brooklyn, New York, provided him with the tools to read, analyze, and comprehend the writings of Kant, Hegel, and Einstein, which he eventually discovered in the public library. His encounter with theories of relativism undermined his confidence in the absolutist, exclusivist, and totalistic Hasidic worldview. Several other men with whom I spoke told me that reading illicit material in public libraries deepened their extant doubts about Hasidic life.

In order to continue to study at the library, my informants had to learn the appropriate ways of acting in this space, which maintained hushed tones and reading and learning were largely silent. This behavior was in stark contrast to the physical routines of learning in the study halls of their yeshivas (institution of Jewish learning, modern Hebrew pronunciation of the plural), where they and their study partners engaged in loud and animated discussions about the precise meaning of ancient texts. As Binyamin absorbed the norms of studying in a library, he picked up elements of the cultural rules outside of his enclave.

For Binyamin, as for many other informants, the interplay between the stages of defection—tears in the canopy, first transgression, and passing—was flexible. These moments were not necessarily discrete; they readily melded into each other. Binyamin, for example, continued to read secular philosophy and question the Haredi way of life for many years, even as he continued to observe the commandments. As he said to me, "Being part of this community is in my *kishkes* [gut]." He found it difficult to continue the religious practices and participate in the Haredi world while doubting its very premises. Leaving the community, however, was fraught with danger. He was afraid of losing his secure way of life, his family, and his community, and, more starkly, he risked punishment from God. During these years, Binyamin was internally, cognitively passing between his Hasidic world and outside society. Even as a teacher—passing on religious knowledge and skills—he continued to ask the same questions.

> BINYAMIN: So when I left London, I started quietly breaking—eating nonkosher or listening to the radio on Shabbos, things like that.
>
> LD: What did that feel like?
>
> BINYAMIN: It was...in the beginning. I felt very guilty, and I felt doing these things was coming from a bad place. I was so depressed I felt I had to break out of this in some way. And I was just like pissed off anyway, so of course I felt bad about it, because in the world I came from that's so wrong. I was deeply conditioned; these feelings were instinctive. On the other hand, I thought, why does it matter? Why do any of these rituals matter? So with time, it became this whole private/public lifestyle that I lived. In the community I acted as pious as I had to, but I found myself sneaking out to eat in un-kosher restaurants, or go to the movies.

Binyamin's depression was rooted in his deep internal conflicts. Depression was common among the people I met for this study: Eighteen of the forty Haredim I interviewed told me of their struggles with depression. All of the causes of depression cited in the medical literature were relevant to my respondents: Trauma, especially in early life, major life changes, stressful events, and low self-esteem are key triggers. Their childhood suffering was inscribed on their bodies and in their brain chemistry, making them more prone than others to adolescent and adult depression (Kramer 1993).

BINYAMIN: So after London, I came back here to New York; I became part of the 770 yeshiva [770 Eastern Parkway in Brooklyn, New York, location of Lubavitch headquarters], and I studied for *smicha* [rabbinical ordination]. But even as I was doing that, I was exploring things. In my head, I thought about it this way: I'm not perfect, and I don't believe anyone is really. So this is...so as long as I'm mainly frum and all that, and I *put on a good show*, maybe I'm just going through a phase, an episode, and maybe at some point, as time goes on, I'll have a change of mind and heart and I'll go back. So I might as well be part of it anyway. Questioning leads to confusion, and who wants that? People want to have peace of mind. Especially if you're in this kind of community that has a secure support system. But all the confusion was just too much for me, I was not progressing in my learning and I was just getting bored, because I found it easy to understand all or most of the studies. You know, I had most of the points down and all that.

So even when I was really frum, I would once in a while go to a museum. I was interested in historical aspects of American life and culture. I was already living this double life; good friends of mine knew this a bit. You know, I would skip davening, here and there, but at the same time, for example, that I may not daven I would run to 770 for the rebbe's *fabrengen* [a joyous gathering for the men, where the rebbe leads the group in old Hasidic tunes and offers words of wisdom and inspiration]. I rationalized this hypocritical behavior to myself in two ways: First of all, maybe I'm just not a good Jew, so what can I do? Or, maybe there really is truth in the Lubavitch way of life. Everyone around me was so adamant that this is the truth. The 50,000 people who are Lubavitchers truly understand, so what do I know?

There were two tracks going in my brain of not believing and believing, and I was aware of the contradiction as it was happening, and I felt intellectually confused, but at least emotionally, I could still bring myself back into the spirit of the community. I had been raised this way, and so that's what I identify and am familiar with. You just can't turn off your past, and this is my past.

Binyamin knew that going to a museum violated community regulations. It was a forbidden place because it offered Hasidim a rare opportunity to explore ideas and artifacts beyond the ideological enclave. Entering the museum, or library, was a decisive physical act of resistance. In visiting these places, respondents mingled with people outside of their enclave, breaking through their social encapsulation as well. Earlier I spoke of three types of boundaries, forms of encapsulation—ideological, physical, and social—that are meant to insulate members of the group from all ideas and artifacts of the larger society.

When Binyamin publicly took part in his community's rituals, he put on a display. He knew he was playing a role, but it was one he knew well and could convincingly perform. He put on a show of acting pious in the frontstage area of his Lubavitch community; he was consciously performing the identity of a Haredi man. As long as he acted the part and publicly engaged in ritual performances, he thought no one would know what was in his mind. Inwardly, however, he sensed his Hasidic commitments were waning. In an effort to reduce his confusion and the anxiety of moving back and forth between two worlds, he sought to get beyond this "phase" by redoubling his efforts to be frum and to feel settled in his community.

In my conversation with Binyamin, he frequently spoke of the cognitive dissonance brought on by passing back and forth between two worlds and living a "double life." He tried to reconcile the contradictions at the core of his being by lamenting his youth ("I am still young"), lack of moral will ("I am not good"), and intellectual waywardness ("maybe I am wrong"). Though he was struggling intellectually, Binyamin hung on to his emotionally familiar world by continuing his practice of Hasidism. As he said, "That's the identity I am familiar with." Binyamin was not ready to come out of the closet and fully own his dissent. Instead, he continued to pass.

The cognitive conflict he described eventually became public, as more people in his private sphere became aware of his transgressions:

BINYAMIN: Yeah, I became known to sneak away. I would sneak away
    to libraries like others might sneak away to a strip club. But at the

same time I would seek inspiration by going to different shuls in Crown Heights.

Binyamin likened his sneaking away to libraries and reading taboo literature to going to a strip club, a sexually deviant act in his community. Both behaviors were illicit. As we will see, unlike most other respondents, who declared some lapses—such as breaking the Sabbath—as more sinful than others, Binyamin did not think in terms of a hierarchy of transgressions. He saw the Haredi system as an all-encompassing set of norms and practices, rooted in the group's master narrative, in which all breaches of the standards are equally abominable.

He continued reporting his internal dialogue, illustrating the argument in his mind between his attempts to remain and his desire to leave:

> BINYAMIN: But given I don't believe in God, what am I davening for? But I like davening anyway, because once I walk into a shul, I feel an emotional connection; it is an outlet for expressing deep-rooted feelings. So in these moments, affinity comes from the kishkes. And when you're in that position, if you're in the God mindset, you can be pretty convincing, like an actor. An actor isn't the character 24/7, especially after an actor is off the project or something. So he's whatever. He's Nick Nolte or Alec Baldwin, but once you're there, when you're in the role, you are totally convinced you could do this, and you're true. It's the *atzma* [the real thing, the essence], you're not being false.

Once again, Binyamin refers to his frontstage behavior in the synagogue as performing a role. Just as in deep acting, however, he became the role he played. In the powerful, emotionally fulfilling space of the synagogue he managed to temporarily convince himself that he still was the Hasidic man he was raised to be. And just as actors leave the set and become themselves, he knows it is his presence on set—in the shul—that elicits his convincing performance. But outside of shul, his questions persisted and they ran deeper than his ready ability to perform in synagogue. Through his passing between two widely divergent worlds, Binyamin gained insight into the power of social and cultural contexts to shape his actions.

Despite his deep questions, when Binyamin was engaging in Hasidic rituals, he could almost convince himself of his religious sincerity. He vividly illustrated the emotional draw of rituals and their power to establish group cohesion, an insight that derives from Durkheim's early study of religious life. Shared religious participation elevates members of these groups into a higher state of awareness they could not achieve alone. The effect of these group gatherings, in which they enact and reinforce the elements of their foundational narrative, is to lift all participants into what Durkheim called a *state of collective effervescence*. In this context, in these moments of intensive participation, the torment of Binyamin's internal struggles between his cognition and his gut was temporally suspended.

Binyamin remained conflicted and continued to pass between two opposing worlds for many years. His passing narrative depicted a long, gradual process, fraught with internal indecision and the discomfort of feeling unsettled. He was not eager to leave the Lubavitch lifestyle behind ("I don't want to erase my past and memory, and so I go on"), but he was still unable to bring his thoughts in line with the Lubavitch worldview.

The discord Binyamin experienced by having a foot in both worlds could not be sustained indefinitely. As time passed, he became aware that others were beginning to perceive his ambivalence and question his long-term commitment.

He told me that while he was studying in the 770 yeshiva, he felt disoriented and torn apart by his ambivalence. His mother, noticing how depressed he felt, spoke with his rabbi's wife. This is how he described what happened:

BINYAMIN: During this period, my beard was coming in heavily, and, according to biblical law, we were not allowed to cut off our beards. So a lot of the students, in all the yeshivas, start pulling out their beards. Even as they were studying intensely, some of the guys— perhaps unconsciously—were starting to pull out their beards, so

I started playing around with my beard, which, as you know, is a publicly visible sign of being a Hasidic man. Tugging on it to pull out the growing hairs was forbidden.

In order to get smicha we were required to pass three exams, all of which I came through well. It was then time to receive the actual documentation, the printed certification that I was now a Lubavitch rabbi and was ready to be sent to another country, thereby further-ing the work of the Lubavitcher rebbe to spread Jewish observance around the globe. But when I went into the rabbi's office to pick up the certificate, he said to me: "Well, you know, Binyamin, I see you're playing around with your beard, so it is clear you still have ques-tions about where you're heading, so you know what? I'll hold on to this document and once you get married," meaning to a good, frum Lubavitcher girl, "then I'll give it to you." But I couldn't guarantee him that I wasn't going to marry whatever girl I fell in love with, Lubavitcher or not. And I was not ready to get married! That was another Lubavitch practice I could not see myself doing. I felt that get-ting married in your early twenties was too early, and I still wanted to be sure that this is the way I wanted to live and all that. So the rabbi and I left it at that.

Binyamin and his rabbi both knew that when yeshiva students played around with their beards, it was the outward manifestation of their wavering dedication to the Lubavitch community. A beard allowed to grow freely is an embodied sign of male membership in a Hasidic com-munity. Binyamin's attempts to remove his beard publicly signaled his doubts and waning religious commitment. Despite his stated desire to settle back into his community, Binyamin's reservations were written on his face and in his comportment.

Binyamin's stage of passing lasted for many years; he felt trapped and unable to resolve his internal conflicts. He wanted to remain safely ensconced in the Lubavitch community, even when he no longer felt in harmony with the underlying tenets of their religious practices and beliefs. No one was pressuring him to continue observing command-ments. Rather, his lengthy period of passing was shaped by his own personal desire to both remain in the community, the only world he had ever known, and reduce his cognitive dissonance.

EHUD

So I experienced a sudden, abrupt transition.

Ehud's narrative provides another good example of the complex ways the various stages of defection might be going on at the same time, or readily slide into each other. His parents, who were proud of his powerful intellect, sent him to a secular high school where he could get the best education possible. They also hired a tutor to make sure he would continue to advance in Judaic subjects, particularly in his study of the Talmud. To be so competent in both spheres, Ehud had to learn to move between what he called "two worlds." Through repeated exposure to the secular society he became fluent in English as well as Yiddish, the language spoken in his home. His full competence in English contributed to his sense of ease as he transitioned each day between secular high school and Talmudic studies. In order to successfully perform his dual identity he learned and practiced the bodily comportment appropriate in each world. He relished this double identity: "I really enjoyed feeling completely comfortable in these two worlds, and evidently I was doing well. I was one of the best students in class, and I was one of the best students in the Talmud."

Nevertheless, a different story he related to me, intended to demonstrate his ease in transitioning from the secular context of school back to his Haredi world, actually revealed his discomfort:

EHUD: I remember once coming out of school, and I was sort of joking with my friends. I was in the spirit of complete immersion in this high school kind of thing, but soon I was going to meet Reb Yankel [his Talmud tutor], and we were going to study in my family's apartment. So in the midst of my joking around with my friends from the high school, the rabbi appeared on the sidewalk next to us. Somehow

I didn't expect him at that moment, although I clearly knew we were meeting after school. So I experienced a very abrupt transition, where all of a sudden I went from one world to the other, changing languages to speak Yiddish with him. I felt so uncomfortable being between two worlds at that moment, and speaking a language my friends did not even understand, that I did not even say goodbye to them. As soon as I joined him, I was now in my other self, the talmid chacham. I was wholly with him. The transition felt sudden and abrupt.

Even in high school, where Ehud said he excelled in both secular and religious studies—and enjoyed them both—he began to feel the strains of his daily move from the person he was in his high school with his friends, and his other identity as a brilliant Talmud scholar. This part of his narrative described his early, painful experience of being split in two, of finding himself questioning Haredi assumptions even as he assiduously maintained its religious ritual practices. His language here, about the "sudden and abrupt transition" he experienced that day after high school, anticipated his struggles for the next decades. This observation served as a harbinger for his own angst-ridden journey. He described his emerging feeling of discomfort and pressure.

> EHUD: I continued studying, fulfilling all the commandments rigorously, and excelling in high school for quite a few years. It was only much later that I started feeling the strain, which many years later grew to the point that I had to do something about it.

Binyamin and Ehud, both of whom emphasized their intellectual abilities and scholarly prowess, remained in this uncomfortable stage of passing for several years. They told me that, although for many years they struggled mightily with intellectual questions and doubts, they nevertheless found it hard to break away from their habitual embodied rituals and communities. Perhaps it was hard for them to give up their identities as pious, brilliant, and esteemed Talmud scholars. Their deep commitment to religious practices and their desire to resolve their doubts and believe fully in God and the teachings of their communities were incompatible with their profound understanding of the relativism of all worldviews.

In contrast, Abby was internally consistent about her desire to break free. She was constrained, however, by various external loci of control, such as her duties as a wife of a Hasidic man.

ABBY

I had more freedom, but I was not feeling free enough.

In chapter 2 we met Abby, whose upbringing in a Satmar family in Monroe, New York, was particularly emotionally and physically painful due to the frequent beatings to which she was subjected. Her first transgression was illicit sexual exploration. She also adopted the tactic of lying to her parents so she could go out into the larger world and watch secular movies. She was eager to escape permanently.

Just as Binyamin used his gendered socialization as a scholar to find and decipher philosophical literature, Abby relied on her internalized definition of adult women as wives and mothers to find a route out of her Satmar community. When she reached marriageable age (seventeen), she went along with an arranged *shidduch* (a match or date arranged by a third party for the explicit purpose of marriage) because it was a viable, appropriately gendered strategy to get out of her parents' house and have her own life. Unfortunately, this exiting path did not increase her comfort or satisfaction with her life. When she married, she was emotionally unstable due to the unresolved traumas of her childhood, her persistent questions, and her overall discontent with Hasidism. In addition, her parents' tense and argumentative relationship failed to offer Abby a model of how to make a marriage work.

ABBY: So in the next couple of years following my marriage, I really tried to make my life work as it was supposed to. I wanted to have a happy life. But I didn't really know what happiness was. I didn't know how to have a healthy relationship. I was not allowed to talk with men before I got married, so I had no idea how to communicate with my husband or resolve issues through discussion. I became a very demanding wife; it was as if I was channeling my mother, who was incredibly demanding herself. I was still always very pent up with anger and resentment toward my childhood because I was constantly abused. And I wanted my husband to be my rescuer. I wanted him to give me all the attention and love that I never got. And he wasn't that kind of guy. It just was not his temperament. He also did not come into the marriage with any idea of how to establish a working relationship; his father worked out of town all week, and so he rarely saw his parents interacting. He was a very nice guy, but he was really a kid, like me. I was constantly trying to get from him all the love and affection I never got, which was really not his job. I wasn't stable enough to be in a relationship. I was not ready to be in a relationship with anybody, not just him.

In these comments, we can we see the consequences of Abby's unresolved pain from childhood, as well as the strain of a marriage between two very young people who did not know each other. Many of my respondents described how the stringent Haredi laws forbidding all interactions between boys and girls before marriage turned them into marriage partners who did not know how to have an intimate—verbal or physical—relationship with each other.

Keeping children away from knowledge of their most intimate bodily organs and how they work created a larger fence around the scriptural laws forbidding premarital sex. When sexual feelings emerge in adolescence, young Haredim would be less likely to act on these desires because they had no context in which to understand them. Instead, these new sensations made them feel ashamed, as if their bodies had become out of control.

When Shlomo interacted with women at the dance club, he described himself as "blown away" by the opportunity to relate socially and physically with women. Abby and other women told me they routinely dreaded their husbands' sexual advances; the men had not been taught the importance of satisfying women, or how to touch women sensually. Their sexual interactions were devoid of genuine care and tenderness.

Abby learned that getting married did not bring her the greater freedom and happiness she had hoped for. She spoke of feeling bored and lonely within her marriage. Her husband studied at the yeshiva all day, whereas she was alone at home with not much to fill her time. She had come from a large, noisy family, and she felt depressed being alone all day. By breaking the taboo against allowing secular media into the home, she was able to use her essentially cloistered situation to her advantage. She bought a computer and began using the Internet. Her illicit explorations on the Internet provided her with covert ways of learning about the outside world.

> ABBY: So I got on to the web, and I started chatting around. I started realizing that there's interesting stuff out there. I started going into chat rooms. I started talking to people, and I felt safe to talk about anything because nobody knows who's sitting behind the screen and talking. And I would talk to people about where I come from, and people would be interested in finding out about me. And I'd be interested in finding out about the outside world. I started talking to gentiles. You know, God forbid you talk to a gentile. We were never allowed to talk to gentiles. And here I had the experience where I could talk to a lot of people, and nobody knew who I was. It's not like I'm meeting them in person, you know. As I started talking to them I became hooked on it. I became almost addicted to the web. I would browse, read up on the news, and eventually I started talking to different people. I was so interested in how different their lives were. I was also interested in religion. I learned there's Buddhism; I learned there is Christianity. There are all these different cultures, and I wanted to know more about them. Eventually I made some friends through this "chatting," and I went to meet these people. It was such an adventure for me.

At this point, Abby experienced a rush of freedom. She felt she was discovering the world. Haredi communities were so protective and insular, so resistant to all "foreign"—non-Haredi—ideas that Abby, like other Satmars, had no knowledge of other cultures or religions. Such knowledge was taboo; the community worked to ensure members had little exposure to the threatening ideas and practices of the goyim as well as Jews who were not Haredim. Earlier, I described Abby's perception that her parents created an environment where she could not ask questions and had to "keep things to myself."

Communicating through the Internet opened up "new worlds" to Abby, and she expressed her fascination and awe at how much there was "out there" that Hasidim had never even imagined. This idiom of discovering or suddenly seeing "the world" was used by over half of my interviewees. Abby's forays on the web fed her curiosity about the outside world during a time she was feeling constricted and bored in her Hasidic world. The anonymity of the web helped Abby feel more comfortable expressing herself, sharing her story. These Internet exchanges allowed Abby to learn about how others lived. She saw, through their reactions to her descriptions of her world, how strange and unbelievable it seemed to others. At home she engaged in these illicit ventures, but in the frontstage of her community she passed as a frum Satmar wife, mainly through her bodily comportment and dress. She wore the appropriate headgear for women in her community: a scarf tied around her head rather than a wig or wig plus a scarf. The costume fit, and she passed.

LD: Were you worried about people finding out about the Internet?
ABBY: I felt safe in my home, and online I felt I could express myself about how sheltered my life was. I had nothing, no radio, no TV, no nothing. Eventually, though, I got a TV in the house. I got a VCR.

Although Abby was still living within the Haredi enclave, she brought forbidden secular media into her house, allowing her the freedom to explore the larger world within the privacy of her home, while still maintaining her public identity as a frum wife. Her husband was resistant to Abby bringing secular media into their household and using it as a means to acquire forbidden knowledge; but his greatest concern was not about his wife's new ideas.

ABBY: He just wanted to make sure that nobody else finds out because that's the biggest thing. Nobody else in the family should find out that we have a TV in the house. I would watch all the different shows. I was really hooked on it. Cause the first time it was something that was outside, and I had it in my own house. I had my freedom. You know, my father's not breathing down my throat, and I'm not getting abused. I realized, though, that although I had more freedom, I wasn't feeling free enough. I was feeling like here I have TV, I have Internet, but everything has to be hidden. I started hating the fact that I can do this, but I always have to pretend.

Community policing of homes to make sure there were no forbidden objects—TVs, computers, VCRs, in other words anything that might bring the "outside world" into Hasidic homes—was a common means of ensuring conformity. Shlomo provided a vivid example of this community surveillance and control. He told me that when community authorities found out there was a TV in his home, they simply broke in and took it away.

In order to remain within her familiar world, Abby's initial rush of freedom had to be hidden. The more she explored options in cyberspace, however, the more she felt the painful contrast between the freedom she experienced in the wide-open space of the Internet and the depressing constraints of her daily life. Over time, Abby became increasingly dissatisfied with being closeted in public; she had come to hate "passing" and playing the part of the frum wife every time she stepped out of her home.

ABBY: I was still living in Monroe, New York, and I was uncomfortable there. I was always afraid that someone would find out about what I had and did in my home. I just couldn't stand it. All my life I was living in fear, and I just don't want to live in fear any more. And I don't think this life is what I want. I started hating that I was shaving my hair[2] and always being told what to do.

I like to be honest and direct, rather than pretending, and I just couldn't take it anymore. I started talking to my husband about how I really wanted to grow my hair. I did not want to shave it every month. But he became totally freaked out about that and insisted it was almost as severe a violation as breaking Shabbes. Since he was okay about the computer, I was surprised to hear how strongly he felt about this. He said it was a very big no-no to grow your hair. And I said, "OK."

But the more I was on the Internet, the braver I became. My parents were not around, no one was beating me, and I realized I could start to take charge of myself and that I do have choices. If I don't like something, I don't have to do it. So all of a sudden, I started to realize I could choose to do what I want. I started wanting to change because I realized that I could. I knew so little about the larger world, though, I could not even imagine what my options were.

I explored the web always wondering, "What does Abby want? What do I want to be? Do I want, for the rest of my life, to live in a community where you have to lie constantly about everything that you do?" I constantly lie, and come up with all these lies so, God forbid, they don't find out.

As I have previously explained, although Hasidic rabbis taught students that the commandments were part of an integrated system, with each being as important as the others, many of my research participants spoke in terms of a continuum of transgressive behaviors. They typically signaled the severity of the offense by comparing it to the intensity of other transgressions. To Abby's husband, breaking the taboo against a married woman growing her hair was as religiously offensive as breaking Sabbath, a violation so severe that many interviewees spoke of it as the worst form of transgression. One woman told me that if someone doesn't "keep" Shabbes (Kahn 1989) it is as if the person was not Jewish.[3] Abby had grown up in a powerfully patriarchal community, and since her husband did not want her to grow her hair freely, she decided against it. Growing her hair would be a visible and flagrant violation of community norms; others at the ritual bath would see her hair and know she had gone astray. This risky behavior could lead to her being rejected by other Satmars. Abby described feeling trapped between the enclave community she had always known and her desire for the world. Her conflict between individuation and community loyalty is typical of the passing stage.

This movement between worlds resembled that of gay, lesbian, bisexual, and transgendered people, Haredi identity changes are enacted and accomplished through the medium of the body. Abby became bolder in her transgressions, eventually choosing to grow her hair out despite her husband's protests. She had less and less desire to pass as "the good obedient wife," and yet she was not ready to strike out on her own. Even as she disinscribed the bodily ritual of married women shaving their hair monthly, she kept her growing hair hidden, so she could continue to pass. It was hard for her to face the threat of losing her husband and the sheltered cocoon of the enclave. She did not fully step out of the Hasidic world until she was prepared to leave her husband, be self-supporting, and create her own independent path in life.

Binyamin and Abby showed how exit routes often began through the gendered roles into which they had been socialized. Abby chose marriage to escape her family and begin exploring the outside world. Binyamin, like some of the other men who had been brilliant students, began his explorations of the outside world by locating taboo literature and discovering entirely new philosophies of life. But these were not the only means of beginning to step out. Others found alternative roads. As Binyamin said, "I would sneak away to libraries like others might sneak away to a strip club."

Shlomo, whom we met in prior chapters, chose precisely the latter route to learning about the secular world. His first major transgressions against Hasidic laws involved nights out with his friends at what he called "dancing clubs." He followed that violation with others, such as breaking *Shabbes,* eating treyf, and embarking upon explorations of his sexuality. His forays into these gentlemen's clubs eventually provided him with an opportunity to be sexually playful with non-Jewish women. The sequence is clear: Once those who wanted to leave the Haredi world broke one taboo, they became emboldened to transgress still further.

A few of my respondents had unusual family situations such that when they began transgressing and eventually passing, they had to do so not only between the outside society and their Hasidic enclave. If one of their parents became Modern Orthodox, for example, moving between the two religiously observant households required passing in three different contexts, each with its own requirements for how to dress, eat, and perform all other activities of daily life.

ALIZA

When we met first met Aliza in chapter 3, we learned of her deeply troubled childhood in an abusive household. As we spoke she suggested that her abuse was distinctly gendered, making her even more aware of women's low status in the community. Her abuse had completely destroyed her self-esteem. As the only girl in a family with four sons, she quickly figured out that her parents valued her, and her education, considerably less than that of her brothers.

> ALIZA: When I was a teenager, I went to Israel and wanted to study in Bar Ilan University [which was religiously observant]. My mother did not think there was much purpose in educating girls; they only needed to learn enough to be able to establish and run a frum household where they would be good wives and mothers. So I never learned algebra, history, geography, or trigonometry. But I still really wanted to go to college, and I felt I could do a good job at it because I knew I was smart enough to catch on to things and learn it fast. But I had no idea how to even apply to college, and no one helped me to figure it out.
>
> About this time, my parents divorced. My mother remained Hasidic, but my dad became Modern Orthodox. I had to figure out what these options meant for me and find myself religiously so when I married it would be with a man who has my same religious orientation. But I did not know what my beliefs were or the level of religious strictness I wanted in my life.
>
> When I returned from Israel, I did not move back into the Satmar enclave in Monroe, but rather to a Modern Orthodox neighborhood, where I moved in with a Modern Orthodox roommate. I became fascinated by her world. I saw her walk out of the house without any socks on. I was like, "Wow, you actually can do that!" Watching her was like a breath of fresh air that made me start to feel so free and powerful. She had been raised to be religious and observe God's

commandments, but she was very laid back about it. Unlike where I came from, she ate things that were kosher but not *cholov Yisroel* [dairy products that are supervised by a rabbi from milking through packaging], like Entenmann's cake. I remember feeling so cool going to shop in a goyishe store in a supermarket on Kings Highway where goyim go to shop, unlike the strictly cholov Yisroel mega supermarket near Kiryas Yoel, in Monsey [a reference to the huge market, catering to Hasidim, I had visited]. In my new neighborhood I shopped with people who were just like the rest of the world.

I felt free, no longer tied down and bound to the senselessness, and craziness, and corruption, and guilt that were my life at home. It was like this whole new world. I could buy Entenmann's and I was not doing something bad, but just something that normal people do. I could go without socks, and I felt so free to be able to do that.

I immediately understood how shopping in a supermarket that carried kosher, but also treyf, foods felt liberating to Aliza. The diverse food she saw opened her eyes to new culinary options, which opened the door to questions about various other realms to explore. Most people who have never met Hasidim, or known Orthodox Jews in general, cannot imagine how strictly religious commandments are taken. When I was working on an earlier version of this book, I showed two of the chapters to a colleague at the university where I work. She was a Unitarian and had been brought up with a liberal and open approach to religious membership. She expressed shock that anyone would believe eating shrimp was a big deal. I understood her puzzlement; she had not learned of the all-encompassing nature of Orthodox Jewish life and the strict adherence to God's laws it demanded. I explained that these rules about food choices were part of a larger system of beliefs and practices meant to separate the sacred from the profane, the observant Jews from all others. By following religious laws, and strictly observing all 613 commandments in the Hebrew Scriptures, they were able to create and maintain, within their communities, a sanctified life. God had commanded Jews to be holy, and their systematic observance of the commandments was their way of following God's mandate. For

Haredim and Modern Orthodox Jews, there was no leeway on these questions. Children were brought up to fear God's punishment if they violated the rules. For the Orthodox, the strictest observance of all the commandments is the only way to ensure Jewish survival in the future.

It is in this context that Aliza's jubilation at shopping at a "regular store with people who were just like the rest of the world" is easy to understand. She had told me that at this stage she was still living a pious life in her neighborhood and was maintaining both a Hasidic and a Modern Orthodox identity. Aliza's words about the regular people in the supermarket implied a dramatic shift in her perspective: She no longer saw Hasidim, who were the only kind of people she knew for the first seventeen years of her life, as the "regular people." The regular people were those who did not care about *cholov Yisroel*, or which particular group of rabbis stamped their seal of kashrut on specially designated foods. In this open, public space, Aliza was able to identify herself as a *regular* person, who was not limited by the strictures of her Satmar community.

Nevertheless, just as we saw with Binyamin, Shlomo, and Abby, living with an unresolved set of dilemmas was discomfiting and challenging. Aliza was trying to live a freer frum life, but she felt confused about where she stood in it all. In contrast to many of my conversation partners, who were eager to get out of the enclave but were bound by external constraints, such as their age, lack of education, job skills, and the dynamics of their personal relationships, Aliza did not want to turn her back on Orthodoxy. But she did not quite fit into any of the worlds she passed between. She still felt like the child who had no place to go.

Many of my respondents, like Aliza, felt extremely out of sorts during this period of passing. She described how she could not assess her own religious position wtihin the continuum of Orthodox communities.

ALIZA: I started to become very unhappy. It started to happen often that I would just like cry myself to sleep, and I didn't know why. I just felt this void and this emptiness, and I didn't have any guidance. I wasn't sure what it was. I felt so alone, not alone in that I didn't have friends, but alone in the sense of belonging nowhere.

Aliza's comments about depression depict a theme that recurs throughout many of my informants' stories. Many were depressed as children in families that abused them and were marginalized from the rest of the community. Their depression persisted through their passing phase, a period of feeling deeply disoriented and unsettled.

Although most respondents passed between two spheres—their Haredi worlds and the larger secular society—Elisheva, like Aliza, traveled betwixt and between three distinct spheres—the larger society, Modern Orthodox communities, and the Haredi world from which she came. Her frequent transitions between these three different realms complicated her attempts to discern what she herself wanted to be.

ELISHEVA

Everything was like this external game to show
my father that I was datiya [religiously observant
in a Modern Orthodox way], to show my mother that
I was a proper Hasidic girl, and to show people
on the street that I was secular.

I am introducing Elisheva in this chapter because her narrative of passing is distinct from nearly all others. Like Aliza, she spoke of passing between three distinct spheres, each with different norms for how she should dress, comport herself, and even with whom she may speak. Until she was five years old, Elisheva's household was intact and strictly Hasidic. That year her parents divorced, and each chose a different way of life, heading in two different directions. Her father moved away from Hasidism toward Modern Orthodoxy, whereas her mother became more punctilious in her observance. When Elisheva was in second grade, her father married a secular woman; the following year, her mother married a Hasidic man with five children. She and her mother, brother, and sister moved into his apartment, where there was very little space. The dynamics in this blended family were tense, and Elisheva no longer had any privacy.

LD: So you mentioned that by sixth grade you wanted to be out of your mother's house and out of the school you were in.

ELISHEVA: Yeah, I wanted to live with my father, but it's just that after he was remarried I think his wife didn't want me to come. For her it was like, you know, some girl, and she didn't feel like dealing with it. Um, even—the truth is even before that, since, like, fifth grade, since I was younger, I wanted to leave my mother's crazy religious house and move in with my father, and he completely refused. For many years he completely refused that I would go live with him.

Whenever I visited him, I always felt like a guest in his house. I felt I had nowhere to go, so first my parents sent me to live with cousins. But I didn't want to sit all day at my cousin's house; they were Haredim like my mother. I preferred to be out of the house as much as possible.

Elisheva described going to the Haredi girls' school, Beis Yaakov, when she lived with her cousins. She developed a routine of spending time at malls. As she described her illicit pleasure in transgressing community norms and going to shopping malls, she was simultaneously revealing how the taken-for-granted Hasidic habit of wearing long skirts faded, step by step. At the shopping mall she had an opportunity to express herself as an individual who was (at least temporarily) not trapped in others' desires concerning her identity. At her mother's home she played the frontstage part of good Hasidic daughter, when she visited her father she followed the norms of the Modern Orthodox community, and on her own she followed patterns she saw outside of her enclave and her father's Modern Orthodox world.

Elisheva passed by manipulating gendered clothing. She was not yet ready to make a statement about her preferences in life by going frontstage in her new garb: It would immediately reify a transformation of identity she had not yet undergone. Although she told me she had started to "loosen up a bit" by wearing shorter skirts and sleeves and not covering her legs, she still tried to keep these violations mostly backstage. She changed out of her Haredi clothing at secular places like malls or at mixed beaches, where she would wear a bikini.

Elisheva was clear by the time she was thirteen that she no longer wanted to be frum, as required by her mother and her community. In her father's house, there were fewer restrictions, but he and his wife did not offer to pay for her education. Her mother's family sent her to a boarding school in a very Haredi neighborhood. She realized then she would need to muster a convincing Haredi presentation of herself in order to secure an education that could lead her to a stable living situation.

> ELISHEVA: In order to avoid trouble at home, I was sent to a Haredi boarding school in ninth grade. At this school, there were a lot of people who were *hozrot b'teshuvah* [women who became Orthodox after being brought up as more secular Jews]. They really do a brainwashing there, telling everyone to be a *hozeret b'tshuva* [singular], meaning, even if they are already religiously observant, they can always come closer to God and more stringently follow the commandments. And I didn't like all that pressure. I was lucky and found some girls that also weren't Haredi at all, who, like me, were forced to be there, and they didn't want to become hozrot b'tshuva either. We used to do all sorts of nonsense together, and that's when I started wearing pants. But hidden, never visibly.

Many of the female respondents transgressed by wearing pants in private, backstage areas. Elisheva knew wearing pants was a major transgression against biblical laws forbidding members of one gender from wearing clothes of the other. When Elisheva spoke of the "sorts of nonsense" she did with her girlfriends, she described how they engaged in bodily transgressions. They enacted their resistance to Haredi norms defining women's appropriate clothing and separating them from men's clothing.

> LD: So where could you privately wear pants in a boarding school where you are always surrounded by others?
> ELISHEVA: Well, if my friends and I ran away from the boarding school for the day, then I'd wear pants. I even was extreme, once, I wore

shorts and a tank top. I have all sorts of pleasant memories and nostalgia. By tenth grade my two best friends there left, and I didn't want to keep studying there.

I returned home, where my father insisted I go to a religious school, even though he knew that I didn't want to be religious at all. He forced a religious lifestyle on me. Not Hasidic—both parents had given up on my remaining Hasidic, but they both at least wanted me to remain religious. So at this point, I no longer had to wear the hat, or perform the role of Hasidic girl. I was strongly forced to be *datiya* [Modern Orthodox], and no longer did I have to also be Hasidic.

LD: How did your life change when you were datiya instead of Hasidic?

ELISHEVA: Well, first of all, dress. I could wear short sleeves, no stockings, no socks. You know, it was a different outfit, different uniform. I could pretty much go wherever I wanted, even though my father tried to supervise where I went, like, he used to follow me sometimes and really stressed me out during that time. So I was living in my father's house, and I learned in a Modern Orthodox school. It was crazy: I had a life that was really split into three. At home [meaning, her father's house, at that point in her life] I needed to look religious. At my mother's house when I used to visit her, I used to have to look *haredit* [female form for Haredi], and in the street, when I used to hang out in the street, I used to exchange my skirt for pants, and I used to act like a secular person.

As she moved between three different worlds, Elisheva was astute enough to learn important things about the secular world that would serve her later when she broke free. I asked her how she learned to act like a secular person.

ELISHEVA: Well, I think because I moved from so many places in so many years it was, like, automatic. I like, absorbed how people were around me, and I became like them, I connected with the things that they connected, I copied them; I didn't show them the gap that was in my knowledge. I just, it was some sort of like, wisdom, like...I was very quickly able to fit in. People couldn't even tell that I was religious, that I still lived a parallel life, you know, in these three parallel existences. My way of presenting myself was all external, everything was like this external game to show my father that I was datiya, to show my mother that I was haredit, and to show people on the street that I was secular.

In twelfth grade I started meeting all sorts of people on the street, all sorts of, like, negative characters. Like you know, people that do not-good things. And so I hung out with this sort of people, you know, like all people that were ostracized for all sorts of reasons. For social reasons, you know. So they, like, wander around the town, and they drink and smoke and get in trouble.

Elisheva was not entirely comfortable in the world of troublemakers, either. She began to despair of ever finding a place for herself. As she told me, "Little by little, I deteriorated into a depression, I really sunk down into it." As we have seen, depression is a common theme in these narratives. For Elisheva, the pressures of wearing three different costumes and playing three distinct roles were overwhelming.

Nearly all defectors in this chapter, as well as others I interviewed, described being in the passing stage for a very long time, over a period of years, sometimes even a decade. Aryeh was unusual in describing himself as somewhat comfortable passing between two worlds.

ARYEH

I was sort of teetering on the edge of being religious,
not being religious. I always knew why I wasn't
comfortable with it. I was never sure why
I was comfortable with it a little.

Aryeh, a young man from a Satmar Hasidic household, told me he had ascertained at a young age he did not fit into his Hasidic community. Unlike most of my other respondents, he never strongly identified with his religious identity, so he approached his first transgressions—violating laws concerning dress and bodily comportment—without the fear of punishment so prominent in the accounts of others. Unlike the others, he did not feel torn between worlds, or that he was living a bifurcated life. He spoke about transgressing and passing in a matter-of-fact way, as if it was not a source of anguish and internal turmoil for him.

Nevertheless, as long as he was a teenager and lacked the knowledge and means to leave his community, he depended on his parents. He was comfortable transgressing in private, so he continued smoking on Shabbes, eating nonkosher foods, and interacting with girls and then slipping back into his Hasidic self when he was back with his family and community. With the exception of his frontstage, public presentation of hair that was longer than normative, he committed his various transgressions outside of the confines of his enclave and continued to begrudgingly perform the rituals expected of him when in the community.

> ARYEH: I never thought, "Oh, maybe this all really does mean something and I'm doing something wrong." I knew I was not. I knew many people who had ceased observing most commandments but felt they still believed in God, or in the Hasidic way of life, and so they were full of guilt. I did not feel any guilt about what I was doing.

Despite his comfort with his transgressive and passing behaviors, Aryeh wondered whether if he stayed much longer in the religious community, he might come to feel some kind of connection to it. He was open to this possibility when he enrolled in a Hasidic high school in Israel that specialized in working with ambivalent Haredim both Hasidic and Yeshivish. The school tolerated rebellious behavior, and it had a reputation for working patiently with each student to help him lose his desire for violating the codes of Jewish law. The school succeeded in turning some of its defiant students back into frum members of the community.

> ARYEH: I was in a Haredi high school, which, as far as my parents were concerned, was so liberal it might not even be appropriately religious, but it was a good place for a lot of people like me. I was comfortable there; the other kids were similar to me. This cool guy ran the place,

and he knew his audience really well. He would approach kids and say, "Hey, you really belong here."

The school had this reputation of being a place where people like me belonged. Going there made the kids comfortable, and the parents were happy, thinking their kids might come out of that place religious. It was a good place. It was very laissez faire...they left you alone a lot. They were very subtle and slow, and it was very good for a lot of people who felt: "Okay, well, I really want to become religious, but I'm just not. And you know, I've got to do it in some way." For me, it just kind of never worked. I spent a lot of that year in Israel sort of finding myself. I'm not sure what that means, but...

The school in Israel provided Aryeh with a social context in which he felt his questioning and rebellious spirit were accepted. He finally felt a sense of belonging there. He knew that the only way he could sustain a connection to his family and community was through becoming more religious himself, and part of him hoped his experience in Israel would lead him down that path. Indeed, his stint in Israel did not become his exit route. Rather, the interest in scholarship he developed in school led him to stay in the community and learn more, despite his ongoing transgressions. He was in that unsettled state of not knowing for sure who he was and what he wanted to be.

ARYEH: I was involved with Jewish things. I was sort of moderately religious in some ways. I sort of did religious type things I guess. I kind of...I had this weird relationship with religion, I guess, for at least a year or two as an undergraduate. And I was thinking about it, and I was sort of teetering on the edge of being religious, not being religious. I always knew why I wasn't comfortable with it. I was never sure why I was comfortable with it a little.

LD: Did you think that those feelings might pass?

ARYEH: Yeah. Yeah, I thought, at some point, especially when I was in Israel for the year, I thought, "Well, maybe I will be religious one day," and this is what kept me reading. As I became sort of more intellectual, I thought, "Maybe one day I'm going to pick up that Jewish book that's going to just do it for me and make it all make sense." And I kept picking up books, but none ever clicked for me. Nevertheless, I kept reading these books, cover to cover. I continued passing with the hope that if only I'd just read the right book, meet the right people, I might develop religious feelings.

When Aryeh returned from his stay in Israel he began to take on the scholarly role expected of brilliant young Torah scholars. Although he was still questioning his religion's teachings, Aryeh made an effort to behave like a proper Hasidic man and worked hard on himself so he could once again identify with his enclave community.

While Aryeh was struggling to find himself and hoping he might find the path back to religion, he passed back and forth between the role and comportment of a young Jewish scholar and a resentful, rebellious spirit who occasionally ate treyf and violated the bodily norms for dress, hair, comportment, and diet. It was not until Aryeh moved out of his parents' home and into an apartment with a friend that his passing behavior ended; he was happy to free himself of the constant battle of trying to live in two worlds. Although he tried to find a religious spirit in himself so he might still belong, he was not plagued by the guilt and fear described by many others.

Sam, a brilliant Yeshivish Jew whom we met earlier was unique; he was not plagued by any ambivalence and never tried, from when he began questioning, to become frum again. He also differed from other respondents in the rapidity through which he passed the interwoven stages of defection. It had been clear to him from a young age that he wanted nothing to do with Orthodoxy. While he was young, his parents exercised control over him to remain in the community, but as soon as he could live on his own, he was primed to step out.

SAM

At this great rabbi's funeral the eulogies were going on and on and I was a rotten little rebel back then.

I was sitting there reading about the senselessness of religion,
but I still looked like I belonged.

When I asked Sam, an erudite, scholarly man in his late forties when I met him, to tell me his "life narrative," he replied, "The one I tell changes all the time. Not always, but, you know." He was the only one I met in the course of this study who seemed aware of, and articulated, the sense that life stories are fluid and are constructed differently according to audience and social context. This was my perspective on narratives as well, so I immediately felt a strong rapport with him. We played Jewish geography and learned we were from the same neighborhood in Queens, New York. His family owned the take-out kosher food store in which my family shopped. Having established the similarity of our early experiences, we both relaxed into the interview conversation.

Sam, like many other respondents, grew up in a family in which his parents diverged greatly in their religious commitments. Neither his mother nor his father had been raised Orthodox, but when his dad was in the army during World War II, he had several profound experiences that changed his life: He experienced anti-Semitism in the service, his younger brother was killed, and he helped to liberate several concentration camps. What he saw in the camps strengthened his desire to affirm his Jewishness. He came back to the United States and joined an Orthodox synagogue.

In contrast, Sam's mother had been raised a secular Jew. The two became engaged before he left for the army, and when he returned, she wanted nothing to do with his Orthodox predilections. Nevertheless, her parents compelled her to go ahead with the marriage. They had a strong moral conviction that it was wrong for their daughter to get engaged to a man and then, when he came back from war, to just say goodbye. They pointed out that during the four years he had been in the army, she collected his salary, and therefore could not leave him now. She was pushed to get married.

Listening to Sam tell this story, the outcome seemed fairly clear:

SAM: So, they married, and it was miserable. Right from the start it was a horrible marriage. And I was the oldest, so my father had high hopes for me. Unconsciously he felt that if I became an ilui [a brilliant Talmud scholar] and a great learned rabbi, it would somehow relieve some of the anguish he retained from his seeing the concentration camps.

So, I was immediately tagged as an ilui and that meant rabbis would come up to him and congratulate him on having a son like me. And for my father, that was heaven. That was the meaning of his life. These people knew him, and respected him, because of me. The rabbis and my father decided to send me to various schools that were right out of the eighteenth century.

As we saw with Ehud, Haredi parents' greatest joy in the world was to have a son who was deemed a *talmid chacham*. Both Sam's and Ehud's fathers felt their suffering in the Holocaust might be diminished by the joy of a son who was an ilu. In all Haredi worlds only men could study in advanced *yeshivot*, and so this venerated role was unavailable to women. As we learned in chapter 2, in one of the books of the Talmud, a rabbi asserted, "Anyone who teaches his daughter Torah [it is as if] he is teaching her *tiflut*." Given women's limitations, they would surely turn the words of the Torah into trivialities.[4] By not teaching women to study sacred texts, the patriarchal order of Haredi life maintained and reproduced itself.

I asked Sam which schools he had been sent to. He described how each yeshiva varied by the particular worldview of the Haredi groups who sent their children to study there, as well as by the intellectual prowess of its students. In this world, knowing what school someone attended provided a great deal of information about his religious origins and perspective. Also, I imagined that I would be familiar with his school since we had grown up in the same neighborhood.

SAM: Yeshiva Torah Va'daas [Torah and knowledge]. It was a small school.

Sam started to explain the meaning of his school's name, and I interrupted him (something I try to avoid in interviews) to say, "You don't have to define any Hebrew for me." I imagine at that moment I was showing off a bit, or just making my bona fides clear to him. I also was surprised, given how much "Jewish geography" we had shared—he was familiar with the neighborhood in which I grew up as well as my synagogue and Hebrew day schools—that he thought he needed to explain the Hebrew to me. Perhaps translating terms was habitual for him, given that he worked at a Christian university.

SAM: The school was in a cellar in east New York. We would study in the *heder* [Jewish school where young boys formally start their Jewish education] from about seven in the morning till about three in the afternoon. Then we had what was called "English classes," which were all the other subjects that did not include the study of Torah and Talmud. And the shul I went to was Haredi—not Hasidic, but Haredi just the same. It was very narrowly construed. Those were the kinds of yeshivas I went to. When I was about eight I was pulled out of this school and was sent to a place that was even stricter and had a narrower curriculum. In my second year of high school I told my parents I was quitting yeshiva altogether and would enroll in a public school. In order to avoid that possibility, I was sent to a yeshiva which was not on the left wing or anything, but compared to where I had been, it was a wide open place. We actually had a half-day of "English," as it were. In the stricter school those two hours of English were taught by eighteen-year-old girls who could barely speak English themselves. I recall these teachers; it's a miracle that I am literate in English.

But all the time I was reading like crazy. I'd read five books a week. Finish two on Friday nights. What else was there to do? I read things like *Tales of King Arthur* and had no idea the Holy Grail had anything to do with Christianity. I just thought the story was fabulous. Lancelot and Arthur and Sir Gawain and the Green Knight; I read every edition of it. I read it over and over. I knew it was mysteriously religious, but I knew it wasn't Jewish. That didn't matter.

Sam's narrative follows the trajectory of Binyamin's account. As we saw, he, too, was marked as a brilliant student who would grow up to become a great rabbi in the community. Like Binyamin, Sam used his talents as a young man with a "great mind" to discover new worlds outside of the enclave. His naïveté about the story of King Arthur, and what it represented, can be attributed to the limited attention given to "English" subjects as he was growing up. His studies were often conducted in Yiddish. Interestingly, Haredi girls were taught to be more fluent in writing and speaking English; that way, when their husbands studied at the yeshivot they could take care of all household affairs. Also, they were the ones who, when they finished high school, taught "English" (as Sam defined it) in the community's high schools.

Although Sam's story traces a similar arc—chronology—of events, Sam's transition through the stages of passing was quicker than that of Binyamin and Ehud. All three started questioning before their bar mitzvahs at age thirteen and spent many years deepening their questions as they continued to read and explore alternative philosophies. Binyamin had a long passing stage in which he tried many times to redouble his efforts to accept the absolutist world of his Haredi community and remain in his settled life. Binyamin did not engage in any conscious violations of the commandments until he was in his early twenties, when he ate nonkosher food for the first time. Sam's trajectory was quicker. He knew as a young boy he did not want to remain Haredi, and he never doubted that stance throughout high school.

SAM: And by the time I graduated from high school, I had read Bertrand Russell. What was his book? *Why I Am an Atheist* or something [the actual title is *Why I am Not a Christian*]. And I can remember reading it, in fact, at a funeral for a rabbi. The eulogies were going on and on, and I was a rotten little rebel back then. I was sitting there reading about the senselessness of religion, but I still looked like I belonged. You know, I was there with a beard, dark short hair, a big black yarmulke, and very slovenly [a typical image of a young man at a yeshiva]. You know—the typical yeshiva boy outfit, the dark pants, the white shirt...

After high school I was sent to Ner Yisroel (light of Israel), a strictly *Haredi* and very distinguished yeshiva for young men in Baltimore. Going there, ironically, was kind of an escape for me. I was able to get away from my parents. So the guys from my yeshiva would go into town and study at Loyola, a Catholic University, at night. It was a very anti-Semitic place at that time. So anyway, I was taking evening courses, which meant a whole lot more to me than anything I studied during the day. I began to act out. I would not study the texts for study hall, and although I spent my days there like a good student, it was a front. I actually sat there reading secular material and writing about my philosophical beliefs. After four years I had had enough.

I have presented several accounts of bright men who used their scholarly skills to find new worlds of ideas and meanings; their exposure to secular ideas led them to question their Haredi life, producing a state of confusion and discomfort. Sam, in contrast to these others, did not remain in a questioning stage for many years. By the end of high school, he was already aware he was passing. From the outside he appeared to fit in. He had the right comportment, facial hair, and clothing of a Haredi man and was using his skills for textual analysis to learn. But he was aware of the ways he was performing embodied resistance, such as reading a book on atheism at the funeral of a distinguished rabbi. In contrast to many of my informants, who said they frequently tried to quell their questions and slip back into role, Sam knew he wanted to leave and accelerated the process as much as he could.

All of my participants experienced a passing stage during which they moved between two or more worlds. They experienced great confusion and unhappiness during these years. It was uncomfortable, especially for those who had grown up in a strict community where there was only one way of being. Clearly, passing was a major stage in all the defectors' narratives. But they varied in terms of the length they stayed in this liminal state and how long they lived with serious doubts. They were different, also, in the depth of suffering they described. Many spoke of serious depression.

The passing stage was described differently by women and men. For the men who had been trained as scholars, as well as the women who thirsted for secular knowledge, it was an intellectual process but also an intense emotional struggle. Women who married without officially leaving the community described how they were able to explore the secular world during the day while their husbands were out studying. Although in the Haredi world men receive more respect and have a greater degree of freedom in their lives, ironically, during the passing stage the women had enough freedom to enter into and explore many dimensions of the secular world.

CHAPTER FIVE

STEPPING OUT

I had never traveled this road before.

"Stepping out," the phase in which defectors left their families, communities, religious practices, and taken-for-granted bodily routines, was intimidating, risky, and required great courage and self-confidence. As someone who left Orthodox Judaism forty years ago, I am especially attuned to the ways in which leaving one's familiar world can be fraught with emotion, guilt, fear, and doubt. All my conversation partners described their fears of the terrible consequences that would inevitably befall them if they failed to observe the religious commandments and, even worse, if they left the community. Hasidic socialization aimed to convince children that they would be severely punished by God if they failed to obey their parents or observe all 613 biblical commandments as they were interpreted in their respective communities. Hasidic children did not grow up with a conception of a loving and forgiving God; instead, they were told that God was harsh and stern and would penalize them for every transgression, even accidental ones.

Esther, one of my respondents, highlighted this point.

The whole religion revolved around trying to escape or avoid punishment. And the fear—like God is a monster, really, to such an extent that if you are not nice today, then you will later have sick children. Similarly, if you don't show proper respect to your parents, you will live in poverty for the rest of your life.

Another respondent vividly described what she had heard about the sequence of disasters that would befall rebels: They would get worms in their stomachs, be hung by their tongues, and sent to *Gehanna* [Yiddish for hell] when they died. The basic message was that if they violated God's laws, he would send them every possible sorrow, sickness, and tragedy.

In addition to these deeply rooted fears, defectors enumerated the countless other risks involved. Many spoke of the profound emotional costs of losing their families and communities. Some feared their parents would disown them. They knew they would hurt their siblings' marriage prospects because families who "lost" a child to the outside world were stigmatized. In the world of *shidduchim* (plural of shidduch) they had less exchange value and would therefore find fewer desirable marriage partners.

Interviewees' personal crises concerning the role of religion in their lives were thoroughly intertwined with bodily, cognitive, emotional, familial, social, and cultural doubts. Throughout their upbringing, they were taught how to use the Hasidic cultural tool kit (comprising values, language, cultural stories, and other skills) as well as embodied rituals as a guide to their actions. Lessons about how to precisely follow God's commandments were so deeply internalized that they guided members' automatic behaviors all day long. Leaving would render them scriptless. The United States has a multitude of distinct social and cultural communities, each with their own widely varying norms and strategies of actions; in order to leave, defectors had to figure out who they might become and what they wanted in their new lives. This task was particularly difficult since their knowledge of the world outside the enclave was minimal. They did not possess the basic skills required to perform the actions that come with living an independent life, such as finding an apartment and a job and comfortably interacting with the non-Hasidic world. Those on the verge of leaving did not yet know where they could go, how to talk with secular people, or how to even dress appropriately. In order to transform their identities, they would have to learn an integrated system of new bodily practices through which they would perform and constitute their new identities.

Leaving the Hasidic world was accomplished through the medium of the body. For Hasidic Jews who defect from enclave communities, identity transformation involves a negotiation between the habitual and internalized routine bodily performances that sustained their religious identities and the extensive range of bodily practices available in the wider society. Accomplishing an integrated sense of self required them to disinscribe—to remove—the internalized, taken-for-granted bodily techniques that had shaped every moment of their waking lives before defection.

The embodied transformations of leaving produced a shift from one socially mediated understanding of the body—that of the Hasidic world—to another, that of the wider society, and of the group that will become their new social context. Whereas Hasidic Jews understand the body as a divinely created vessel that is to be disciplined through strict subordination of self to God's laws, the contemporary secular understanding of the body constructs it as a vehicle for self-expression and personal exploration. Thus, as Hasidim began to defect from their communities and establish new identities outside their enclaves, they engaged in a continuous negotiation between the corporeal performances that sustained their former identities and the extensive range of bodily practices available in the wider society.

Formerly Orthodox Jews who changed their diet, hair, shaving practices, and clothing as they left the community negotiated their new identities, playing out new personal and religious orientations toward the self on the bodily canvas. They rejected the gendered Haredi framework for bodily action (including the assumption that such rules and regulations have divine origins) and instead adopted the wider society's notion that fluidity in appearance and performance is perfectly acceptable. This process is much deeper than a noticeable change of dress; it is hard to uproot automatic, taken-for-granted ways of being and acting in the world. Exiters leave a community wherein their bodily practices are regulated and divinely justified to join a society wherein they must pick and choose—from a wide variety of options—those bodily practices through which to define their new identities.

Interviewees' stories illustrated that as they rejected the disciplined bodies required by a transcendent authority, they began to invoke a discourse of personal choice, an individualistic approach that challenged the collectivist orientation that characterizes a Haredi upbringing. Defecting required a strong sense of oneself as an independent being who is not bound by the traditions and duties of his or her community. This embodied shift in identity was not without its challenges. The deeply ritualized character of Haredi embodied practices creates what social theorists Anthony Giddens and Bryan Turner refer to as a strong sense of ontological security—a comfortable sense of being in the world—and of being a member of the group (Giddens 1991; Turner 1984, 1992). As defectors began to reject the Hasidic mandates for culturally distinctive dress, hairstyles, and bodily comportment, they experienced a sense of dissociation from their bodily routines and from the identities established by the repetition of traditional practices, leaving them vulnerable to existential anxieties that threatened their sense of self-identity.

My conversation partners' accounts of stepping out of the enclave highlight the interwoven motifs of emancipation and ontological vulnerability. This chapter illustrates how difficult it was for these members of enclave communities to move beyond their feelings of insecurity and helplessness and toward a stronger sense of liberation, empowerment, and independence. This movement is not necessarily always in one direction—out. Sarah's narrative, for example, shows how setbacks, such as severe depressive illness, hinder defectors' path outward.

GENDERED EXIT STRATEGIES

Male defectors whose culture encouraged them to be scholars started their exit by using the analytic skills they had acquired growing up. As teenagers, they read widely, seeking alternative philosophies and worldviews. By probing secular literature, they came to understand that the realities of their enclave world were relative and not absolute. This newly acquired knowledge revealed to them the tears in the seemingly solid canopy that was supposed to protect, stabilize, and give meaning to their lives as Hasidim. Their new critical perspectives provided a basis for challenges to the totalistic worldview of their enclave community.

Over time their questioning turned into strong doubts, but, until they had the resources to leave, they spent years in the discomfiting state of cognitive dissonance, torn between the only world they had ever known and the lures of larger society. Many of these men sought to resolve this tension by bringing their bodily habits in line with their new ideas. Ehud vividly described how he ceased observing the religious obligations incumbent on men in their community.

E H U D

But I had no choice. I really had to do it.
I couldn't live with the contradiction.

As we have seen in previous excerpts from Ehud's narrative, he was struggling internally between his deep emotional commitment to an exacting routine of the gendered bodily practices of his Yeshivish community and his cognitive doubts about the absolute truth of the community's worldview. He had uttered the phrase "then the chicken happened" in a passive voice, as if the event was external to him. Perhaps this language allowed him to avoid taking full responsibility for that first transgression. As we continued our conversation, he recalled how the contradictions in his life ultimately became intolerable and he felt the need to bring greater congruence and peace into his being. He could no longer silence the arguments in his mind and he hated the hypocrisy of passing. He decided to cease performing the male ritual of putting tefillin on his arm and head every morning in order to pray.

EHUD: The next thing I did was I stopped putting on the tefillin every day, which was very hard. I felt like I was committing bloody murder. I mean, I was really, uh, I don't know…cutting off one of my limbs or something. But I had no choice. I really had to do it. I couldn't live with the contradiction. Why was I putting on the tefillin? I was betraying it all by eating treyf, anyway.

Ehud's extreme statement in which he compared his ceasing to observe the laws of kashrut with murder, indicated how deeply his identity and his sense of himself as a moral being were intertwined with observing religious precepts. The language here is extreme; perhaps he felt as if he was killing off his past by ceasing to perform the commanded ritual practices. The more Ehud felt disoriented and frustrated with his ongoing internal conflicts, the stronger was his push out of the community. He could no longer silence the arguments in his mind, but he could put an end to feeling hypocritical by changing his daily activities and establishing consistency between his ideas and his behavior. His words indicate deep ambivalence about his choices: "Cutting off a limb" and "committing bloody murder" signal how painful it was for Ehud to remove the markers of his Haredi identity and substitute a more secular one.

He told me he had lived with these contradictions as long as he had because, like many others I met, he felt guilt about the impact his defection might have on his parents, especially his father, whom he loved and respected deeply.

LD: Was he angry at you?

EHUD: No. No. No, he wasn't. He was such a strong person, but I sensed he was wounded. I always experienced him as a man who knew exactly where he was headed, why he was doing what he was doing, full of energy and determination. He lived through many, many things, and brought up a family and provided for them. He was an admirable man in whom I never experienced any weakness. But one Sunday when I was twenty-four or twenty-five, we were walking, and I told him I had stopped putting on tefillin. At that moment he turned to me and said: "So what are you telling me? Are you telling me that I was misguided, all of what I did when I brought you up? Are you telling me that this is all, this is...I was wrong to do this, the way I brought you up?" And this was hard for me to take.

146

His statement was pretty dramatic, because he was sixty-five and dying of cancer. And he was full of energy, and he died of cancer, so that was very hard. He suffered a lot. It was a horrible thing. But another aspect which is more germane to this interview is that he never made his peace with neither mine nor my sister's leaving the religion, which he experienced as a betrayal. And although both of us knew he was deeply hurt about this, neither of us had really had the ability or the courage or the resources to have a heart-to-heart conversation with him, especially after we learned he was dying of cancer. There was no longer any need or possibility to start this conversation. It wasn't even relevant. I don't know, but there were so many things left unspoken when he died.

I felt extremely sorry that I caused him so much pain, but I couldn't see how I could have not done what I did. But when I heard a tape which he left, which included a very simple request for my sister and me: "Please come back," I was devastated.

Ehud's sorrow over hurting his father left him with a heavy burden of guilt. He had sought to end his emotional turmoil by bringing his practices into alignment with his thoughts. Despite feeling certain that he could no longer continue to live a contradiction, Ehud continued to feel internally tormented by the painful emotions resulting from his father's deep distress and pain.

EHUD: So, I felt stuck. I could not settle down, but kept groping to figure out who I was and what new identity I wanted to adopt. At that point, after my father's death, I started a sort of spiraling, a downward spiraling for a year or two where I was sad all the time. During that period I had a hard time being myself, knowing what I was, what I wanted to be, where I was, what I was doing with myself, and just who were the people I wanted to hang out with.

LD: Were you in a depression?

EHUD: Well, to an extent I was still functioning but in other ways I wasn't functioning. I was spending very, very lonely evenings hanging out in bars, you know, or in restaurants or just taking long strolls, walking around feeling like a complete misfit and was overwhelmed by my utter loneliness. I remember being very miserable; yes, I'd say I was depressed. To cover over this pain I read a lot, tried to play some music, and to paint...I don't know. I was an existentially tormented twenty-five-year-old boy, really, in New York, all by myself.

Ehud told me that meeting new people, particularly those outside of the Jewish community, provided a social context in which he was able to re-establish a settled life. He told me his new friends were almost exclusively non-Jewish, a drastic change from his earlier life:

> EHUD: It's like I was putting on a new skin. You know, I underwent like a transition, after a seemingly endless period of feeling torn. I felt I had spent *arbaim shana bamidbar* [forty years in the desert, an allusion to the biblical narrative of the ancient Israelites][1] until I met some non-Jewish friends who helped me learn about secular culture and the various skills I would need to create a new identity.

Ehud's statement about putting on a new skin was meant to suggest he had shed his old Haredi self and was emerging into a new one. The use of the term *new skin* provides a metaphor for the embodied process of defection. As he shed his old practices and the Haredi identity he created and accomplished he *simultaneously* performed new ones. For example, instead of wearing a beard, he was now shaving. Instead of wearing the white shirt and black pants uniform of Haredi men, he donned colorful and sometimes patterned shirts and blue jeans. Ehud's choice of words revealed the embodied nature of his defection. As he began to break out of the restraints of the all-consuming routinized practices of his community, he grew "new skin." Our skin is the visible, physical representation of who we are; as he took on a new identity, his new round of bodily practices simultaneously created that identity and performed it. Through the performance of his new secular embodied routines a new sense of self developed—"I am a person who...[now] eats treyf"— signifying his breaking through the constraints of Haredi life and developing the physical practices that would be part of his newly embodied identity. He described his years with his non-Jewish friends as a period in which he continually searched for clarity about who he really was. His close circle of friends was, for him, a substitute for the religious community he had just left. They spent a great deal of time together. Their group activities provided him with opportunities to learn about the world outside the enclave.

Knowing that I too was a defector, Ehud relished telling me in detail about all the treyf food he had eaten at that stage:

> I learned to discern fine wines. I started cooking and started appreciating the cheeses from around the world and learning about good food, including all the treyf food. You name it, I ate them all. Snails and mussels and oysters and everything. It was quite interesting. It took a while for me to really get used to eating pork roast, yeah. I ate pork. I did it. I don't know if I felt guilty or not. You know, what is guilt? I don't know. It's hard to say whether I was doing anything wrong, because I was not harming anybody. But I did feel a great and very deep sense of loss. Absolutely. But there was nothing I could do about it; I just had to do what I did.

Ehud, like my other respondents, found it difficult to figure out who he was outside his community, where his role had been clearly defined. He did not know how to fit into the larger society. His depression was related not only to his feelings of guilt, but also to his loss of a stable sense of self and the difficulty of constructing a new one. As respondents stepped out, they had to engage in a process of cultural learning that would equip them with the knowledge, skills, and bodily practices that would become routine aspects of their new identities.

Ehud's description of how he finally left Orthodoxy emphasizes the embodied nature of the changes he had to make. He used the phrase "growing a new skin" to describe the feeling of shedding his old self and taking on a new identity that would develop as he learned new, secular routines and techniques of the body. Establishing a new friendship circle provided him the social context he needed to learn a new way of life. I imagine that he was better able to come out as a non-Haredi when he was away from Jewish communities: There were no reminders of the life he used to live. Those who might have been offended by his transgressions were no longer present. Hanging out with goyim provided him a safe space where he could try on new ways of being in the world, drop his former embodied rituals, and learn the new ones that would become the embodied basis of his new identity.

LEAH

I wanted the world!

Leah, like Ehud, also used her gendered upbringing to find a path out of her Hasidic community. Women's gendered socialization into the roles of wife and mother and the community's emphasis on early marriage for women had the unintended consequence that women who desired to leave could find and marry a fellow doubter. Then the two of them could exit the Haredi community. Strategically, these women sought partners who similarly desired to leave the community or at least were tolerant of their exploration. This pathway to stepping out allowed women, ironically, to use their socially limited roles to expand their horizons. There were also a few men who used marriage as the path of least resistance in their process of defecting.

> LEAH: I wished I could leave the house by myself, but where would I go? I just couldn't figure it out financially, and I couldn't figure it out emotionally, like how would I leave. I didn't have the wherewithal to pack my bags and leave. I didn't know where to go, and I didn't have a lot of friends from the outside world.
>
> I knew I was not ready to get married, but after exploring my alternatives I realized my only viable option was to marry and become established. The boy I was introduced to [Ben] was from my world, but he, too, was seeking to defect. He had already begun to violate the rules. I thought he could be just right—like me, he did not want to be religious, but he still could pass; he knew how to walk into my father's house with a yarmulke and suit and say Good Shabbes, and make small talk.

I guess we helped each other leave. We married right after I graduated from college. Although I loved him at the time, I felt it was obvious that I was not ready for marriage, and I thought my parents
were just idiots for not seeing this. But they were relieved to see me
get married and become someone else's responsibility.

Leah and Ben provided each other with the ability and confidence to
challenge all the truths they had been socialized to believe, and to leave
the community together. Referring to her marriage, I suggested her husband was her exit ticket, and she concurred. She told me how she knew,
even before she married, that it was unlikely to work out, but at the
time it was good for both of them. Together, Leah and Ben moved to
a place in Brooklyn that was farther than walking distance from their
parents' home, ensuring their families could not visit them on Shabbes.
Leah knew this distance gave the couple space to establish their own
lives, without the obligation to perform religious identities.

> LEAH: Yeah. We were not religious anymore, so that was great. But I
> thought his desire to leave Orthodoxy would also include his willing-
> ness to transcend the gender barriers we had grown up with. When I
> didn't take his name and he was okay with that, I thought he would be
> cooperative about my other feminist ideas; but when it came to house-
> work he refused. When I left my Hasidic world, I sought liberation. My
> husband, however, was loath to give up all the male privilege with which
> he had grown up. He would not do any housework, although we were
> both working full time. We had lots of fights about that, and I guess I was
> not yet liberated enough at that time to assert myself and challenge him.[2]

Their marriage helped both of them to leave, but over time it became
increasingly obvious to Leah that they were not a good match; they
were going in opposite directions. Whereas he was content with ceasing
to observe the commandments and stay in the apartment, Leah wanted
to break free of all restrictions. As she said: "I wanted the *world*!"

And so the world opened up to her. She divorced her husband and
moved into the East Village, a move that took her even farther from the

Brooklyn enclave in which she grew up. However, her narrative emphasized her lack of knowledge of how to behave in this larger world. She had no experience meeting men, or dating, and described herself as having no idea how to interact with "regular" people. When she began to meet men, she felt she had no idea what to say to them. In contrast to her shyness, they seemed so much more sophisticated and worldly. She felt they looked down on her naïveté.

Ehud's new cultural lessons about how to behave in the secular society began when he met non-Jewish friends. Leah pursued a similar strategy for learning about the new culture. She sought out people who could help her shed her old automatic habits and teach her new social and cultural skills. She described a new friend who served as her model and guide to behavior in the secular world.

> LEAH: I remember I met this one woman where I was working, and she was just like very forward. She would be very sexually forward with people, such as saying to a man at the bar: "Hello. Come here. Let me take a look at you." I was so shocked it was like my jaw hung down. This woman was just sort of like *Sex in the City*. So even though in my mind I wanted to be free and cool, I still acted like yeshiva girl. And so it was…I'd be like dumbfounded.
>
> And I remember once she took me to a bar, and we went around talking to the people there. She was a much older woman than me, but she said, "I like you," and so she took me on as her project. I thought it was great, because I didn't have to say very much. And so we went to bars together, and she taught me how to smoke. Cigarettes were a cool prop in bars; she taught me how to hold my cigarette in one hand and a cocktail in the other.

Although Leah presented herself in our conversation as having fully left Hasidic life at this time, as she began to explore the world of dating in the East Village, a bohemian neighborhood, she believed she still carried and presented herself like a "*schleppy* [awkward, clumsy, and unattractive] woman." She was still dressing according to the Hasidic idea of a modest woman and had not yet learned how to interact with men. Although Leah had fully stepped out of Hasidism into a community with vastly different gender norms, her self-presentation revealed the powerful, lingering impact of her strict upbringing. Over time, she met other women at the bar, but they seemed "other" to her; they resembled the actresses in the television show *Sex in the City*, a model of womanhood that challenged everything she had been taught about appropriate female behavior. She sensed how difficult it would be for her to find a place for herself in this new world, just as she had known she would never fit into the Hasidic model of womanhood. Getting along and making friends in the secular society, however, was a challenge; she found it difficult to disinscribe her internalized habits and her feelings of awkwardness in the presence of men.

Leah's desire for "the *world*" led her not only into neighborhood bars, but to years of traveling abroad, where she was not expected to say very much because she did not know the language of the groups she met. Her interactions were limited, and so everyone thought she was sweet and she felt the same about them. No one asked her questions about who she was and where she came from; they simply saw her as a young woman from New York. As she traveled and observed various cultures she came to understand how people everywhere did what they had been raised to do; all social groups required some measure of conformity from their members. Leah came to see everyone was simply repeating the habits they had learned through socialization. She told me that in all places "there was a craziness about habitual lives," and that insight helped her put her Hasidic upbringing into a broader context. "I started understanding things differently, and it made me feel a little bit better about myself, where I came from, and who I was. I started to figure it out, and I think contextualizing a little bit, like okay. Orthodoxy is not the worst thing, each group has its own rigidities."

Leah's travels taught her about cultural relativism and that other cultures, too, were conformist. She also came to see the patriarchy of Hasidic life as a more universal pattern, which helped her become a bit more forgiving of the world in which she had grown up.

ARYEH

I really felt as if I had stepped out of it.

In the last chapter we met Aryeh, a young man from the Satmar enclave in Kiryas Yoel. His story demonstrates it was not only women who found their way out of the community through marriage, It was his exit route as well.

Aryeh, like many other respondents, had been raised Satmar in the Kiryas Yoel enclave in New York. As a teenager he felt restricted and sought friends who were similarly rebellious. He began to hang out with "the wrong kinds of friends," who were more sophisticated and open-minded. Nevertheless, he was careful to maintain his religious practices whenever he was on the front stage, within view of the prying eyes in his enclave. He began rebelling more visibly, however, when he was about fourteen. At that point he told his father.

> ARYEH: I really could not take school anymore. It was just something that I could not see myself doing. I just said I did not want to go back to school. My dad had seen me occasionally come home from there crying because of all the fights in school. The atmosphere was terrible. It's almost like—there were different groups and you had to fit in. So my dad offered me the opportunity to go to school in Baltimore. That school was Haredi, but not Hasidic, so they were looser than what I was used to. They were in a city. So imagine: I went from a real Satmar isolated place to a real city. I lived there in the dorms.

Several of my respondents told me that when they could no longer get along in their school or home, they were sent to religious boarding schools. Their parents wanted to avoid their becoming un-Orthodox so they tried another approach, thinking their kids might get along better outside their native communities. Aryeh told me he loved the new school in Baltimore. It opened his eyes and mind as he met different people and engaged in new activities such as playing basketball (which in his community was seen as a waste of time that could be devoted to studying Torah), which he had never seen before. The school had an open atmosphere, and the young men were allowed to dress in diverse ways. He felt freer and less isolated than he had in the ghetto of Kiryas Yoel. Until:

ARYEH: But when I got to be about nineteen, there was a lot of pressure on me to marry. I wasn't ready to get married; I wasn't even into girls then. I was doing things with the guys, hanging out, playing pool and going to clubs. But what happened was I had a younger sister who was eighteen, and all her friends were getting engaged. When a girl gets to be about nineteen or twenty, it becomes uncomfortable and embarrassing for her not to be married. And in our community you had to get married according to your birth order. So in order for her to have a shidduch, I had to get married first.

A man in our community suggested he would arrange a meeting with a nice girl who lives close by. He said she was very cool, and she's open-minded, and she is into hanging out. He assured me she was not like the usual Satmar girls. At first I said I was busy and working hard, but the second time he approached me, I thought, yeah, why not? And we went out on a date. I think the date was arranged. I did not want anyone to see us, so we went to a restaurant in Monsey, which is a more mixed Jewish community. We had a reservation in a restaurant. I came alone in my own car because she was being dropped off by a friend. We had a good dinner, but she was very shy. I saw in her eyes, though, that she is open-minded. She was not happy living in Monroe.

After we ate, I drove her home, which I didn't know was a big no-no. It was my first date ever. So when I told my mom I had taken her home, she was shocked. She was like, "Oh, my God." My father was looking at me thinking, "Driving is one thing, but taking home a girl in Monroe!!! You're lucky no one saw you."

Aryeh's parents were upset because they knew it was forbidden for unmarried women and men to be alone in an enclosed space such as a room with a door closed, or a car. They were concerned that if others saw him driving with a young woman in his car they would see him as irreligious, making it harder for him to establish a shidduch with a woman who had high social standing in the community.

Arranging meetings between young men and women for the purpose of marriage is a ritualized, embodied process. The boy and girl are given strict instructions about how to comport themselves on the date. They should never, ever touch or be in a position where they might start touching each other; consequently, they must meet in a public place. Being alone with a member of the opposite sex to whom you are not married is forbidden in order to avoid any temptation of illicit sex. That is why Aryeh's parents reacted so strongly to his story of driving the girl home from their first date. Had they been seen, the stigma would have been worse for the girl than the boy, in accordance with the community's firm guidelines for women's modesty.

Aryeh was happy to take note of her openness to the larger society; she told him she had an older sister who had also left. They went out a few times, and then they began to feel pressure to get married. Long engagements could lead to transgressions of sexual boundaries, so their families wanted them to marry as soon as they could. He told me he was cool with that because he had a sense that she, too, did not like where she lived. She seemed eager to explore the outside world.

> ARYEH: When we got married, my whole life changed. I had never wanted to have peyos, because that is the defining look of Hasidic people. She wanted to stop being religious just as much as I did, so I promised her that after we got married I would take them off. I will get a normal haircut, and my hair is going to be normal like any normal person. So the day after we married they just came off. At that moment, I really felt like I had stepped out of it [meaning the Hasidic world]. I was married. I was cool.
>
> LD: Like it was a symbolic manifestation of your freedom.
>
> ARYEH: My peyos was something that was really my symbol of being a Satmar. And they just came off. I had planned to cut them off. I did not like them; they bothered me and were in my way. I just wanted to look like a regular person. She was cool with it. We planned that

after our wedding we would take the day off. That was the day I got a regular haircut and a shave, and I stopped wearing tefillin, which is a daily must. For a Hasidic guy to miss a day of tefillin is the biggest sin. They can never forgive themselves. But that day, I really chose to step out of that whole world. We moved to another town to start our own lives.

Aryeh, like Ehud, understood that ceasing his daily practice of wearing tefillin was a huge step in exiting. Unlike Ehud and Binyamin, he was not a luminous scholar, so his exit strategy did not arise out of his discovery of new ideas that challenged the absolutism of Haredi life. Instead, Aryeh, like Leah, met someone who also wanted to leave the Haredi world, and they provided a mutual support system as they stepped out of their former lives.

This book argues that identity changes, for many people, are enacted through the medium of the body. Aryeh's narrative illustrated how important that move was for him. At the first breath of freedom he felt, he changed his appearance, disinscribing the markers of Haredi masculinity. Changing his bodily practices was both a sign of, and contributed to, his sense of being different and, finally, free.

CREATING DISTANCE

Entering new social spaces to learn the ways of the world outside the enclave helped the defectors break away from Haredi life. Getting married provided some respondents with the opportunity to do so. It offered young adults a way to represent themselves as coming into adulthood within their communities and taking on their appropriate gendered roles as adults. When these couples married, they moved far enough away from their parents to preclude them from walking over on *Shabbes*. Over time, some sought to move farther away and immerse themselves in other cultural places.

As we saw, Leah had stopped observing commandments while she was still living in her parents' house. She took pleasure in sneaking out and hiding her transgressions from her family members. In essence, her acts of bodily resistance occurred while she was still "in place." In contrast, Sam and a few other respondents felt the need to travel a long way in order to find the freedom and private space in which they could shed their old selves, literally, and create new identities in places where they felt safe.

SAM

I will never again in my life live in that world.

Earlier, I recounted Sam's description of his passing between the advanced yeshiva he attended during the day and the Catholic University where he enrolled in night courses. His daily journey was between two radically different social and religious groups, each with its own competing metanarratives about who and what they were, and how they came to be that way. He quickly figured out how to present and comport himself appropriately in each setting and managed to pass for four years.

There was not a moment during this time, however, that Sam wavered in his clear desire to escape the Haredi world and step out into the larger society. In contrast to Ehud, whose extended passing behavior was due to internal conflicts, Sam's narrative did not reveal strong internal conflicts or external constraints that held him within the bounds of his community. Passing, for Sam, was not a struggle between competing selves. During Sam's last few years at the yeshiva, his aversion to Haredi life revealed itself through his acting out in study hall where, instead of studying ancient texts, he spent his days reading secular material. He hesitated to take his resistance any further, however; he knew little about the wider society and realized he would feel deeply unsettled when he left. The process of leaving was not only cognitive—he had made that change years earlier—but also, and equally important, it was embodied.

He knew after three or four years of studying simultaneously in a yeshiva and a Catholic University that he had "had it." He knew he wanted to leave, but it took some time to actually step out.

SAM: When I finally did walk out, I felt really lost. I had nowhere to go, and I lost literally every friend I'd ever had. At that time I had only Haredi friends, and they could not deal with my leaving. They were all gone in one day…in one minute.

I will never again in my life live in that world.… It was just the most profoundly life-giving, moving, rooted kind of place. And leaving it was going into exile. It was like finding yourself washed up on a foreign shore. Robinson Crusoe. That's how I thought of it. There's nobody there.

Sam's story of departure was a tale of long-desired freedom and a deep sense of loss. Once he stepped out, he knew he would never return. He felt thoroughly isolated and overwhelming alone with no one to talk to and nowhere to go. He told me that his profound concern about breaking his ties to his community made him remain there for so long, despite intellectually accepting atheism at the age of thirteen. Reservations about losing such roots were a common and powerful theme in respondents' narratives, even among respondents that did not speak of trauma.

SAM: Literally, I had to start everything over. I had no support system. My friends—even the ones I felt I had actually been able to talk to, they were all frum. None of them left, but many of them would have loved to escape, as I did. I mean, some of them were acting out, and many were questioning. I remember walking on 72nd Street one night with a girl I was dating very chastely. I probably had been on two or three dates with her. I liked her. We went out a couple of times, for drinks and so on, maybe a movie. One evening I saw one of my friends from yeshiva leaning all over this blonde waif, this clearly not Jewish waif, in the doorway of a restaurant, and he was not wearing a yarmulke, and clearly he was just taking advantage of every opportunity that the city offered, that New York had, which were a lot. This was the era of the sexual revolution. So it was clear many of my frum friends were questioning and breaking the norms, but none of them left. When I walked away, it was just me.

When I left the Haredi world, I went to Israel, a society where the majority of people were just like me—non-religious Jews. Traveling six thousand miles from home gave me the distance and space I needed to carve out my new identity.

Sam had decided to break away from Haredi life when he was young. From that time until he became mature enough to live on his own, he had never doubted this decision. Over those years, the accumulation of his questions, doubts, and the new ideas he had learned at the library strengthened his resolve to leave. But, as all other respondents told me, Sam knew the dangers of leaving. He knew deep in his gut how challenging stepping out would be.

> SAM: I knew all the time I would eventually leave. I could see the light at the end of the tunnel. It was a matter of my having the courage and the belief that I could get along without it. And that was it. You know, when you leave, you give up everything, just everything. I know this might sound weird, but leaving meant losing everything I had in my life before, including my group of friends, the girls I knew, and even my health care coverage. And I went to Israel. That was my period of slipping out. My father had no problem with my going to Israel, but my goal was to be free—I was not known there and could do what I want.

In contrast to those defectors who had some support in leaving, such as a role model who helped pave the way, and those who got married in order to leave, Sam was completely alone when he decided to step out. As he said, "I felt really lost. I had nowhere to go, and I lost literally every friend I'd ever had." Not only did Sam face the fears and anxiety of leaving described by all my other informants, but he was also further devastated by the hypocrisy of his friends who shunned him. They themselves were also transgressing and passing; however, they chose the safety and familiarity of remaining in the only world they had known.

Sam's description of the great courage it took to leave his Haredi world was familiar to me personally. I appreciated his self-awareness of how much inner strength it took for him to defect, especially when he had nowhere to go, no support system, and no idea of how to set himself up in the larger society. Even if he knew how to secure a place for himself, he emphasized he did not know how to behave, comport himself, and dress in the larger world. He had no idea of what behaviors were normative in the world outside of his Haredi enclave.

As a Haredi man, he had always simply dressed in the uniform of his peers: a white shirt and black pants. When he left, he had a great deal of cultural learning to do. For example, he found it hard to choose colored shirts, wear a tie and how to match the two. Similarly he did not know how to order food or wine in a restaurant, converse with others, or begin meeting women. His painful awareness of his lack of knowledge of the larger society echoed remarks by Leah and Ehud. They all were defecting from a world where their daily routines were established through routine bodily techniques and cultural skills and tools. All three described stepping out into the larger society as if they were foreigners who, in order to survive, had to quickly learn to get along in new social and cultural surroundings.

Sam's choice to spend time in Israel provided him with a ready opportunity to make all the personal changes he desired. Israel was a safe haven where he was unknown; it was a backstage space where he could experiment with various ways of changing his habitual body routines as he developed a new identity.

> SAM: I spent about six months in Israel, part of it on a kibbutz [an Israeli communal settlement, often agrarian in nature]. At that time, there was fewer Haredim there than now, and life on the kibbutz was very different from where I came from. It seemed everyone on the kibbutz were sexually loose and maybe even promiscuous. I stayed there and had a great time. Then I traveled. I just hitchhiked around, working sometimes so I had money to travel.
>
> I loved being there. It was the first place I ever landed where I was completely anonymous. No one knew me, and I greatly enjoyed my newfound privacy. How could I not at that point? I slept on the beach. I got a job washing dishes at a hotel. *And I began to claim my new identity* [Sam's emphasis].

So by the time I got back to New York in November or December, I was no longer Shmuel, the biblical name I had been given, but Sam. I came home as Sam and Sam I remained. When I returned, however, I did not have a place to live, nor a job to pay for it. I moved back in with my parents temporarily.

Changing his name was a powerful way of symbolizing Sam's new sense of individuality and of his taking control of the construction of his own identity. Many of my interviewees similarly switched from their Hebrew or Yiddish names and instead chose to be addressed by "English" ones. Their desire to shed their Jewish names and use their legal ones instead symbolized their desire to individuate and separate themselves from the people who knew them only by their Jewish names. Some of my respondents actually had to create a secular name since at birth they were given only a Hebrew name.

Sam told me he began to feel stifled after he returned home and desperately wanted to be free. He felt he could not be his new self in his parents' house in his old community. About a month after he returned from Israel he traveled to New Zealand. He sought a place halfway around the world to find the distance and freedom he needed to consolidate his new identity by "doing secular," meaning, enacting the identity of a secular person, one whose routine, demeanor, comportment, and bodily practices performed his identity as a secular person in a secular society. Israel was a Jewish state that followed religious law in numerous ways: The Orthodox Rabbinate had control of all matters of civil life, such as marriage and the annual calendar, which ran according to Jewish laws about observing Sabbath and holidays.

Although he began to break free in Israel, he sought a secular milieu in which to fully disinscribe all elements of his Haredi identity and take on the different bodily routines he observed in his new environment.

SAM: By the time I came back to New York again, there was no question anymore about my being frum. Going to New Zealand was the real sort of birth for me. From that point, I've simply been myself, whatever I wanted to be and not what anyone else told me I should be. That was it. That was a real breakthrough.

Nearly all my interviewees discussed the difficulties of taking on a new identity. It is easy to understand why Sam traveled halfway around the world to be reborn. Identities are always constructed in social contexts. In order to disinscribe elements of his Haredi identity and take on the bodily practices of a secular person, he needed the freedom offered by being far from home. All of my respondents described their lack of knowledge about how to live a life outside of the enclave and the challenges it posed to their exit. None of them was able to leave when they were young and started questioning. All took time—often years—between their first transgressions and stepping out of the community. Some left when the accumulation of pressures of passing became too great. Others, however, narrated precipitating events that gave them a push to finally leave.

PRECIPITATING EVENTS

BINYAMIN

A messianic fervor erupted.

Binyamin spent years passing and struggling with his deep internal conflicts about whether to leave the Lubavitch community. He tried redoubling his efforts to convince himself the Lubavitcher worldview was correct, even though his understanding of relativism made it hard for him to accept absolutist certitudes. He was emotionally connected with his community and, like other informants, knew the great risks of leaving. Sam left after the strains of years of passing, dissembling, and feeling self-alienated built to a breaking point. In contrast, Binyamin's narrative highlights a particular point of time and a specific set of issues that finally propelled him to cross the borders into the larger society.

When Binyamin was in his early twenties, and accustomed to transgressing and violating commandments, the Lubavitcher rebbe, Menachem Mendel Schneerson, the leader of his Hasidic community, suffered a series of strokes. Nevertheless, he continued to gather his community together for *fabrengens*, where he expounded on the ancient texts and led his large (more than 1,000 families) congregation in *niggunim* (wordless, soulful tunes). The men in the community relished those joyous and inspiring get-togethers in which, as the niggunim got increasingly intense, the group reached a higher state of awe and exultation—what Durkheim termed "collective effervescence"—that none could have reached on their own. Binyamin loved these collective rituals and described himself as "running" to them.

After his first stroke the rebbe continued to host fabrengens and lead the group in wordless tunes. But his health deteriorated with each successive stroke until he could no longer speak, lead the community in collective rituals, or fulfill his role as spiritual leader. It was perhaps time for him to step down and appoint another rebbe to lead his community.

Succession in Hasidic communities is typically handed down within families, generally to the rebbe's sons. But since there were no sons in the family, leadership was passed down to a son-in-law, which was how the most recent Lubavitcher rebbe—Menachem Mendel Schneerson—acquired his role. Schneerson and his wife had no children; there was no son or son-in-law to anoint. He had not spoken about appointing a successor, which was a part of his duties. As he became more ill and less able to function, knowing there was no appointed successor, many members of the community deduced he must be the *Moshiach* (messiah), who was supposed to arrive and redeem the world. For Binyamin, this messianic fervor highlighted and underscored his thoughts about the irrationality of his religion. The detailed and dramatic story he told was so powerful that I have chosen to represent his account in the way he told it to me.

BINYAMIN: When I was in my early twenties and living back in Crown Heights [the primary Lubavitcher community], the whole messianic fervor exploded, came out big-time. Even though we all thought the rebbe was infallible and almighty, his sickness revealed his vulnerability and weakness. He was confined to a wheelchair. So there was a two-year period when the rebbe was not well. Knowing he had no successor, some of the outspoken members of the community used this time to develop the idea that the rebbe must be the Moshiach. The news spread across the community, leading to a state of collective excitement and anticipation.

I mean, these messianic hopes were always there, but they remained contained during the rebbe's leadership. But after he became ill, this spirit came out big-time. This was happening around 1991. The whole Lubavitch community knew and took for granted that the rebbe was the Moshiach, but they were unsure about how to treat this fact: Should they pass this information on to other *Hasidic groups*, and, should we openly refer to the rebbe as Moshiach? Since we all knew he was the smartest person and a great *tzaddik* [a pious and righteous man], who was complete in all of his qualities. One of these essential qualities was he was the Moshiach. Over time, the focus became on the messianic part of the rebbe and the community's certainty he was the redeemer.

I felt outside of all this excitement and fervor; this leader worship did not feel Jewish, and it started becoming repulsive. I mean, I had been questioning since my childhood, and I doubted this whole idea of the rebbe as messiah to begin with. Who says the rebbe is the Moshiach anyway? You're debating if you should publicize that the rebbe is the Moshiach or not? Who needs this whole Moshiach thing to begin with? When I expressed these doubts, people would say, "This is not a human being. This is an avatar. This is a conduit of the divine itself, so you know, how could you question all that?" But my point was, even if you want a better world, why are you focusing on a person, on a human being? And implicit within that is he is a human being, he is mortal, a view that contrasted with the general attitude among the Lubavitchers who thought the Rebbe will never die. Any mention of his mortality was heresy to the Lubavitchers, but in my brain, since I was already critiquing, I knew he had to be mortal.

So once he died in 1994, I no longer needed to stay committed to this community or stick around. But I remained there for a while because the whole episode was so fascinating. I was riveted by watching how people who tried to reconcile the conflicting ideas that he was a mortal man, with the idea he is the Moshiach, were going to reconcile his mortality with his being the Moshiach? What's going to be at the end of all this? I wanted to find out... it was like a narrative. I wanted to see where the story was going, what's the final chapter. And the final chapter is that he died, and the Moshiach was not revealed. The rebbe's death removed all obstacles to my leaving. It was not the cause, but seeing the community's behavior around the whole thing heightened the skepticism I had felt for years. It just blew the lid off the whole thing and resolved my internal debates and struggles. This made my leaving much simpler, and so I left; I was no longer a member of any religious group.

Binyamin's ambivalence about leaving dissolved as soon as he saw the emperor had no clothes. The Lubavitcher community was entirely focused on the rebbe: All Lubavitchers had photos or paintings of the rebbe in several places in their homes, with a prominent one in the dining room so he could symbolically bless their food. Over the years I have heard comments from many Jewish people who felt the Lubavitchers were idolizing him and turning him into an idol. The Bible forbids all forms of idol worship. Many Jews see the fact that every Lubavitch household had numerous representations of the rebbe on their walls as a blatant disregard for the first commandment. For Binyamin, the rebbe's death undermined the group's self-understanding and their entire way of life. Although earlier he had spoken about leaving as emotionally wrenching, by the time he actually left Binyamin no longer had any attachment to the community, and his actual stepping out was without any hint of doubts.

For Binyamin, the precipitating event was based in his community, rather than a personal and internal crisis. For other defectors, however, the precipitating event was a serious crisis in their own lives. Sarah told of the long, multistaged, and circuitous route she took before she actually shed her old clothes, literally and metaphorically, and learned to create a life in the larger society. The details of her story reveal a great deal about Hasidic life and how difficult and painful it was for her to challenge the system.

SARAH

Suddenly, God is not in Long Island...

As a young Hasidic woman, Sarah, despite her painful childhood, tried to do what others expected of her. Her deep depression rendered her incapable of making her own decisions, so she agreed to marry a man she barely knew. From the beginning of her marriage, Sarah told me, it was clear neither of them knew how to establish a satisfying emotional or sexual relationship. She reported that her marriage was utterly devoid of emotional connection; each month, after she went to the *mikveh*,[3] she dreaded her husband's sexual expectations. She was obligated by the commandments to be available to her husband during her ritually clean times, but she hated their sexual dynamics because he approached their intimacy with no concern for her feelings or satisfaction.

Ironically, it was through fulfilling her embodied, gendered role of birthing children that Sarah became exposed to the wider culture. Her midwife's waiting room had books and magazines about anatomy, pregnancy, and birthing, as well as copies of *Ms.*, a feminist magazine. This reading material introduced Sarah to the concept of patriarchy and contained articles demonstrating the far-reaching effects of patriarchy in all dimensions of social life. Reading this new material, she acquired a language that allowed her to analyze the Hasidic world. Her newly emerging feminist consciousness helped her understand how her uncle, a judge in the religious court, had the support of the religious community and therefore was able to excommunicate her father without even discussing it with her mother.

During her second pregnancy, Sarah secretly took her young son with her on excursions to explore New York City. Her repeated transgressions in this regard—entering forbidden spaces outside the enclave—conformed to the pattern of passing I have previously discussed.

Sarah described her children as the best part of her life. Nevertheless, she worried that her deep unhappiness made it impossible for her to care for them properly. She sought counsel from a rabbi, who told her she was just experiencing postpartum depression after her second child was born. She tried alternative forms of therapy, but nothing helped her feel better. Her anxiety and pain were palpable as she described this series of events:

> SARAH: I was just miserable. I was still wondering where I am going from here. Was I going to have to continue my life like this, living with a stranger and having to do what he wants me to do, and having a lot of babies? I just couldn't see myself doing that, but Hasidic women were not allowed birth control pills either. How could I tell anyone I'm on birth control pills? We were brought up to give birth to as many babies as God would bless us with. Who would I go to for these pills? You know, you can't just go to a doctor and ask for it. My husband is going to see the doctor bills, and he would notice something new being paid for. So I felt that option was closed. If you had a medical condition and the doctor said you would be in danger if you kept having babies, then you could get permission from a rabbi for birth control. But no rabbi was going to give you permission if you did not have a medical condition. So, what should I do, go find a medical condition I don't have? Okay, yeah right. So by the time my daughter was two, it was horrible, it was just so horrible; I was so depressed.

Sarah understood that she, like all other women in her community, had minimal control over her own body; the laws regarding intimacy, like all others, were created and interpreted by men. In all Haredi communities only men were trusted to interpret the Hebrew Bible, its 613 commandments, and the subsequent sacred texts: the *Mishnah*, the *Talmud*, and the *Shulchan Aruch*, the most frequently consulted and authoritative guidebook to correct Orthodox praxis. These commandments and their interpretations were rooted in the assumption that women were not equal to men in all things, except the one thing only women could do—give birth and rear children. Haredi interpretations of the proper sex/gender system rested on essentialist, permanent differences in women's and men's physical, intellectual, and moral qualities. Simone de Beauvoir (1949) expressed this dynamic perfectly: "Women are other."

In Haredi communities, this otherness of women can readily be seen by examining the multivolume sacred text, the *Mishnah*, which was redacted and sealed between 200 CE and 220 CE. The *Mishnah* consists of six "orders" that are distinct from each other by virtue of the questions they ask and seek to answer. The *Mishnah* is composed in the form of a question about a biblical passage posed by one of the seventy sages who gathered to redact and save for all eternity the oral tradition they dated back to Sinai. The questions were followed by lively discussions among the sages about how to interpret particular biblical passages and what guidelines for action they could derive from them. The orders of the *Mishnah* each seek to interpret and apply biblical laws concerning issues that were important in their times: planting seeds, observing holidays, determining who is responsible for damages, how to remain holy, the meanings of purity, and women. The presence of an entire order of laws dealing with questions concerning women provides evidence for de Beauvoir's assertion that men have always seen women as "other" (1949). The sages were puzzled by these "others"— the women—who, among numerous other issues, bled monthly, entering a state of ritual impurity that, if not carefully managed, could transfer to their husbands or other men. In order for women to end this state and be permissible "unto" their husbands, they had to immerse in the *mikveh*, the ritual bath, and follow the complicated series of bodily rituals needed to restore them to their state of ritual purity.

Sarah explained to me how her husband asserted control over her sexuality. He carefully kept track of the days of her period and the ensuing seven days during which she was still considered ritually impure and physical contact between them was forbidden. It felt to Sarah as if her husband had an internal clock; he was always aware of where she stood in her menstrual cycle. On the appropriate day, according to Jewish law, he would ask Sarah to prepare herself to immerse in the *mikveh*. By performing these embodied rituals, she once again became "permissible"—sexually—to her husband and was obligated to have sex with him when she returned from the ritual bath. Sarah confided that she had come to dread those days when she had to engage in loveless and joyless sexual intercourse with a man who was not concerned about her feelings.

Patriarchal control over women was enforced by all men in her Hasidic enclave. Although Sarah wanted to choose whether and when she became pregnant, no doctor in her community would prescribe birth control without the approval of a rabbi, who authorized it only when a woman's life or health was in danger. Sarah, who was in a terrible depression, knew she was incapable of taking care of more children. She considered going outside her community boundaries in search of a secular doctor, but she had no independent income to pay for these doctor's visits.

> SARAH: I remember just feeling like I just wanted to open this door, roll out, and have it be over. I felt I couldn't live like this anymore. And it scared me because here I have kids I love, and I hated being unable to properly care for them. Finally I went to see a psychiatrist, who was outside the community and not religious, and spoke honestly to him. I really opened up and told him everything. This doctor actually told me he admired me! I couldn't even understand what he admired. All he saw was a depressed, almost suicidal person who just wanted to die. And he said, you're married to the wrong guy. I give your marriage a 10 percent chance; if you decide to continue with it, it's just not going to work out.
>
> And I needed to hear that, I needed to be validated from somebody there, somebody outside, not a rabbi—just don't give me rabbis anymore, 'cause all they're going to tell me is "go pray."' I prayed enough. The psychiatrist gave me medicine to calm down. I have no clue what it was, but it would help me relax. I think it might have been an anti-anxiety kind, because that sort of slows you down a little bit and puts you to sleep. That's what I wanted.

Sarah went home with these medicines and wondered if she would take them and whether they would actually help her relax. But she knew feeling more relaxed would not help with her emotional and sexual relationship with her husband. She told me she felt stuck: She was desperate to leave her Hasidic community, but she could not imagine where she would go. Feeling trapped in an impossible situation, one day she took nearly her entire bottle of pills at once, wanting nothing more than to sleep deeply. She was fortunate, however, to have a close friend, Esti, who was more open-minded than the other people in her community. After swallowing the pills, she called Esti and told her what she had done.

Esti immediately came through for her. She called the ambulance and went to stay with Sarah until the ambulance arrived. Esti later told Sarah that Sarah had been unconscious when she arrived. Her friend had saved her life. Her mother referred to this event as the time "the bomb dropped on Williamsburg Brooklyn, N.Y." When I asked Sarah what her mother meant by "the bomb," Sarah explained that Jews were forbidden by God to commit suicide. The prohibition was so strong that suicides were not allowed to be buried in a Jewish cemetery. Her mother knew the entire family would be stigmatized by this event, which "spread through the community like wildfire." Esti called Sarah's sister after she called the ambulance. Her sister told her mother. After that, Sarah said her suicide attempt became the talk of Williamsburg.

Taking a bottle of pills as an ambivalent attempt at suicide was a huge biographical disruption, just as her dad's excommunication had been. Her call to her friend was a cry for help; it signified Sarah was not actually ready to die at that moment. Sarah woke up in an emergency room where her stomach was pumped. Members of her family came to visit her while she was still dazed from the pills. They kept asking her about what she had done, what she was going to do afterward, and if she was going to stay with her husband. She sensed they were more concerned about their standing in the community than about her health or mental condition. They pressured her to remain with her husband and fulfill her proper roles as wife and mother.

Sarah's beloved father visited her in the hospital and saw that she needed some space away from her family and their constant pressure to force her to be someone she no longer was. He arranged for her to be transferred to a private mental hospital far away from her home. Ironically, her confinement in a psychiatric facility provided her with a safe space in which she was free to experiment with new, illicit activities and foods. As she laughingly said about the first time she ate nonkosher food at the hospital: "Suddenly God's not in Long Island anymore!"

Yet, even as she freely engaged in taboo behaviors Sarah was so deeply ambivalent about leaving that even in the hospital she continued to dress and carry herself as she had been brought up to do. She wore skirts that fell way below her knee, blouses that covered her collarbone and elbows, and the requisite stockings.

Experiencing the freedom given to her in this private hospital, Sarah gradually understood she had no idea about her own individual likes and dislikes. She could not articulate what activities she enjoyed. The hospital staff provided her with support and good suggestions for learning about herself. They encouraged her to cut out of magazines pictures of things she liked in order to learn who she could choose to be outside of the enclave.

> SARAH: I had amazing therapists. Each and every one was the most understanding person, and to me it was so shocking that there are understanding people in this world. I just couldn't understand where I came from. Why was there no understanding of me there? And there, everybody was so loving, so understanding, so validating. Their idea about the magazines was the best thing for me to sort of get to know what I like, what I dislike, who I am in some ways.... It was an unbelievable experience! I'll never forget it.

Hasidim bring their children up to have a sense of themselves as members of their particular community and to live according to its precepts. The locus of control is the community, which has no room for individualistic assertions of personal will. By leaving the community and changing their routines of physical practice, defectors started to create new, individualized identities. Sarah had not yet individuated, but the suggestions of the hospital staff helped her make progress in defining her own identity.

Eventually the staff felt Sarah was ready to leave the hospital, and they offered their support to help her begin a new life.

> SARAH: When I left the hospital I stayed with my father for a few months. I wanted to find a job, but I was not sure where to even begin looking. I thought if I went to the mall, I may get lucky because the only thing that I might know is how to sell clothing, and I could always learn more about that. I got a job at a fine women's clothing store, but all the while I worked there I was concerned women from the Haredi community might come in and call me by my Yiddish name, Saraleh, which I no longer used.
>
> In order to get this job I had to learn to dress a little differently, so the customers would not stare at me as if I had come from another planet. I started to wear pants and more modern clothing. With my employee's discount I was able to buy some nice clothes at this store where I worked. The other girls taught me how to put outfits together. I began learning about this new world. But I could tell I still was not doing very well. And I felt scared, everything at work was so new, so foreign to me. The whole culture was different from the one I came from.

By working at a women's clothing store, Sarah became aware of the great amount of cultural learning she needed to do in order to fit into the society outside her enclave. She learned new skills for interacting with others and for embodying her new identity. She told me she had felt terribly awkward about her appearance and behavior. In contrast to the other women working at the store, she was unfamiliar with the little gestures and manners that smoothed everyday interactions between strangers. Her socialization did not include instructions for politely greeting and talking with people she did not know, especially those whose way of life greatly differed from her own. Hasidic women were not expected to have many interactions with people outside of their enclave, so there was no reason for girls to learn those skills.

Sarah confided to me that her boss occasionally chided her for being rude to customers, an adverb she had never heard before. She became aware that there were basic assumptions and skills shared by the customers and other employees that she clearly lacked. She had not been raised with the cultural knowledge that would provide her with the social graces needed to interact politely with those who had such different ways of comporting themselves. Her customers' ways of asking her for items in the store, mannerisms, and general demeanor were unfamiliar to Sarah. Her coworkers and customers had their own ingrained assumptions and habitual behaviors, rooted in their socialization in a cultural and social world radically different from her own.

In describing how she felt others perceived her at the time, Sarah used the words "butch mannish," and "coarse." As she said:

> You know, I, like other Hasidim from my community, would talk very sort of like…butch mannish, maybe a bit coarse. We just did not have the polite manners of the women coming into the store. Like, Hasidim generally don't open the door for the next person. You have to be there to see it. I continued to feel I don't fit into this genteel world of delicate clothes and the women who bought them. I felt as if I was not here. I felt like an immigrant who did not know anything about the new society they had just entered.

"Butch mannish" is often used to signify a "masculine" type of lesbian. She felt her presentation of self was too coarse for the upper-middle-class, well-mannered women who came into the clothing store. Observing the differences between the qualities inculcated in Haredi girls and those expected of women in the larger society created for Sarah a sense of shame and marginalization.

Nevertheless, she worked hard to resocialize herself by acting in ways that approximated secular culture's prescriptions for feminine behavior. She changed her comportment, demeanor, clothing, and mannerisms in an effort to fit in with the other women at the shop. Her struggles reminded her of the numerous adaptations immigrants must make when they arrive in a new culture. They, too, have to learn new ways of talking, dressing, eating, and getting on in their new society. As she became more adept at embodying the social norms of white middle class women, she felt a surge of confidence in her new identity. She expressed this feeling quite powerfully:

> SARAH: All of a sudden I had an image that I was about to be born.... I felt as if I was in the womb trying to get out and find my way, trying to find some peace. I knew I was really going to emerge and just get going.

Rebirth provides a powerful image of coming out of narrow straits and emerging into the larger world. This was the goal of all defectors. In many ways, Sarah's narrative was distinct from most of the others. She was one of the very few who spoke of various forms of social support that helped them make the passage to another social group and culture. The encouragement and assistance Sarah received from her friend and the nurses and therapists in the hospital helped her begin to formulate who she might become outside of the enclave.

Like Binyamin's, Sarah's story reveals a precipitating event—her suicide attempt. Her narrative also showed the extent of cultural learning required to create a new identity in another social context and the importance of others' support. This time, when Sarah once again emerged from the womb, it was as an individual, with the right and ability to create a new identity. She was determined to further individuate and learn who she was and how she wanted to live.

Rutie's story, in contrast, did not focus on a dramatic and life-threatening event, but, like Sarah and Binyamin, she experienced an ultimately liberating precipitating event. She recognized that strangers, such as therapists outside their enclave communities, were better able to see the signs of the strict social control and lack of freedom in their Hasidic patients' lives. These therapists' understanding and support validated respondents' desires to become independent individuals who could create lives of their own choosing. In a session with Rutie and her parents, her therapist's backing was essential to Rutie's departure.

RUTIE

*It was the first time it occurred to me that I had the right
to make a decision.*

When we met Rutie earlier, we saw that her questions about Orthodoxy
had begun at a very young age. One of her strongest objections to Hasidic
life was the lack of interesting and intellectually challenging roles for
women. She had no interest in the one option allotted to women in her
community—that of wives and mothers. She did not want to get bogged
down in the details of everyday life with a large family. Instead, she preferred a life of the mind. In her comments we can see how powerfully
gender, religion, embodied practices, and identity are interconnected.

> RUTIE: I didn't want to be religious, and I didn't want to be a woman.
> And those two things were related for me. I think I wouldn't have
> minded being an Orthodox man, but I definitely didn't want to be
> an Orthodox woman. Being an Orthodox woman meant being gar-
> rulous, stupid, coarse [the identical term used by Sarah], involved in
> unimportant material aspects of life, having a lot of kids and dedicat-
> ing her life to raising them. I was so unattracted to the role, and to my
> mother, and to the girls in my class. I mean there were different ways
> of living as a non-normative Haredi woman or a girl, but I didn't
> like any of them. For example, there were the boy-crazy girls, and
> there were the goody-goody girls. I did not fit in with either group.
> Instead, I think I was pretty seriously male-identified. I didn't par-
> ticularly want to be any kind of woman, but I was much more OK
> being a woman outside the Orthodox world than in it. So definitely
> a big part of my identity crisis was the female part. That's why I was
> cross-dressing—wearing pants, short hair, and hiding my developing
> breasts by binding them. I longed to write, to study, and to be an
> intellectual. I had no interest in the lives of any of the women I knew.

Although at a different life stage (prior to marriage), Rutie, like Sarah,
spoke of her desperation to leave her restricted enclave. Instead, she

was bogged down in constant arguments with her parents. After a few years, her exiting was similarly facilitated by a talented therapist who, in Rutie's case, was seeing her together with her family.

RUTIE: When we were meeting with the therapist, I remember very distinctly saying: "The reason we're here is because I don't want to be frum, and my family wants me to be frum." Wait, let me get that right. I remember exactly what I said [laughs], "We're here because we're having problems communicating." That's what I said. I don't know where I learned to talk like that, but that's what I said.

I was only fifteen years old at the time. So I think at our third or fourth session, we came in, sat down, and the therapist told us: "I've been thinking about it, and I think I'm going to have to terminate this therapy. This is going to be our last session, and it's not really going to be a session, it's going to be a way of saying goodbye. Let's just have a conversation, and I won't charge you for it."

We were shocked because we all sort of liked him. Someone asked him "why?" and he said, "I can see what the main problem is in this family. The main problem is Rutie doesn't want to be frum, and you all want her to be. And that's not a psychological problem; that's a theological problem—that's a religious problem. And I'm a therapist and not a rabbi. So this is really not my province."

I thought that was the greatest gift that anyone could have given me. It was the first time it occurred to me that I had the right to make a decision—as a free agent and as a person with my own relationship to this tradition who could decide for myself whether I wanted to maintain it or not. His statement was the clearest possible depiction of what was going on. I remember my feeling of lightness and relief.

The therapist asked me what I would do next, and where I would go. I thought I'd go to a friend's. She also was beginning to question, and she had created a life that was highly unusual for a woman who grew up Hasidic. She was twenty-five, not yet married, and had shocked people when she defied community norms by moving out of her family's home as a single young woman. Our religious tradition required children to live with their parents until they married.

Girls were seen as especially vulnerable outside the shelter of the Hasidic enclave.

Rutie's courage to become a new "self" and make her own decisions about how she wanted to relate to her religious tradition and its practices was boosted by her therapist's analysis of the situation. Psychotherapists are skilled at reading family dynamics, naming the undercurrents, and helping individuals extricate themselves from relationships that stifle and harm them. Her therapist understood that Rutie's parents sought to constrain her behavior by insisting she remain in their Hasidic community, although she clearly no longer wanted to be frum. The counsellor she saw validated her desire to individuate, create her own identity, and choose her own way of life, encouraging Rutie to become a "free agent." Rutie had never before received such strong legitimation of her wish to be free. Until this family visit with the therapist, Rutie had never been allowed to articulate her own feelings or communicate her unhappiness with Hasidic life. Expressing such thoughts had serious consequences for those in the community. Before, she and her parents had argued a lot, but they had never directly confronted the fundamental issue. The therapist cut through everything to point out the proverbial elephant in the living room.

Although her parents expected her to come home after this meeting, Rutie decided to go to a friend's house. It was, for Rutie, a safe haven where she could stay as she sorted out what she might do next. Like other defectors, Rutie had great fears of leaving the enclave. She genuinely did not want to hurt her parents, and she feared that her family's excellent reputation in the community would be sullied by her actions:

RUTIE: I never treaded this road before. On one hand, it was terrible when I became non-Orthodox because it was like a big fall in this distinguished family. I knew other similar cases in the community where parents felt deeply shamed by their offspring's defection. One example was the granddaughter of a distinguished, respected, and well-known rabbi, who was one of the most respected and sought-after rabbis at that time. I don't know if you heard of this case. [I had not.] I was always fascinated when I learned of prominent and highly esteemed Haredi families who lost children. I don't mean to imply that our family had that kind of stature, but we certainly were known and respected.

I was intrigued to hear Rutie use the word *lost* when referring to the experiences and feelings of parents whose children had stopped being frum. When I think of losing a child, I think of parents whose children had died, or disappeared. Rutie's use of this term, approximately thirty years after she had defected, revealed how deeply the assumptions and language of her former social context remained embedded within her. She might have used a positive term emphasizing the children's newly gained freedom. Her use of the word *lost* in this context represented the Hasidic perspective, which viewed religious defection as a great loss. No matter how many years passed since a defector's exiting the community and her current life, Hasidic worldviews and language still might come out at certain times.

Rutie was not only afraid of her family's potential embarrassment and stigmatization if she left. She, like other defectors, had no idea how to actually accomplish exiting, learn the requisite new cultural skills, and create a new life:

> RUTIE: It wasn't clear to me how you left. I mean how you physically did it. Where you went. How you got money. How you even had the right clothes to go. I mean it was in New York; it's a big, dangerous city, and I didn't know a soul outside of my community. I was lucky to find a place to stay with my friend Chana for a few months. She helped me find a job and enroll in Brooklyn College, the one school some more liberal Haredi parents might have allowed their daughters to attend.

Living with her friend in a safe environment and rapidly gaining new knowledge about the "world," Rutie found herself in a situation where she could decide for herself what to do next. Her account, like those of Sarah and others, illustrated the great importance of social support in empowering members to leave their strict communities. The therapist intervened with her parents, legitimating her desire to individuate and pursue a life of her own making; her friend offered social as well as practical support. This friend provided Rutie with a roof over her head and a safe haven that made it simpler to leave her parents' home—she had somewhere she could readily land. She also helped Rutie enroll in college and find jobs and introduced her to new, secular friends with whom Rutie *eventually* established a new home and began to carve out a new, freer sense of self. Her story contrasts starkly with that of Sam, who spoke of being betrayed by all his friends, his utter lack of any support in leaving, and his need to go overseas in order to make his transition.

The presence or lack of social support in exiting and transitioning into a new life was a critical factor in defectors' accounts of their experience of exiting. Most exiters did not have role models or assistance from others in finding their way to a new life in a world they had previously not known. They all described numerous fears, dangers, and other obstacles to the stepping-out process. The strength and self-confidence that enabled them to leave, despite numerous impediments, were vital to their finding their way and settling down in the larger, secular world.

CHAPTER SIX

YOU CAN'T TURN
OFF YOUR PAST

It's from the kishkes, from the gut. You just can't turn off
your past, and this is my past.

I began the introduction to *Becoming Un-Orthodox* with a story of
how I began to see tears in the sacred canopy surrounding my family.
My father developed a narrative around the loss of my mother. Her
death provided the context for his constant assertions that, as a reduced
family, we all had to stay together. I knew I had to leave; I had surmised
it somewhat as an eight-year-old, but by the time I was seventeen it was
crystal clear. In order to create my own life—note the rampant individualism in these words—I had to be free of his constraints as well as
those of Orthodox Judaism. Leah wanted "the world"; I needed to be
free! I worked hard to learn ways I could go beyond that sad statement
about our diminished family and not be bound to it as my mantra or
guide for how I should live. When Rutie spoke of the sadness felt by
families who had "lost" their children to the secular world, I had an
image of them as a different kind of "diminished family" with all the
duties and obligations thereof. One of my father's expectations was
that all three of his children would live at home until they married.
This approach was common in all Hasidic communities; the irony was
we were Modern Orthodox, and he was a strong believer in the principles of Modern Orthodoxy. As I close the book, I return to my story,
showing how I, too, stepped out. Like my respondents, I thought my
decision to leave was thorough and permanent. Nevertheless, like the
defectors with whom I spoke, I have learned that I, too, could never

fully uproot my early foundations. They remained part of me no matter what my conscious volition intended.

When I left my father's house after a year and a half of commuting to college, I was able to move into the dormitory at Barnard College. I ceased passing between what I thought of as "my real self" and my routinized performance of a young Orthodox woman. I got a ride to the subway the morning I left; I was emboldened that day by my father being out of town. Like the others I have represented in the chapters of this book, I, too, was afraid to leave. I did not worry about being punished by God; I had already learned that was unlikely. Nevertheless, it was challenging to give up the security of a roof over my head and a steady supply of food and to risk losing my family. I did not know then how big a loss leaving the community would be. Nevertheless, when I got out of the car that morning, the refrain of an old song from The Who's rock opera, *Tommy*, rushed into my head: "I'm free, I'm free!" In my mind, I heard it as they sang it. It was a moment of pure joy.

Several of my conversation partners described the various forms of support that helped ease the challenges of leaving. I was fortunate to have had support from several sources. Early in my second year as a college student I was struggling to make a clear decision about separating myself from my father's expectations. I went to see a rabbi from my Orthodox high school whom I trusted, Rabbi Haskell Lookstein. When he saw how depressed I was, he immediately understood my situation. It was important to me then to have his validation, to be told by a well-known Modern Orthodox rabbi that I had to leave, despite my father's adage. Somehow, his approval helped free my conscience. I began to make plans to move out on my own.

I wanted to remain at Barnard, but I had no financial support. I was fortunate that the college acted as a community, and several people worked together to help me make the transition. During this period I was privileged to talk with the president of the college, Martha Peterson, a gift I still savor. I explained to her that I wanted to continue my education but that I had been cut off from my family's funding. She, like my professors, recognized I was a strong student. The college provided me with a scholarship that defrayed some of the costs of my education, and they helped me get federal college loans, which carried a low interest rate. Although it was the middle of the academic year, they also helped me find a single dormitory room. It was my first genuinely private room; at my father's house, he in effect "owned" my room. I found a job, signed up for spring semester courses, and savored my hard-won, delicious freedom.

I began to build a new life in which I could choose which, if any, rituals or holidays to observe. I had left the Orthodox world and could carve out my own path. Nevertheless, it is clear from my professional life that I continue to be fascinated by frum people and their communities. Two of my three books have focused on Orthodoxy: The first was a study of women who became Orthodox; this book studies men and women who defected from Ultra-Orthodoxy. Despite sensing that I had left Orthodoxy behind, I obviously have remained involved—in one way or another—with Orthodox life. During my research for this book I talked with several other defectors, who, like me, maintain a connection to their roots, Jewish texts, lives, and communities. Their fields ranged from the study of ancient texts to postmodern cultural studies. Others remained connected through various jobs within the community, or through participation in cultural events.

REMNANTS OF THE PAST

As I wrote this book, I thought about how Orthodox imprinting remained with me and my conversation partners throughout our lives. Our early socialization and absorption of Orthodox practices, were deeply inscribed within our bodies and shaped our everyday taken for granted bodily routines. For me, it was not hard to give up any of the religious ritual practices; I was happy to be free of their demands. But something about my roots in this world has always stayed with me. Binyamin and other respondents expressed his same feeling of never being able to fully escape his origins. As he said, "It's from the kishkes, from the gut. You just can't turn off your past, and this is my past." Who we have been is always a part of who we are now; it is inscribed in our very beings. Our Orthodox backgrounds were deeply and solidly planted in us; elements of this former life have had a way of surprisingly showing up in our current lives, no matter how much we think we have abandoned them. My research has shown me neither I, nor my respondents, were able to fully leave behind our early socialization or throw away our entire cultural tool kits and the corresponding set of gendered embodied practices and routines.

Neuroscientists have recently emphasized the ways experience effects changes in the biology of our brains. Building on this insight, I can say that defectors' earlier experiences and practices have been hardwired into their psyches. We could almost say they have become part of our "psychic DNA."[1] The cultural tool kit and its embodied representations continue to remain entrenched in our deepest selves. Do you remember the old cliché: "You can take the girl out of New York, but you can't take New York out of the girl?" The metaphor is apt for the ways, both intensive and occasional, into which the past rises up from our roots and reinserts itself into our present lives.

These habitual modes of comportment formed the basis from which we branched out to transform our identities. Changing these taken-for-granted physical routines was an essential step in creating a new identity. We did not simply make an intellectual decision to change our lives. Rather, the newly learned routine of embodied practices was the medium through which we transformed our sense of who we were in the world.

LANGUAGE

Language provides a framework for how we see and talk about the social world, and elements of this cultural tool kit may remain deeply embedded within. When Leah was expressing her critique of Hasidic patriarchy, she referred to it as "sinful," a word I was surprised to hear from her. Even as she described her antipathy toward the treatment of women within Haredi enclaves, she used the language of her former world. Sarah described to me the stages through which she left. Speaking of a time when she had already moved out of her Hasidic enclave, she reported: "Pants I didn't wear yet; I still wore a skirt, but I started wearing shorter skirts." I want to call attention to the structure of her sentence: English syntax would have called for a sentence that had the subject before the object, as in "I did not yet wear pants." Instead, Sarah inserted the object before the actor and the verb, clearly translating from a Yiddish syntax and vividly illustrating how the structure of the grammar she learned growing up continued to inflect her current speech. Her language further revealed the gradual, emotionally charged, step-by-step manner in which defectors disinscribed the taken-for-granted habits of the Haredi world they had left.

Another linguistic symbol, which would be obvious to insiders (even former ones), was the particular, contemptuous way in which another respondent, Aryeh, used the word goyim. This made me wonder whether he still viewed non-Jews and Jews who were ignorant of their religious obligations as less developed than themselves. When I asked him if I was picking up anything in his tone of his voice, he replied:

Non-Orthodox Jews were kind of just not there for us. I didn't think much about them. They were just irrelevant. The non-Orthodox are not doing what they were supposed to do, or they just didn't know what to do, but we had the right perspective. We were living the right way, and they weren't.... It was subtle. It was never, "They're evil, they're horrible, and they're terrible." But the message was clear. I grew up with those constant reminders: "You guys are special. You guys have it right. No one else has it right. You guys are the princes of Israel," they would say. And the implication was that everyone else was lesser.

Aryeh's negative attitude toward goyim was inculcated in him from birth. The negative valuation Haredi Jews applied to all others served as one of their strategies for maintaining solid, high boundaries between themselves and those who did not follow their way of life. Despite having left Orthodoxy himself, Aryeh's tone reflected the condescending views he had heard all his life, suggesting to me that he still retained some of these ingrained perspectives.

The staying power of defectors' former automatic patterns of action produced some ambivalence about stepping out completely. Aryeh told me that although he felt he had indeed exited from his Hasidic world, he continued to occasionally experience a sense of ambivalence.

> ARYEH: When I showed up for medical school orientation, we were all asked to tell each other about ourselves. When it was my turn, I hesitated, but then I told people about how I had grown up. I wanted people to know that about me, because I feel I am still evolving, and I wanted to avoid social awkwardness as I got to know my classmates. If I wavered in my stance, I would want them to know my background, and that way they can understand.
>
> LD: As we've been talking, I noticed that you have talked a lot about anxiety. Do you experience any feelings of loss, regret, or guilt?
>
> ARYEH: About?
>
> LD: Your transitions.
>
> ARYEH: Yeah. I try to counteract those feelings now, but they are not always under my control.

In addition to defectors retaining the language and syntax of their Haredi lives, their narratives further revealed the staying power of the habitual, taken-for-granted physical routines learned in their earlier lives. The all-consuming and numerous Hasidic bodily practices were inscribed on defectors' bodies and formed their essential core. It is not surprising, then, that many of my conversation partners told stories illustrating some enduring ambivalence about stepping out completely.

GENDERED EMBODIED PRACTICES

CLOTHING AND BODILY COMPORTMENT

Hasidic laws that ensured women's "modesty," such as the detailed instructions for how to dress, continued to affect several of the women we met earlier: Aliza, Sima, Leah, and Sarah each told me they continued to wear skirts in public for at least several years after leaving.

Aliza described the first time she wore pants in public as a moment of great transformation that was both private and public: Breaking the community's rules for women's bodily practices was an emotional experience that publicly proclaimed her separation from her Hasidic roots.

Both Aliza and Sima had already left their communities and were participating in secular society. So ingrained was their sense of bodily comportment and modesty as defined by their old enclaves, however, that it took some time before they were able to change their clothing and outwardly reveal, even as they were constructing them, their new identities. The routine performance of particular bodily practices constitutes and maintains individuals' identities; a public presentation of a radically changed appearance reinforced to the defectors and those with whom they came in contact that they had changed their basic identities.

Esther, a strongly secular woman who had established her distance from her former Hasidic identity by disinscribing Hasidic bodily practices and adopting new ones, was surprised to discover she still retained deep feelings about women's need to dress "modestly." Esther was used to wearing pants, short sleeves, and going about without the protective garb of female Hasidic identity. But when she became a student in drama school, she felt the expectations for female appearance there went far beyond her comfort zone:

ESTHER: I was interested in studying drama, but I had no background. But all my friends went to the school to audition. And I thought, "What the hell, I'll give it a try, it'll be fun and I'll have friends there." And, they accepted me! I was in shock that they accepted me when I was not sure I belonged there at all. They accepted my friends, too, so I thought we'll be like a little gang there. But I had a terrible year there; it was terrible; I had a really hard time. Maybe my friends had an easier time because they were boys, but me with my background, to be an actress, it wasn't a good fit. I had a very hard time with the exhibitionism there. I hated the way that my body was treated and the coarse language that was spoken there. I felt it was not a positive environment, not a good place for me to be.

One teacher especially didn't like me. She knew I had come from a religious home and got a kick out of it; she was always talking about my chest, my tush, and other body parts, and I used to cry. She gave me such a hard time and really harassed me. So there were five of us ex-Hasidim who started there, and by the end of the year, three of us had left. I left at the end of the year. Once again I became very depressed; I just didn't know what to do.

Esther's gut reaction to the open discourse about her body and the need to display it at school reflected her original socialization about tzniyus. In the Hasidic world, the norms for "modesty" shape every aspect of a woman's presentation of self: all the subtle and obvious details that constitute a particular female Hasidic identity. We saw in earlier chapters that Hasidic women's bodies are subject to so many restrictions that most of my women interviewees had not been told the names of their body parts, or anything about the physical transformations that accompany adolescence. All expressions of sexuality are limited to marriage. Understanding the social and cultural context from which Esther's feelings about her body were derived helps us understand why she was so uncomfortable at the drama school. Her teacher frequently referred to parts of her body that she had earlier not even been able to name herself.

Esther's story reminded me of one of my own lingering vestiges from the past. As I said before, I had grown up Modern Orthodox. My mother did not follow the strict Haredi practices of entirely covering her hair and body at all times. She wore shorts, bathing suits, and sleeveless blouses. I followed her standards, and when I left Orthodoxy I felt I could dress any way I desired. As an adult I have been surprised to find that I retained some lingering feelings over women's proper forms of dress.

On Valentine's Day during my first year at the University of Kansas, my husband and I went out to an elegant hotel bar where hundreds of students had congregated with their dates, or to perhaps find a date. I remember feeling shocked by the skimpiness of the dresses and great height of the heels the young women wore. Nearly all of them wore strapless dresses, many cut in a low and revealing style. I wondered what message they were trying to communicate and how they felt about themselves when they appeared in public scantily clad. As I thought about my reaction, I realized that I myself would never feel comfortable in a dress, strapless or not, that revealed so much cleavage. Although I had no religious compunctions, I still found the students' outfits went "against my grain." Once again, an element of my earlier ideas about comportment appeared nearly forty years after I had left.

Aryeh told a similar story indicating the residual effects of his internalized religious practices:

> Sometimes when I am walking in the hospital where I work I suddenly start wondering whether I am doing anything wrong at the moment. One day I caught myself putting my hand to my head and realizing I was not wearing a yarmulke. Immediately feelings of guilt and shame washed over me. I tried to calm myself down. I said to myself, "Listen, it is Wednesday...it's not Shabbes. So, you're not wearing a yarmulke, but it is not a big deal."
>
> So, yeah, I will catch myself sometimes overcome with this sort of fear. I get the feeling like I'm doing something wrong, and there is an impending sort of judgment in it. But when I say oh, "Let it pass," I can deal with it. So yeah, I do sometimes feel a level of some kind of guilt. It's not guilt in terms of you're doing something wrong from heaven, but it's guilt in leaving tradition, and feeling a loss of that strong sense of identity. Yeah, I do feel it. I'm fighting...I'm actively working against that, but it still stays with me.

Aryeh's expression of guilt and shame reminded me of Sima's statement about the shame, nakedness, and exposure she felt the first time she wore pants. Their upbringing in Hasidic communities had taught them at a young age that any mark of difference—between them and their peers, or their parents and the community—was shameful and could result in marginalization. The term *shande* (shame) also was applied in Hasidic communities to families in which a child defected. The concept of shame was utilized in a variety of ways in Hasidic life and was one technique for socializing children to conformity.

Despite Aryeh's not having worn a yarmulke for a few years, when he suddenly perceived the absence of his kipa, the old guilt and fear came rushing back. He felt he had experienced a momentary lapse in his sense of identity. His description of this experience is evidence of the ongoing presence of his earlier embodied practices: Although the incident he described happened years after his leaving, it showed how the strong compulsion to enact Hasidic bodily rituals was still deeply embedded within him, on occasion catching him unaware.

RELIGIOUS PRACTICES

As we have seen, many Hasidic defectors construct new identities by changing their bodily routines. As individual agents, however, they sometimes make conscious choices to retain some elements of their former bodily techniques and cultural tool kits, even as they are learning new strategies of action from a more secular tool kit, usually by continuing to engage in certain practices, rituals, or celebrations that were part of their Hasidic lives. Although exiters no longer identify with their Ultra-Orthodox roots, their Jewish identity remains important as they find new, syncretic ways of practicing Jewish rituals and maintaining their identities as Jews.

The food we consume becomes a part of us; as in the popular saying, "You are what you eat." Strict observance of the laws regarding kashrut is a private and public symbol of a frum life. Defectors' accounts of their post-leaving dietary habits revealed the staying power of this element of Hasidic life. This embodied foundational element of their old Haredi practices was hard to completely abandon. In some cases, people continued to limit their intake of certain foods, or avoided mixing foods that were forbidden to combine. Ehud, for instance, cannot imagine mixing meat and dairy: "I couldn't drink a glass of milk with a roast beef sandwich." Similarly, Esther also maintains some food prohibitions and prefers to patronize kosher stores and restaurants:

ESTHER: Mind you, for all my hang-ups about hating the way I had
    to do all these things, I still don't eat pork and shellfish, because it's

psychological. I don't know why. I just can't. And I do tend to eat in kosher restaurants disproportionately, not because I keep kosher, but I kind of feel like, "Oh, you know, it's my choice of eating in the Jewish people's shop or the other one," and I typically choose the Jewish kosher one, simply because it's kosher.

In both of these cases, religious food prohibitions continued to structure their eating habits long after they had defected from Orthodoxy. Food habits are important markers of individual and cultural identity. Early socialization into particular food habits can remain embedded in defectors' psyches, forever structuring their relationship with food. A formerly Modern Orthodox friend of mine saw a lobster in a restaurant and immediately said, "That is disgusting," in a tone of deep revulsion. This is especially the case when the early socialization associates certain foods and food practices with sin and punishment, as is the case in Haredi communities.

In addition to gut-level responses to certain foods, defectors told stories of how deeply and fundamentally their food habits were embedded within some of their religious practices.

> BINYAMIN: In the beginning when I was officially not religious anymore, I still kind of did a few Jewish things. Like every now and then, I would make some sort of gesture, like I would light Chanukah candles. You know, I still kind of think I should be doing that. I forget most of the time, and I'm not very concerned with it, but I think in the beginning I lit Shabbes candles when I lived on my own. I thought, "Oh, that's nice. Maybe I'll just light candles."

An interviewee named Rochel told me she still never goes out on Shabbes, even though she breaks the rules at her home by turning the lights and TV on and off. Rutie told me she always lights candles on Friday night, even if she is serving a nonkosher meal. Her house is filled with numerous Jewish ritual objects. For example, she has a beautiful collection of handmade *Menorot* (plural for *Menorah*, the candelabra for *Chanukah* candles). Hanging in the various rooms are tiles from Israel decorated with various symbols of Jewish life such as the Ten Commandments, a prayer for the peace of Jerusalem, and several images of that city. Most respondents, like Rochel, kept at least a few Jewish ritual objects in their homes, such as a Hanukah menorah, or a *mezuzah* [a decorative case holding a parchment of the section in the Hebrew Bible affirming the unity of God] on their doorframes; which indicated to all passersby that this is Jewish home. During our conversations, many of the defectors spoke of their occasional desire to observe a commandment (such as lighting candles on Shabbes) but in most of these cases they did so in their own way. For example, one woman told me how she transformed the traditional candle lighting ritual by lighting candles many hours after Shabbes had already begun. She knew it was forbidden to light fires on Shabbes, but she created her own way of following this commandment.

ONGOING FEELINGS OF LOSS

Although my respondents knowingly violated the commandments, several spoke of feelings of guilt that sometimes arose after they "sinned." Remember how Aryeh felt shame and guilt when on an ordinary day he became aware he was not wearing his Yarmulke? Sarah's first experience of going to the movies brought up similar feelings.

> SARAH: At one point, actually, when I was already out [of the Hasidic community], I went to the movies for the first time. And it was in the village, and I went to see *Chasing Amy*. I can't even tell you the story, but all I remember is what it looked like, the huge screen and how fascinated I was, and all the chairs…and walking out that night, really thinking that on the next block, this huge truck is going to come and hit me, and I will die right then and there because I went to the movie theater. We had always been told God would punish us for our sins, and so I believed I would inevitably be punished.

Nearly all of my interviewees described how their dread of God's wrath and punishments were emphasized in their socialization at home, in school, and in the community. Sara's use of the trope "when I was out," [in an ironic tone], indicates her awareness that those who come out as gay, lesbian, bisexual, and transsexuals must have to go through many of the same processes as did the defectors. As I discussed in the first chapter, gay, lesbian and gender queer people also challenged their dominant cultural metanarrative, transgressed, passed and eventually changed their bodily routines, an essential aspect of this identity transformation.

Sarah's fear of punishment when she transgressed by seeing a movie for the first time was common. When respondents described their first violations of the commandments they expressed their deeply internalized fear of punishment. I sensed some ambivalence in these accounts. During my conversation with Ehud, for example, his ongoing fluctuating feelings were palpable. He told me that he sometimes yearned to set aside his differences from Haredi life, as did many of my respondents, and his profound critique of its worldview, just to feel the comfort of a community. The power of being sheltered within an enclave community was a strong attraction of Haredi life, one my conversation partners missed the most.

EHUD: You know, I remember when I was here several years before working for my Ph.D. I was really struggling with these things and whether I like to hang out with Jews or not. And I haven't gone to any Rosh Hashanah or Yom Kippur service for years. I really hadn't been going. I mean, you can imagine what that means for me. I mean, I know half of the Torah by heart. I can just recite it. As a teenager I often chanted the Torah portion of the week at services. So on Rosh Hashanah I would hang out and walk around the synagogue, so I could listen to the blowing of the Shofar [Ram's horn, whose sound is supposed to awaken Jews to repent] as the new year began, but I never walked in. I had enough conflict in me that as I approached the door to the synagogue, I could not bring myself to walk in. I knew it would not be the right place for the new me. I didn't want to be with Jewish people and say the prayers. I didn't believe. I didn't want to lie to myself, and yet I just missed it so badly. I was just miserable without... without experiencing it, without living it, without singing it, without being with Jews. My goodness, I was just so miserable.

LD: I'm interested. What did you miss about it?

EHUD: That what you miss when you lose a leg, you lose a finger, you lose a hand. I feel…maybe that's what it must feel like. It's just such…such a big part of you. You know, you're expressing yourself, your emotions, everything. What do I miss about it? It's the language and tunes that I had grown up with. That is where you really feel comfortable. That's where you've been for all your childhood and a big part of your life as an adult, so you miss it. It's so rich and warm and familiar.

Ehud's expression of his feelings resembled those of Binyamin. Jewish rituals, language, and song had been so deeply inscribed from the earliest stages of their lives that it pained them to leave it all behind. As we continued to talk and I noticed how he held his head in his hand for much of our conversation, I came to feel Ehud was a tormented soul who could not find a place for himself. He longed for the familiar tunes that enveloped him and the others in his community in a transcendent experience of unity, but as an intellectual, he could not simply walk into a religious service. His statement that he felt that part of his body had been torn off showed how strongly he identified with his former life and how tortured he felt by his irresoluble ambivalence.

Like many others, Abby spoke eloquently about how deeply she missed some aspects of her former Hasidic life. When I invited her to elaborate, she stated:

ABBY: I miss the community aspect, the close community and the singing on Shabbes. I still like to do that. So when I get together with friends and have a Shabbes meal [as a cultural rather than religious ritual] I like the singing of the traditional songs around the Shabbes table. It is something that deeply resonates within me. So, yeah, I miss the deep bonds I had within the Satmar world.

There's no such thing as a homeless Hasidic person. You never see that. That everybody sticks up for each other, despite all their religious craziness. I mean there are a lot of good people there. I don't look at Hasidim and say, "They're all nothing." There are a lot of good people there, a lot of people who would welcome me despite my looking like a "goy." Although my parents were not very good, there are others in the community who were very loving and accepting. You know, it happens to be that the way I was raised was totally crazy, but there are a lot of things that are very beautiful about Hasidic life. There is togetherness. You never feel like you're alone.

I myself have found that I miss the sound of collective singing and the tunes sung in my synagogue when I was young. When I do go to services on the High Holidays my choice of where to go is complicated. On the one hand, my philosophy is more in line with Reconstructionist Judaism. But I cannot get used to English services. Only the Orthodox have services entirely in Hebrew, but I resent having to sit behind a *mehitza* (the division between men and women in all Orthodox synagogues). I have cousins who belong to a Hebrew, Orthodox *egalitarian* synagogue in Brookline, Massachusetts; I immediately felt comfortable going there—it felt right to me.

We have seen from these examples how elements of our inbred bodily practices and original cultural tool kits can never be fully abandoned. Social identity is negotiated through cultural and material practices; those that became constitutive of our identity during our formative years could not be completely replaced even as we acquired the cultural knowledge and routines of the body that we incorporated into our new identities. The choices we make and the practices through which we reconstruct our identities in later life are always built upon the deeply internalized routines that are foundational to our sense of self. Even when people leave the social and cultural contexts in which their daily routines were taught and upheld, they do not completely discard all the elements of their primary socialization.

Defection from Orthodoxy was significantly more complicated than I, or my respondents, had ever anticipated. Although we decided to leave in order to be free of religious strictures and encumbrances, my respondents and I found we were unable to entirely disinscribe aspects of the embodied selves we had incorporated in our youth. Even as we seek to create new identities, some elements of the old ones hang on and show up in surprising ways when we least expect it.

CONCLUSIONS

This book relies on the case studies of defectors from Hasidic enclaves to illustrate that identity changes are made through the medium of the body. In situations of biographical disruption, when a person moves out of one culture and starts to learn the basic elements of a new one, the body is the medium through which old identities are disinscribed and new identities are played out. Social interaction occurs between individuals who assess each other's comportment, demeanor, dress, routine bodily practices, and diet—to learn about that person and the culture from which she or he comes.

Becoming Un-Orthodox illustrates how much we can learn about a culture by observing the details of how members dress, comport themselves, and perform their identities in everyday life. The social, cultural, and physical environments in which people live are literally embedded in their physical beings. Humans play out the fundamental values, norms, and assumptions of their culture by embodying its conventions in the minutest details of their everyday lives, such as how we walk, conduct ourselves, and present our physical bodies to others.

Human bodies are not generic; rather, they bear the markers of culturally constructed differences. Religious groups rely on symbolic as well as physical markers to differentiate themselves from all others. Within conservative religious communities, assumptions about gender distinctions are woven into the fabric of everyday life. Hasidim believe God designed women and men to be physically different to signify and sanctify their distinct roles. As they perform the duties of their gendered roles—whose guidelines were commanded by God— their routine physical practices become incorporated into each one's sense of self and imprinted on their bodies. The complimentary roles assigned to women and men provide a vivid example of embodiment at its most basic level. Fundamentalist religious groups believe that men and women's paths in life are rooted in their biology and cannot be changed. Biology is destiny.

Throughout this book I have used the idea of embodiment to describe how cultural values and assumptions become imprinted within us, inscribed upon our bodies. Sociologist Peter Berger brilliantly wrote about how all aspects of social life—including religion—are created by people. In his words: "Society is a human product and nothing but a human product," although over time, people forget that these norms were once created and therefore could be re-created (1967). By forgetting our own role and agency, all social norms and institutions become "reified," meaning, made to seem more "real" through the implicit message that their society has always been that way.

The social construction of gender has differed throughout time and across the globe. Nevertheless, gender is fundamental to the organization of all societies, cultures, and religions. Sociological studies of gender and religion, however, have often not paid attention to the bodily practices through which religious tenets are enacted. Marie Griffith's book *Born Again Bodies* (2004) is a notable exception. Her book provides an overview and analysis of the Weigh Down Workshop, the nation's largest Christian diet organization, and other historical examples of Christian fitness and diet culture. My book differs, however, in that I am focusing on individual representations of changing bodily practices, not in the service of God, but as a way of breaking away from God's commandments. In this book I pay less attention to institutions, programs, and literature. These cultural and social guides to behavior are offered to members of religious communities. There are no similar guides for defectors. Instead of focusing on institutionalized religious directions for exercise or life, I have focused on the process through which individuals, in shedding one identity and learning another, perform that transformation through the medium of their bodies.

The process of exiting one's primary role and the community in which it had meaning has been studied by Helen Rose Ebaugh, in her groundbreaking book, *Becoming an Ex* (1988). As a former nun,

Ebaugh sought to understand the underlying dynamics occurring when a person leaves her primary role and identity. She compares and contrasts the narratives of a variety of exes, such as widows, transsexuals, retirees, mothers without custody, and ex-convicts, among others. This book similarly seeks to understand the unanticipated, often abrupt, and sometimes extreme discontinuities in roles that arise when one leaves a known way of life and embarks on a new one. This book is distinct from this earlier work, however, in two significant ways: First, rather than seeking a generalized process that could apply to all exiters, this book focuses on understanding, in-depth, one particular case of identity transformation, that of Hasidic defectors, in order to see what light they can shed on other similar processes. Second, by studying those who leave a religious group whose primary concern is appropriate observance of bodily rituals, I have been able to highlight the critical role of the body in all identity transformations. In 1988, when Ebaugh's book was published, sociology had not yet developed an understanding of embodiment as the basis of all social interactions. Upon reflection, I now wonder how Ebaugh, who herself shed a "habit"—both literally and metaphorically—and learned new modes of dress and comportment, left out the essential role of the body in her study of her own and others' exiting process.

The learning and unlearning of culture that defectors describe is further elucidated by Ann Swidler's dynamic conception of culture, which reveals the simultaneous processes involved in unlearning (what I call disinscribing) the ingrained habits of one's culture and learning the practices that will contribute to their membership in a new one. This study adds to Swidler's concept of cultural tool kits an emphasis on the equally important internalized norms for bodily comportment in shaping individuals as social actors. The tool kit is a repertoire of practices that "cultivates skills and habits in its users" (1986, 94). Like Ebaugh, however, Swidler did not explore or consider the system of entrenched bodily habits that are as essential to our lives as are cultural tool kits.

Swidler's concept of "settled lives" and "unsettled lives" (2003, 89) provides a useful schema for portraying some aspects of how a person moves out of a world where everything is familiar and comfortable (settled lives) to the unsettled state of doubt and questioning that anticipates defection. Before my respondents started experiencing tears in their sacred canopies, and even early in their stage of first transgressions, the Hasidic community provided them with a framework in which they lived reasonably settled lives. The lives of frum Jews are physically replete and culturally rich with tools, guidelines, and bodily practices that provide a strong framework for a settled life. In this context, each aspect of religious life—its culture, modes of social organization, and routine physical practices—reinforce the others, such that if one of these elements unravels, the rest are likely to follow suit.

Specifically, when my conversation partners found contradictions between their lives and the idealized model set forth in their communities, or were exposed to attractive alternative ways of life, they questioned the rightness of the Hasidic worldview and system of practices, which no longer made sense to them. When they did not receive satisfying answers, their lives began to feel "unsettled," out of harmony with their cultural milieu. Their life experiences contradicted the fundamental, taken-for-granted worldview and practices of their religious communities, thus revealing the holes in the sacred canopy that, until that moment, safely shielded them, with their entire communities, from the threat of alternative cultures.

As those leaving Hasidic worlds began to try on the new selves they might become, they were slowly developing a new repertoire of skills, habits, and routine bodily practices that would help them feel at home and begin to resettle their lives again in the larger secular society. Once they saw the holes in the sacred canopy that maintained the Orthodox community's way of life, they began to explore new ways of creating an alternative identity. Completing the exiting process involved discarding some of the tools that sustained their lives in Hasidic enclaves and replacing them with practices that are rooted in the new social and cultural settings they enter.

Most of the literature on identity, and on changing identities, focuses on the mental processes involved and the social context in which this change in concept of self is happening. Within the sociology of religion, faith statements have been the major focus of studies of religious conversion and exiting. This particular focus derives from the Christian understanding of religion in which the most fundamental sign of sincere commitment is a statement of faith. In the world in which I grew up, exacting performance of bodily rituals was the mark of religious dedication.

The predominance of Christians in the United States and in the sociology of religion shapes the fundamental assumptions of the field. I remember being invited to attend a special conference held on a Sunday at a university center on religion. The first person to speak that day greeted us with, "Good Morning and Welcome. And, can someone tell me *why* we are here on a Sunday?" I understood the question to mean: Why are "we" working rather than attending services? I felt uncomfortable about being rendered invisible among my colleagues. I spoke into the breach. "I certainly have no problem being here on a Sunday!" The others in the group laughed, nodding their understanding, and the conference began.

It is this generalized invisibility of Jews in the frameworks adapted within the sociology of religion that I hope to reduce with this book. My intention is to show how the study of Jewish ritual bodily *practices* brings a new analytic focus to the study of religious transformation. This study of defectors from Haredi—Ultra-Orthodox—Judaism shows that among those who stay in the community, their daily lives derive order and meaning from performing God's hundreds of rituals *of the body*. Attention to the embodied nature of human subjectivity—as if the two were really separable—opens the field to new questions and the development of new concepts.

The body as the medium of identity changes is not limited to Haredi or Orthodox Jews. Literature on gays, lesbians, bisexual, and transgendered peoples reports how their redefinitions of their identity also depend on changing embodied practices as the medium and mechanism of identity transformation. Immigrants from radically different cultures also have spoken of the bodily changes that were an essential part of their strategy for learning how to be in a new social-cultural context.

Becoming Un-Orthodox relies on case studies of those for whom bodily rituals are their primary mode of religious expression to illustrate that research resting on the definition of religion as a matter of faith has failed to see how deeply embodied, habitual, and taken-for-granted practices are fundamental to, and shape, all aspects of social and cultural life.

APPENDIX I

Theoretical Framework: Narratives, Embodiment, Religion, and Identity

Culture, identity, gender, and the body are inextricably intertwined. We can learn a great deal about a culture by watching the ways in which its participants, female and male, young and old, comport themselves. This can be seen in their dress, the appearance of their hair—on their heads and faces—how they move their bodies, what they do and do not eat, their demeanor, and where they direct their gaze. In every cultural context, the prevailing values, norms, and rules become internalized as habitual, embodied practices. The performance of these daily physical practices creates boundaries between members and nonmembers of a particular group and serves to reinforce that group's metanarrative— the grand, overarching foundational story defining who the group is, from where they came, and the practices that maintain it. This all-encompassing cultural account shapes the self-concepts, constructions of identity, and bodily routines of group members. Performing these bodily routines, or embodied ritualized practices, is the primary way adherents constitute, maintain, and represent their identities within their communities. Through regular repetition they become internalized as the culturally appropriate, habitual, and taken-for-granted ways that members of a group act in daily life.

When there is harmony between a person's life story and her community's cultural metanarrative and its accompanying bodily techniques, she can live a settled, comfortable life that follows culturally expected patterns. In contrast, when individuals no longer want to follow their culture's norm about comportment, or their experience of themselves falls outside of the group's own self-understanding and their own identity narratives are out of sync with the worldviews of their group, they become "unsettled" and feel out of harmony in their communities.

Like culture, religion is inscribed on the bodies of its members. We can analyze the nature of religious communities by paying attention not only to the stories leaders and members tell about who they are, but, more important, to the visible ways the religious ideology, norms, and values are internalized and performed by members of the group. The body is not only the location for the inscription of cultural or religious norms, but it is also the site where identity is created and maintained through routine embodied practices. Similarly, gendered identities, as Judith Butler (1990) has astutely pointed out, are achieved through a person's repeated bodily performance of gender-appropriate actions and appearances. Through what we do every day we not only perform, but also become, gendered beings. Religion is one important social institution that prescribes, enforces, and perpetuates distinct constructions of gender among its adherents. In *Becoming Un-Orthodox* I use the concept of identity as performance to illustrate the ways distinctly gendered religious bodily rituals create and perpetuate religiously prescribed gendered identities.

This book explores questions at the intersection of religion, gender, identity, and bodily practices. By analyzing my interview transcripts over a period of years, the centrality of the theme of embodiment became apparent, and I probed how it intersects with these central components of strictly religious communities. Although many studies have examined the intersection of religion and gender, or religion and gendered bodily practices, few have addressed how religious identities are constructed and maintained through the performance of religiously prescribed gendered bodily rituals. Incorporating all four of these categories together in this analysis and demonstrating how deeply they are interconnected enables me to use each to help illuminate the others. Religious communities prescribe gender norms, which are enacted through distinctively gendered bodily rituals, whose performance creates and maintains a religious identity.

As children are socialized into a religious community, they learn and internalize the routines of bodily practices that are the physical markers of their religious identities. The more a religious community differs from the dominant, mainstream culture, the greater is its need to isolate—encapsulate—its members physically, socially, and ideologically. Physical encapsulation is expressed through the numerous boundaries created to keep members in and outsiders out: Examples include distinctive food practices, the creation of alternative sources of information and media, and prescriptions concerning comportment, demeanor, and dress. Social encapsulation serves to reduce contact between members and outsiders. It is the means through which strict religions create strong bonds among members to ensure their isolation from all others. Ideological encapsulation reinforces the community's metanarrative by presenting it as ultimate truth and by limiting exposure to the potentially polluting ideas of the larger society.

Despite the powerful forces creating deep bonds among members of a religious community, and the strict religious socialization of children into the community's way of life, not all children grow up to become conforming members of their community. Just as identity is enacted through bodily actions and representations, so too can identity be transformed through deliberate changes in those bodily habits that maintain religious identities. Resisting prescribed religious rituals by changing bodily practices or questioning the group's metanarrative can produce a crisis of identity for those who had previously been safely ensconced within and under their group's sacred canopy (Berger 1990).

When individuals experience contradictions between their own thoughts, actions, and beliefs and those of the group, they may seek to resolve this identity crisis by redoubling their efforts to conform to group norms and maintain their place in their religious community. Others who struggle with these contradictions, however, may not succeed in reconciling their doubts and no longer feel comfortable performing all aspects of their group's bodily rituals. Ultimately they may seek ways to leave their religious enclaves, an enormously challenging task emotionally, psychologically, and practically.

Becoming Un-Orthodox investigates the tumultuous biographical disruption of leaving a strict, insular, and isolated religious community, in this case, that of Haredi[1] Judaism. My narrative in this book is based on multiple close readings of the forty interviews I conducted with adults in the United States who identified themselves as "ex-Orthodox" or "exes." Like other stories of biographical disruption, respondents' accounts emphasized the great extent to which their defection split their lives into two parts: before and after.

This juncture offers a particularly meaningful occasion in which to ask someone to tell her life story. In times of significant identity transformations, former interpretations of events, learned through socialization into a particular culture, no longer work to establish meaning and provide norms of behavior. When an individual experiences the trauma of questioning and ultimately leaving the only world she has ever known, with its shared, taken-for-granted worldviews and bodily practices, she is uniquely situated to create a new life story that will make sense of this separation and her subsequent search for a new social context that will ground her identity and provide guidelines for the next stage of her life.

In this book, I argue that leaving a religion is more than a cognitive matter of "losing faith." For defectors from Orthodox Judaism, the most significant break comes not from questioning religious precepts, but by ceasing to participate in those ritual actions that create membership in the group. Hasidic defection is accomplished through the medium of the body. The emphasis on ritual practices in Haredi life—as opposed, for example, to declarations of faith—suggested these rituals would make a particularly strong case study for analyzing the centrality of the body in shaping, maintaining, and shedding religious—and other cultural—identities.

CONSTRUCTING IDENTITY THROUGH NARRATIVE

The central concern of this book is with narratives of displacement and resettling, or exiting and reconstruction of self. In contemporary U.S. society, the therapeutic narrative trope, "I was at the end of my rope until I found the help I needed," is articulated in twelve-step communities as well as in other healing contexts. In his book, *Triumph of the Therapeutic,* Philip Rieff (1966) demonstrates that in late modern societies, theological language and narratives have been replaced by therapeutic narratives: those that tell of a person's struggle to find himself, and the power of therapy to help people heal their minds and make sense of their lives.

Becoming Un-Orthodox is the narrative I have created from the stories that were co-constructed in my conversations with forty defectors, who, like me, had abandoned the strictly Orthodox Jewish communities in which they were raised. Over the past twenty years, there has been an outpouring of writings—in all fields—on the nature of narratives. In the social sciences a narrative approach calls our attention to the researcher's role in co-constructing the stories created in interview conversations and in choosing the themes, illustrative quotations, and the central argument that shapes this book.

In writing about these narratives, I, like many contemporary sociologists and anthropologists, have adopted a self-reflexive approach, allowing the reader to evaluate my interpretations by explicating my involvement throughout the research process. Further, throughout the book, I often show my role in the process of narrative construction by highlighting particular interactions between my informants and me in which, for example, they interrogate my knowledge of their world so they can know how much I might understand without explication. These interactions reveal that respondents did not simply "have" a narrative that I, as a researcher, could "get." Rather, by calling attention to the dynamics of the interview, I show the specific ways my informants interacted with me as a woman and as a codefector, albeit from Modern Orthodoxy rather than a Haredi community. The interview narratives that emerged from informants' conversations reflect their engagement with a particular person (i.e., me) and in a distinct place and time. If those factors were varied, a different account might have emerged.

Narratives are not the life events themselves. Rather, they are reconstructions and reinterpretations of these occurrences that are shaped by social contexts, those in which the speaker was socialized, as well as what I bring to it myself. The language respondents used is a combination of the one they learned in their childhoods as well as the newer ways they have learned to speak after their defection. Our social contexts play a powerful role in shaping the language of our accounts and how we represent the events of our lives. As philosopher of religion Paul Ricouer wrote: "As the past is remembered, it is interpreted and reinterpreted in the light of the person's knowledge and understanding" (Ricouer 1980, 183). Within these reconstructed accounts, storytellers tend to try to reduce the dissonance caused by a major displacement by reinterpreting the sequence of events and generalizing the current situation backward, such as "I have always been this way" (or, "I have always been suspicious" or "I have always considered myself religious," and so on). This narrative trope appears in many respondents' accounts as one mechanism through which speakers represent continuity in their lives. These stories seek to place events in a sequential order with a clear beginning, middle, and end.[2]

Each time a person provides a narrative account of his life, he is recreating his identity through the very telling. Sociologists, anthropologists, and cultural critics recognize that in a society continually in flux, our narratives of identity are fluid, and can vary greatly in different situations. They argue that contemporary individuals do not have a fixed, immutable identity; rather, we can have a plurality of "narrative identities." These variations are possible because personal identities do not exist solely inside us; they emerge in interaction between two particular individuals, and the ways the two conversation partners interact create possibilities for creating distinct forms of self. The context of the interview, the dynamics between the conversation partners, and the social contexts in which each grew up shape how the life story is told.

The power of narratives can be seen particularity clearly in interviews about life trauma and hardships. Sociologist Catherine Kohler Riessman (1993) argues that "telling stories about difficult times in our lives creates order and contains emotions, allowing a search for meaning and enabling connection with others." Biographical disruptions offer a particularly meaningful occasion in which to ask someone to recount her life story. Analyzing these accounts of biographical disruptions and the events that follow provides insight into the ways people organize their life stories temporally and logically to ensure their accounts establish coherence across past, present, and future. During these times, former interpretations of events, learned through socialization in a particular culture, no longer work to establish meaning and provide norms of behavior. When members of a community who previously felt in harmony with their group's assumption, norms, and practices begin to feel out of sync within their cultural context, they experience the uncomfortable feeling of being unsettled. This uncomfortable feeling is anxiety-provoking and anomic; people have abandoned the norms that formerly guided their lives but have not yet developed a new set of beliefs and practices in which to ground their new identities. Their challenge is to create a new identity, grounded in different bodily practices and social contexts.

Focusing on embodied practices provides the researcher with a distinct angle from which to observe the representation and performance of an identity reflecting the culture's central beliefs, worldviews, values, gender ideologies, and attitudes toward the body. People's physical presentation of themselves—their clothing, hair, diet, comportment, and public activities—is part of the embodied practices that simultaneously create and reveal a particular identity within a group, as well as reveal the boundaries between themselves as members of one group versus another.

RELIGION, IDENTITY, GENDER, AND EMBODIMENT

All religions, to a greater or lesser extent, shape members' embodied, gendered identities through their prescriptions for religious rituals and roles. Individuals belonging to different religious communities are required to engage in a variety of bodily practices—rituals performed by and enacted upon the body—that create, maintain, and display membership in the group. Through socialization into their religious community, they learn and internalize the group's norms, beliefs, and values and how to perform the group's rituals, including the corporeal rites through which the religion becomes embodied. Within strict, enclave religious communities, such as some Muslim and Haredi Jewish groups, numerous rituals and laws involving bodily practices occupy members throughout the day and are central to the presentation and ongoing construction of their religious identities.

The extent to which religious bodily rituals shape members' identities and their daily routine practices varies along a continuum from nearly total control to a loose set of guidelines. Different groups within the same religion, and individuals within the same religious group, fall on different points along the continuum and comprise a great diversity of religious bodily practices. Even those who only engage in religious bodily practices when in a weekly or annual religious gathering engage their bodies nonetheless. Consider a Catholic adherent participating in a weekly Mass. Upon entering, she crosses herself, then sits down in a pew. Before entering the pew from the aisle, she kneels and crosses herself again. Throughout the service, she sits, stands, and kneels at appointed times, recites or reads portions of the liturgy in unison with others present, and crosses herself before and after every prayer. She stands to greet and shake hands with other parishioners during the passing of the peace. At the culmination of the service, she proceeds forward to eat and drink the bread and wine provided by the priest. She genuflects—a bodily ritual in which a person bends down on one or both knees—as an act of adoration when receiving the Eucharist sacrament. As the service ends, she crosses herself again before leaving. Communion provides an excellent example of a gendered religious practice: The priests who are sanctified to perform this ritual are all men.

Charismatic Christian worship services are actively embodied; during the frequent singing in the service, those in attendance may stand, sway, clap, or dance. During corporate prayer, worshippers are encouraged to speak in tongues—known as glossolalia. If the congregation wants to dedicate a certain portion of prayer time to someone in particular, they gather around that person and lay hands on her. In some churches, the leader may call people to come to the front who are in need of physical or emotional healing. The pastor lays hands on the person and prays, upon which the person may be slain in the Spirit and fall to the ground.

Meditation, a bodily practice that can be done alone or in a group, is a ritual that often takes place outside of weekly gatherings. The practice entails ritualized techniques for maintaining a particular position on a *zafu* (meditation pillow) and sitting still for a certain amount of time. Walking meditation is another way of practicing this bodily ritual, as is focusing on one's breath. Through regular practice, the intensive focus on the breath as it moves in and out offers a means of integrating the mind and body and achieving deeper levels of consciousness.

Hasidic Jews' bodily practices are extensive, and, unlike meditation, they do not end after about an hour of *sitting*.[3] They are all-consuming, every day, throughout the day. Hasidim are required to engage in a variety of bodily practices—rituals performed by and enacted upon the body—that create, maintain, and display membership in the group. As children are socialized into this religious community, they learn and internalize the group's norms, beliefs, and values and learn how to perform the group's rituals, including the corporeal rites through which the religion becomes embodied. Within strict, enclave religious communities, such as the Shakers, some Muslim groups, and Haredim, numerous rituals and laws involving bodily practices engage and shape nearly all aspects of members' lives. The performance of these Jewish religious rituals is a constant reminder of the group's metanarrative concerning God and his commandments given to the Jewish people and is central to the display, presentation, and ongoing construction of religious identity. Enclave communities regulate members' embodied practices by inextricably linking them to acceptance in the group.

Students of religion from a variety of disciplines have intermittently analyzed the role of the body in religious rituals across time and space, often focusing on how particular social groups set themselves apart from others by cultivating distinctive bodily practices (Bartkowski 2005, 11; Kanter 1972). The Shakers, whose celibate way of life was studied by sociologists Meredith McGuire, Rosabeth Moss Kanter, and others, had a prescribed routine guiding all aspects of daily life, including the exact order for getting out of bed and dressing each morning (Kanter 1972;

McGuire 2008). Regulations concerning appropriate dress, diet, and other rituals of embodiment are central to building and maintaining commitment in Utopian communities. In the process of adapting and conforming to the rules of group comportment, members relinquish elements of their individual freedom (Kanter 1972). In this book, I add to this discussion by highlighting the way the bodily practices are involved not only in signaling group membership to others, but also in constructing and reinforcing identity changes.

The repetition of quotidian bodily practices is not only symbolic of religious orientation, but it also contributes to the constitution and cultivation of long-term religious identities within religious communities. Saba Mahmood's study of the Mosque Movement in Cairo illustrates how the repeated performance of bodily rituals actually builds a religious and ethical orientation. Here, everyday bodily practices are at the core of shaping religious identity; they do not just symbolize a modest individual, but also perform the work of creating one:

> Bodily acts—like wearing the veil or conducting oneself modestly in interactions with people (especially men) do not serve as manipulatable masks in a game of public presentation, detachable from an essential interiorized self. Rather they are the critical markers of piety as well as the ineluctable means by which one trains oneself to be pious. While wearing the veil serves as first and foremost a means to tutor oneself in the attribute of shyness, it is also simultaneously integral to the practice of shyness: one cannot simply discard the veil once the modest deportment has been acquired, because the veil is part of what defines that comportment. (Mahmood 2005, 158)

Mahmood's research shows how bodily practices are essential for the cultivation of an Islamic subjectivity; identity is both constituted through and the result of bodily performance. When a person changes her behavior in this realm she enacts not only a transformation of self but also her relationship to the larger community. Thus, bodily practices are not only visible signals of an interior identity; they actually create one. In the words of Judith Butler, "Identity is performatively constituted by the very 'expressions' that are said to be its results" (1990, 25). Applying Butler's ideas to Hasidic life, we can see that the very performance of Hasidic rituals constructs a Hasidic identity. Her analysis illustrates the way gendered religious roles are accomplished through the performance of those Haredi male and female identities they signify. In the Hasidic world—both Yesivish and Hasidic, cosmic significance resides in every detail of everyday life, and repetitive observation of commandments is viewed as a means of building belief (Fader 2006).

When converts join a new religion, their transition is assisted by the group's script, which provides a new metanarrative, values, norms, and guidelines for behavior. As they become members of the group, they take on new bodily practices through which they establish, mark, and perform membership in their new religious communities (Greil 1977; Greil and Rudy 1984, and others). Since the 1960s and 1970s, the growth of new religious movements produced volumes of scholarship on the conversion process, focusing primarily on why people convert and trying to create a generalized account of the stages of conversion. In this research literature, less attention has been paid to processes of defection, although a book by Janet Liebman Jacobs, *Divine Disenchantment* (1989), focuses on leaving "cults," while others focus on denominational switching.

In recent years the subject of leaving a religious community has received little attention. No books analyze people who leave Haredi communities, nor any other strict enclave community. *Becoming Un-Orthodox* adds to the literature on conversion and defection. By analyzing my interview transcripts over a period of years, the theme of embodiment emerged loud and clear, and I probed into its intersections with gender, religion, and identity. Through my conversations with ex-Hasidim I became aware of the ways bodies, gender, identities, and religion are intertwined in complicated ways.

Those who leave intensive religious communities must transform their bodily practices as a way to accomplish their changed identities, thereby establishing and presenting a new sense of self. Since religions are embodied in their members, all those who leave enclave religious communities must disinscribe the community's imprint on their bodies and simultaneously carve out new physical practices and ways of being in the world. Just as Hasidic lives are created, re-created, and performed through the medium of the body, exiting this community is dependent upon changing internalized, habitual techniques of the body and learning new bodily practices available in the wider society.

APPENDIX II

Interview Guide for Those Who Have Left Orthodoxy

Please describe for me, in as much detail as you can, what kind of Orthodox community you grew up in, and the processes through which you came to leave it.

In what context did it occur?

What was going on in your life?

—Source of exposure to a different kind of life

Are there any books, ideas, or events that influenced you in this path?

—Ideas/questions: cognitive dimension

—Emotions: emotional dimension

Did you talk to anyone about what you were going through?

How did that person (those people) react?

Over how much time did this transition occur?

(If this has not been covered in the above: To what extent did you rebel against Orthodoxy before you made the decision to leave?)

Did you think those feelings might pass? How did you deal with them?

Were there any role models for you in this process?

What aspects of Orthodoxy were most difficult for you?

Were there any aspects that felt easy? Or that you enjoyed?

What part of your former life was the most difficult for you to leave?

Did you face obstacles to your leaving? Describe.

Did you have any assistance in leaving? Describe.

Do you feel that you have been on a journey? Describe.

Has there been any spiritual dimension to this journey?

How did you feel about yourself as you were making this transition? Or other feelings in general?

Were there particular milestones in this transition?

How do you understand what it means to be Jewish? Is it biological or inborn, is it a religion, a culture, an ethnicity? Please elaborate.

EFFECTS OF LEAVING

In what ways is your life different now? (Make sure to get details about everyday life.)

Are there aspects that remain the same?

Is there any particular term by which you name/describe yourself?

What aspects of secular society are easiest to live within? Are there any that are difficult?

To what extent do you feel you have integrated into secular society?

Are there any changes in how you view Jewish tradition?

Jewish law?

The Orthodox world?

The secular world?

Other Jews? And other Jewish denominations?

Non-Jews?

What does being Jewish mean to you now? How is that similar to/different from before?

Were there any aspects of your former Orthodox life that were particularly easy to leave? Or particularly difficult?

Are there any aspects of your family's and/or community's traditions that you still continue to practice or that you still have feelings for?

Do you have any sense of God now? Is it similar to/different from your previous sense of God?

What is your current relationship to Orthodoxy in general? To your family (including siblings and extended family)?

Have any of your relationships changed? Which ones, and in what ways?

What has been the emotional dimension and impact of this change?

Do you see yourself on a spiritual path now?

Do you engage in any religious or ritual practices?

Describe in detail.

Are these similar to how you lived before, or different? Elaborate.

What do these mean to you?

Do you have regularized rituals you do that you don't consider Orthodox but that you see as religious or spiritual in some way?

Are there ways in which you can see your religious/spiritual/ritual behavior changing in the future?

Are there major areas in your life now about which you have questions?

Do you have any objects that are or have become ritual objects for you in your current life?

Is there anything different about your looks and how you present yourself to the world? Describe in detail.

What about any changes in your name or in how you introduce yourself to others?

When asked to describe yourself, what do you say when you're meeting someone for the first time and that person says, "Well, tell me something about yourself you think it is important for me to know"?

Has your sexuality changed in any ways through this process of leaving? Describe.

Have your politics changed in this process?

What about work and what you do?

What about your economic life? Earning? Spending patterns?

Are there things you spend money on now that you would not have spent money on in the past?

Are there things on which you used to spend money that you no longer do?

Do you have a sense of what your morals are? How are they similar to or different from before? What about your values?

Do you have kids? How are you raising them? If not, what do you imagine about how you would raise them?

Has this transition had any effect on your health, both physical and mental?

What about on your leisure activities? Your engagement in general with the secular world, arts, and culture—both high- and lowbrow?

Do you still feel any connections to Orthodoxy? In what way?

How do you feel when you think about Orthodoxy and your upbringing?

Do you experience any feelings of loss? Regret? Guilt?

Have you moved geographically through this process? What has that been about and how has that been for you?

Do you have a sense of your role in life? Is it similar to/different from how you used to see it?

Do you have a sense of optimism or pessimism about your future? About the future of the world? Has that changed through this process?

Do you belong to any groups? Describe.

Is there a particular community with which you identify?

In general, do you like belonging to groups or not? In what way is this similar to/different from when you were growing up?

Do you have a support system? Who is in it (not just names, but types of people)? What was most helpful in their support?

Who are your three closest friends (types of people)?

(If not already answered) Do you still have any contact with the Orthodox world? In what ways? Do you have dialogues with people about your leaving?

The following questions are generally answered by this point in the interview, but in case they're not, I have them here to be sure to get to them. But if the person is a good narrator, the answers will have come up in the first part of the interview when I try to get the person to tell me in a very open-ended, full way, their story about leaving.

GROWING UP/CHILDHOOD/FAMILY

Tell me, in as much detail as you can, about your upbringing.

Tell me about your family, nuclear, extended. Describe your relationships with your family members.

Religiosity in the family?

Primary language spoken at home?

Parents' education and occupations?

Describe your neighborhood/community.

Was your community integrated or segregated from mainstream secular society and culture?

Did you have secular media in your house (TV, magazines, newspapers)?

Did you have any exposure to current events, secular books, non-Orthodox Jews, fashion, fads?

Did you have any impressions of secular society when you were growing up? What about secular Jews?

Friendships as a child?

When did you become aware that there were other ways of living, even among Jews, than Orthodoxy?

What value do you place on personal happiness? Is this different from the way you were raised?

Were there any particular communities with which you were affiliated as a child? Any other groups?

Basic demographics:

Age

Sexual orientation

Occupation

Do you know any other people who have left Orthodoxy? Are you particularly drawn to them? Are there any you can refer to me for interviewing?

GLOSSARY

atzma	essence, real thing
ba'alat teshuvah	(pl. ba'alot teshuvah) a woman who adopts Orthodox Judaism as an adult
ba'al teshuvah	(pl. ba'alei teshuvah) a man who adopts Orthodox Judaism as an adult
Bar mitzvah	"son of commandments"; an adult with religious responsibilities; a ceremony in which a thirteen-year-old boy is initiated into religious adulthood.
Beis Din	Rabbinical Court
	Ashkenezic and Sephardic forms of the word for blessing
Brachot, brachos *bracha*	first two words are plural for blessings, the latter is singular; the variations in spelling reflect modern Hebrew (the first word in each pairing) as well as the more heavily Eastern European accent used by the Haredim
cholov Yisroel	milk that is watched and closely supervised from the moment of milking the cow—which is done by a religious Jewish person—through processing and packaging. This term also refers to all products made with dairy. Modern Orthodox drink milk without this extra supervision, but Haredim only drink or eat cholov Yisroel
Dati, datiya	male singular and female singular for religiously observant; meant to refer to Modern (Centrist) Orthodox people
Daven, davening	pray, praying

fabrengen	Yiddish. A word used by the Lubavitcher Hasidim: a festive, joyous gathering between the former rebbe and his male followers in which the rebbe expounded on Hasidic philosophy and led his Hasidim in singing wordless tunes
frum	strictly observant of all Jewish commandments
Gehenna	original Greek formulation (Hebrew is gehinnom). In Jewish, Christian, and Islamic Scripture, this is the destination of the wicked.
goyim	Hebrew plural form for non-Jews. Also in Yiddish, an adjective referring to qualities, mannerisms, and objects that belong in the non-Jewish realm. The term reflects a critique of the non-Jews
Halacha, halachic	the body of religious laws that governs both the religious and secular behavior of observant Jews; actions and objects that are in accordance with Jewish law
Haredi, haredit	singular term referring to an "Ultra-Orthodox" male and female.
Hasidim	(pl.) a sectarian groups of Ultra-Orthodox Jews who congregate around a particular rebbe
Hasidism, Hasidus	the Hasidic way of life
heder	school for young boys
Hozrot b'tshuvah, hozrim, hozeret, hozrot	refers to those who were not brought up Orthodox and who chose to follow this way of life (female plural, male plural, female singular, male singular)
ilui	Hebrew noun meaning above, elevated, or enlightened
kaddish	prayer for the dead
kashrut	the kosher laws that regulate the dietary behavior of Orthodox Jews
kiddush	ritual blessing over the wine, part of the Shabbat meal
kipa	head covering worn by Orthodox and Haredi men
kishkes	guts
lernen	studying Torah

Litvak	literally referring to Jews who originated in Lithuania. Commonly used to refer to those who are Yeshivish Haredi, not Hasidic
mehitza	the partition in an Orthodox synagogue that separates the women's section from the men's
mikveh	(pl. mikvaot) ritual bath in which Orthodox women immerse themselves a week after completing their menstrual cycle
Mishnah	text codified in CE 200 that is the compilation of Jewish oral law
Mitzvah, mitzvahs, mitzvot	singular for commandment; followed by the anglicized form of making the word plural and the modern Hebrew pronunciation.
Moshiach	Messiah
nagel vasser	water poured from a cup over the hands on arising
niddah	menstruant or state of ritual impurity resulting from menstruation
niggunim	wordless tunes
peyos	curly hair sidelocks worn by men and boys in Hasidic communities.
Rebbe	the title for a rabbi who is head of a community or movement, as in Bostoner Rebbe or Lubavitcher Rebbe
schleppy	Yiddish for frumpy, slovenly, or awkward.
Shabbat, Shabbes	first is the modern Hebrew pronunciation for the Sabbath. The following term is the Ashkenazic pronunciation
shande	shame
Shidduch, shidduchim	singular, plural. Matches or dates arranged by a third party for the explicit purpose of marriage
shtiebl	small synagogue
shul	synagogue
Shulchan Aruch	Hebrew. The authoritative code of Jewish law originally composed by Rabbi Yosef Karo of Safed (in Israel) in the 1560s that remains authoritative to this day
siddur	prayer book

Sifrei torah	Torah scrolls
smicha	Rabbinic ordination (in Orthodox Judaism it is available only to men)
sofer	Jewish scribe who can transcribe Torah scrolls, tefillin, and other ritual documents.
shtetlach	Yiddish plural for the small ghettos where Jews lived in Eastern Europe
taharat hamishpacha	laws of family purity governing sexual relations between wives and husbands
Talmud	series of texts, dating from CE 200 to 600, that are a commentary on the Mishnah
Talmid Chochom	wise scholar
tefillin	Phylacteries; leather straps connected to a box containing sacred scrolls that Orthodox Jewish men wrap around their arms and heads for their weekday morning prayers
Torah	Jewish Bible; the corpus of Jewish law, lore, and rabbinic commentary, which is the central organizing element of Jewish religion and tradition and which is considered by believers to be divinely inspired (Heilman, 1976, 289); the traditional Jewish philosophy, learning, and way of life, as in "the Torah things I learned"
Torah im derech eretz	Torah together with the ways of life of the surrounding people
treyf	unkosher
tzniyus	modesty
yarmulke	skullcap
Yeshiva, yeshives, yeshivot	Hebrew for single instititution of Jewish education; Ashkenazi pronunciation of the plural; modern Hebrew pronunciation of the plural
yeshivishe velt	"yeshiva world"
yichus	social capital, having important connections and lineage
Yiddishkeit	Judaism, Jewish way of life
Yorei Shamayim	fearful of God
Zemiros, zemirot	tunes sung at Sabbath meals

NOTES

1. I am aware that the term *defector* is highly charged; other researchers have chosen the term *exiter* to describe people who leave their primary role identities (Ebaugh, 1988). I chose this term deliberately, however, because my respondents all spoke of making a difficult and conscious decision to abandon the Haredi world, knowing that their defection put them at risk of losing everything and everyone in their prior lives. They did not simply exit or leave; they were self-reflexive apostates who disowned allegiance to the community in which they grew up. To avoid repeating the same term in a paragraph I use other words, such as *exiter* or *those who left*.

2. I have borrowed this phrase from the well-known book by Peter Berger, *The Sacred Canopy* (1967).

3. The term *biographical disruptions* refers to ruptures so profound, so significant, that they shatter people's culturally derived expectations of their life course, affecting them so deeply that they might say: "That divided my life," or "I always think of my life as divided in two—before and after."

4. Whereas Haredi communities insist on erecting high boundaries between themselves and the outside world, Modern Orthodox groups allow involvement in the secular world through work, culture, education, sports, and other activities.

5. Yeshivish are also referred to as *Litvak* (Yiddish for Lithuania, referring to those studying in the many outstanding rabbinical academies that were built in Europe over a century before World War II).

6. Some of these laws might be followed by particular groups of non-Hasidic Haredim.

7. Described in the *Shulchan Aruch* (Hebrew literal meaning is "set table." The name refers to the most authoritative code of Jewish law, written

by Rabbi Yosef Karo in 1563 in Safed, a northern Israeli town). Aruch haRav 4:1 Helichot Netilat Yadayim (The Laws Regarding the Sanctification of the Hands).

8. The term *the Divine* is that of an outsider's perspective. Community members would have said *Hashem*, literally the name, as their way of referring to "the Divine."

9. Some are able to trace their family line back to the original founding of their community in Eastern Europe.

10. *Disincribe* is a neologism I created because I could not find an adequate word that describes how individuals remove cultural and religious markers from their bodies.

11. Although I find Swidler's concept of a cultural tool kit to be useful, it is limited in its failure to pay attention to bodily practices as part of a group's repertoire of behaviors.

12. Here I have adapted Freud's famous expression to suit this context.

13. The term for the qualities that match a person's biological sex is *gender*.

14. *Genderqueer* refers to a questioning of the male-female gender binary, which separates sexual desire or behavior from sexual orientation and considers sexual desire to be unrelated to a specific gender. It also refers broadly to gender or sexuality identifications that fall outside of heterosexuality.

CHAPTER TWO

1. Psychiatric literature, such as *Listening to Prozac*. 1993. Peter Kramer has reported that early childhood traumas result in permanent changes in brain chemistry.

2. "Ultra-Orthodox Shun Their Own for Reporting Child Sexual Abuse," *New York Times*, May 9, 2012.

3. It is important to mention (although it is beyond the scope of this work) that research has been done on child abuse in the fundamentalist Christian community, particularly concerning how to discipline children.

4. Tractate *Sota* 20:a. Quoted in Rabbi Moshe Kahn, "Jewish Education for Women," *Ten Daat*, III, no. 3, pp. 9–11.

CHAPTER THREE

1. During the years between the end of World War II and the present, Orthodox rabbis and communities have moved toward increasingly stricter interpretations of the religious laws.
2. By asking me whether I "knew" Flatbush, she was not asking me about a geographical location but about whether I was aware that in the Flatbush neighborhood of Brooklyn, the dominant Jewish community was Modern Orthodox.

CHAPTER FOUR

1. In this book, I have sometimes used excerpts from a wide variety of people, and at other times I have used longer narratives. In this chapter, I have chosen to use longer excerpts from my interviews. Passing was described as a long and anguished stage; to fairly represent my respondents, I wanted to represent their narratives and the tangled emotions with which they lived. I thus needed to show them through the many sides and phases of this experience.
2. Many Hasidic communities require women to cover their hair completely; shaving it was one way they avoided risking exposure. In addition, when women dunked in the *mikveh* (ritual bath in which Orthodox women immerse themselves one week after completing their menstrual cycle) for ritual purification, there were supposed to be no barriers between her and the water. A head without hair ensured complete immersion.
3. *Keep* is a word the Orthodox use to refer to their religious observance, as in, "I keep kosher."
4. This Talmudic passage indicates how the power of patriarchy—and some misogyny—led men to think that they were much more intelligent than women and that women were too light-headed to understand the intricate complexities of the ancient texts.

CHAPTER FIVE

1. This is how it is described in the Jewish tradition and the ancient texts. Rashi, the great eleventh-century scholar of Hebrew Scripture, had asked, "Why did it take so long?" After all, the desert is a small place. It does

not take forty years to pass through it. He then explained that it was a psychic matter. You had to be in the desert to shed your old skin, in this case, their slave mentality. That generation who came out of Egypt was not allowed to come into Israel; they had to die in the desert so a new generation of free men and women could be born, and they would enter the Holy Land.

2. Leah's difficulties in getting her husband to do any of the housework, let alone half, are common to many working women, who therefore work "a double shift" (Hochschild 1989).

3. The *mikveh* has to contain a certain amount of rain or other naturally occurring water (a woman can use the ocean as *a mikveh*, for example). After a woman's period ends and seven days pass without bleeding, she is required to immerse herself completely three times in the *mikveh*, which ended the period of ritual impurity brought on by her menstrual flow.

CHAPTER SIX

1. I heard this term from my friend Rabbi Neal Schuster, who used it as we were discussing the conclusion to this book.

APPENDIX ONE

1. Although many people refer to Haredim by the English word *Ultra-Orthodox*, Haredim resist this term because it implies they are going over and beyond what is required.

2. In my first book, *Tradition in a Rootless World*, which focused on women who became Orthodox as adults, I found they, too, made statements reconciling their current lives with their pasts, such as "I was always interested in Orthodoxy."

3. The term used for meditation in some groups.

REFERENCES

Aalten, Anna. 1997. "Performing the Body, Creating Culture." In Kathy Davis (ed.), *Embodied Practices: Feminist Perspective on the Body*, pp. 41–58. London: Sage.

Abu-Lughod, Lila. 1986. *Veiled Sentiments: Honor and Poetry in a Bedouin Society*. Berkeley: University of California Press.

Ammerman, Nancy T. 2007. *Everyday Religion: Observing Modern Religious Lives*. Oxford: Oxford University Press.

Andrews, Molly, Corinne Squire, and Maria Tamboukou. 2013. *Doing Narrative Research*. London: Sage.

Arthur, Linda B. 1999. "Introduction: Dress and the Social Control of the Body." In Linda B. Arthur (ed.), *Religion, Dress and the Body*, pp. 1–7. Oxford: Berg.

Barker, Eileen, 1984. *The Making of a Moonie: Choice or Brainwashing*. Oxford: Blackwell.

Bar-Lev, Mordechai, Abraham Beslau, and Nechama Ne'eman. 1997. "Culture Specific Factors Which Cause Jews in Israel to Abandon Religious Life." In Mordechai Bar-Lev and William Shaffir (eds.), *Leaving Religion and Religious Life*, in David G. Bromley (ed.), *Religion and the Social*, 7: 185–204. Greenwich, Conn.: JAI Press.

Barnes, Ruth, and Joanne B. Eicher. 1992. *Dress and Gender: Making Meaning in Cultural Contexts*. Oxford: Berg.

Bartkowski, John P. 2005. "Faithfully Embodied: Religious Identity and the Body." *DisClosure* 14: 8–37.

Barzilai, Sarit. 2004. (Hebrew) *To Storm a Hundred Gates: A Journey into the World of the Newly Secular*. Tel Aviv: Yediot Aharanot.

Becker, Gaylene. 1997. *Disrupted Lives: How People Create Meaning in a Chaotic World*. Berkeley: University of California Press.

Becker, Howard S. 1986. *Writing for Social Scientists: How to Start and Finish Your Thesis, Book, or Article*. Chicago: University of Chicago Press.

Bellah, Robert N., Richard Madsen, William M. Sullivan, Ann Swidler, and Steven M. Tipton. 1985. *Habits of the Heart: Individualism and Commitment in American Life*. Berkeley: University of California Press.

Benmayor, Rina, and Andor Skotnes. 2005. *Migration and Identity*. New Brunswick, N.J.: Transaction Publishers.

Benor, Sarah Bunin. 1975. *Becoming Frum: How Newcomers Learn the Language and Culture of Orthodox Judaism*. New Brunswick, N.J.: Rutgers University Press.

Berger, Peter. 1969. *The Sacred Canopy: Elements of Sociological Theory of Religion*. Garden City, N.Y.: Anchor Books/Doubleday.

Berger, Peter, and Thomas Luckmann. 1967. *The Social Construction of Reality*. Garden City, N.Y.: Anchor Books.

Berger, Ronald J., and Richard Quinney. 2005. *Storytelling Sociology: Narrative as Social Inquiry*. Boulder: Lynne Rienner Publishers.

Biale, David, Michael Galshinsky, and Susannah Heschel, eds. 1998. *Insider/Outsider, American Jews and Multiculturalism*. Berkeley: University of California Press.

Bobel, Chris, and Samantha Kwan. 2011. *Embodied Resistance: Challenging the Norms, Breaking the Rules*. Nashville, Tenn.: Vanderbilt University Press.

Boje, David M. 1998. "The Postmodern Turn from Stories-as-Objects to Stories-in-Context Methods." *Research Methods Forum* 3 (Fall): 1–4.

Bornstein, Kate. 1995. *Gender Outlaw: On Men, Women, and the Rest of Us*. New York: Vintage.

Bourdieu, Pierre. 1977. *Outline of a Theory of Practice*. Cambridge: Cambridge University Press.

Bourdieu, Pierre. 2005. "Belief and the Body." In Mariam Fraser and Monica Greco (eds.), *The Body: A Reader*, pp. 87–91. London: Routledge.

Bourdieu, Pierre, and Loïc J. D. Wacquant. 1992. *An Invitation to Reflexive Sociology*. Chicago: University of Chicago Press.

Brinkerhoff, Merlin, and Kathryn L. Burke. 1980. "Disaffiliation: Some Notes on 'Falling from the Faith.'" *Sociological Analysis* 41: 41–54.

Bromley, David G. 1997. "Falling from the New Faiths: Toward an Integrated Model of Religious Affiliation/Disaffiliation." In Mordechai

Bar-Lev and William Shaffir (eds.), *Leaving Religion and Religious Life*; *Religion and the Social Order* 7: 31–60. Greenwich: JAI Press.

Bruner, Jerome. 1990. *Acts of Meaning*. Cambridge, Mass.: Harvard University Press.

Bury, Michael. 1982. "Chronic Illness as Biographical Disruption: Towards an Integrated Perspective." *Sociology of Health and Illness* 4(2): 167–182.

Buss, Diana. 1989. *Essentially Speaking: Feminism, Nature and Difference*. New York: Routledge.

Butler, Judith. 1990. *Gender Trouble: Feminism and the Subversion of Identity*. New York: Routledge.

Cahill, Spencer E. 2006. "Building Bodily Boundaries: Embodied Enactment and Experience." In Dennis Waskul and Phillip Vannini (eds.), *Body/Embodiment: Symbolic Interaction and the Sociology of the Body*, pp. 69–82. Hampshire: Ashgate.

Charmaz, Kathy. 2006. *Constructing Grounded Theory: A Practical Guide through Qualitative Analysis*. London: Sage.

Clifford, James, and George E. Marcus. 1986. *Writing Culture: The Poetics and Politics of Ethnography*. Berkeley: University of California Press.

Coakley, Sarah. 1997. *Religion and the Body*. Cambridge: Cambridge University Press.

Cohen, Steven M. 1988. *American Assimilation or Jewish Revival?* Bloomington: Indiana University Press.

Cohen, Steven M., and Arnold Eisen. 2000. *The Jew Within: Self, Family, and Community in America*. 2000. Bloomington: Indiana University Press.

Colbert, Don. 2002. *What Would Jesus Eat? The Ultimate Program for Eating Well, Feeling Great, and Living Longer*. Nashville, Tenn.: Thomas Nelson, Inc.

Connell, R. W. 2001. "Bodies, Intellectuals and World Society." In Nick Watson and Sarah Cunningham-Burley (eds.), *Reframing the Body*, pp. 13–28. New York: Palgrave.

Connelly, Michael, and D. Jean Clandinin. 1990. "Stories of Experience and Narrative Inquiry." *Educational Researcher* June/July: 2–14.

Cortazzi, Martin. 2007. "Narrative Analysis in Ethnography." In Paul Atkinson, Sara Delamont, Amanda Coffey, John Lofland, and Lyn Lofland (eds.), *Handbook of Ethnography*, pp. 384–394. London: Sage.

Cregan, Kate. 2006. *The Sociology of the Body: Mapping the Abstraction of Embodiment*. London: Sage.

Creswell, John W. 2007. *Qualitative Inquiry & Research Design: Choosing among Five Approaches*. Thousand Oaks, Calif.: Sage.

Crossley, Nick. 2006. *Reflexive Embodiment in Contemporary Society*. New York: Open University Press.

Czarniawska, Barbara. 2004. *Narratives in Social Science Research*. London: Sage.

De Beauvoir, Simone. 1949. *The Second Sex*. New York: Knopf.

Davidman, Lynn. 1990. "Women's Search for Family and Roots: A Jewish Religious Solution to a Modern Dilemma." In Thomas Robbins and Dick Anthony (eds.), *In Gods We Trust*, pp. 385–407. New Brunswick, N.J.: Transaction Press.

Davidman, Lynn. 1991. *Tradition in a Rootless World: Women Turn to Orthodox Judaism*. Berkeley: University of California Press.

Davidman, Lynn. 2000. *Motherloss*. Berkeley: University of California Press.

Davidman, Lynn, and Arthur L. Greil. 1993. "Gender and the Experience of Conversion: The Case of 'Returnees' to Modern Orthodox Judaism." *Sociology of Religion* 54: 83–100.

Davidman, Lynn, and Arthur L. Greil. 2007. "Characters in Search of a Script: The Exit Narratives of Formerly Ultra-Orthodox Jews." *Journal for the Scientific Study of Religion* 46(2): 210–216.

Davis, Kathy. 1997. "Embody-ing Theory: Beyond Modernist and Postmodernist Readings of the Body." In Kathy Davis (ed.), *Embodied Practices: Feminist Perspective on the Body*, pp. 1–23. London: Sage.

Davis, Murray. 1971. "That's Interesting! Towards a Phenomenology of Sociology and a Sociology of Phenomenology." *Philosophy of Social Science* 1: 309–344.

Dershowitz, Alan M. 1997. *The Vanishing American Jew*. Boston: Little, Brown.

Douglas, Mary. 1980. "The Abominations of Leviticus." *Purity and Danger: An Analysis of the Concepts of Pollution and Taboo*. New York: Routledge.

Douglas, Mary. 1982. "The Effects of Modernization on Religious Change." In Mary Douglas and Steven M. Tipton, (eds.), *Religion and America: Spirituality in a Secular Age*, pp. 25–43. Boston: Beacon Press.

Douglas, Mary. 2005. "The Two Bodies." In Mariam Fraser and Monica Greco (eds.), *The Body: A Reader*, pp. 78–81. London: Routledge.

Downs, Alan. 2012. *The Velvet Rage: Overcoming the Pain of Growing Up Gay in a Straight Man's World*, 2nd ed. Boston: Da Capo Lifelong Books.

Durkheim, Emile. 1995 (1915). *The Elementary Forms of Religious Life*. Trans. Karen Fields. New York: Free Press.

Dwyer, Susan Corbin, and Jennifer L. Buckle. 2009. "The Space Between: On Being an Insider-Outsider in Qualitative Work." *International Journal of Qualitative Methods* 8(1): 54–62.

Eakin, Paul John. 1999. *How Our Lives Become Stories: Making Selves*. Ithaca, N.Y.: Cornell University Press.

Eakin, Paul John. 2008. *Living Autobiographically: How We Create an Identity in Narrative*. Ithaca, N.Y.: Cornell University Press.

Ebaugh, Helen Rose Fuchs. 1988. *Becoming an EX: The Process of Role Exit*. Chicago: University of Chicago Press.

Entwistle, Joanne. 2001. "The Dressed Body." In Joanne Entwistle and Elizabeth Wilson (eds.), *Body Dressing*, pp. 33–58. Oxford: Berg.

Fader, Alaya. 2006. "Learning Faith: Language Socialization in a Hasidic Community." *Language in Society* 35(2): 207–229.

Fader, Alaya. 2009. *Mitzvah Girls: Bringing up the Next Generation of Hasidic Jews in Brooklyn*. Princeton, N.J.: Princeton University Press.

Featherstone, Mike. 2001. "The Body in Consumer Society." In Jessica R. Johnston (ed.), *The American Body in Context: An Anthology*, pp. 79–102. Wilmington, Del.: Scholarly Resources Inc.

Featherstone, Mike, Mike Hepworth, and Bryan S. Turner. 1991. *The Body: Social Process and Cultural Theory*. London: Sage.

Feldman, Deborah. 2012. *Unorthodox: The Scandalous Rejection of My Hasidic Roots*. New York: Simon & Schuster.

Flax, Jane. 1990. *Thinking Fragments: Psychoanalysis, Feminism and Postmodernism in the Contemporary West*. Berkeley: University of California Press.

Foucault, Michel. 2005. "The Political Investment of the Body." In Mariam Fraser and Monica Greco (eds.), *The Body: A Reader*, pp. 100–104. London: Routledge.

Franzosi, Roberto. 1998. "Narrative Analysis—Or Why (and How) Sociologists Should Be Interested in Narrative." *Annual Review of Sociology* 24: 517–554.

Freud, Sigmund. 1913. *The Interpretation of Dreams*. New York: Macmillan.

Friedan, Betty. 1964. *The Feminine Mystique*. New York: Dell.

Gans, Herbert J. 1979. "Symbolic Ethnicity: The Future of Ethnic Groups and Cultures in America." *Ethnic and Racial Studies* 2: 1–20.

Gans, Herbert J. 1994. "Symbolic Ethnicity and Symbolic Religiosity: Towards a Comparison of Ethnic and Religious Acculturation." *Ethnic and Racial Studies* 17 (October): 577–591.

Gaster, Theodore. 1959. *The New Golden Bough*. New York: Criterion.

Giddens, Anthony. 1991. *Modernity and Self-Identity: Self and Society in the Late Modern Age*. Stanford: Stanford University Press.

Glaser, Barney G., and Anselm L. Strauss. 1967. *The Discovery of Grounded Theory: Strategies for Qualitative Research*. Chicago: Aldine.

Glazer, Nathan. 1972. *American Judaism*. Chicago: University of Chicago Press.

Goffman, Erving. 1959. *The Presentation of Self in Everyday Life*. Garden City, N.Y.: Doubleday.

Goffman, Erving. 1963. *Stigma: Notes on the Management of Spoiled Identity*. New York: Simon & Schuster.

Goffman, Erving. 1967. *Interaction Ritual: Essays on Face-to-Face Behavior*. Garden City, N.Y.: Doubleday.

Goffman, Erving. 2005. "Embodied Information in Face-to-Face Interaction." In Mariam Fraser and Monica Greco (eds.), *The Body: A Reader*, pp. 82–86. London: Routledge.

Goldscheider, Calvin. 1986. *Jewish Continuity and Change: Emerging Patterns in America*. Bloomington: Indiana University Press.

Goldscheider, Calvin, and Alan S. Zuckerman. 1984. *The Transformation of the Jews*. Chicago: University of Chicago Press.

Greil, Arthur L. 1977. "The Modernization of Consciousness and the Appeal of Fascism." *Comparative Political Studies* 10: 213–238.

Greil, Arthur L. 1984. "Social Cocoons: Encapsulation and Identity Transformation." *Sociological Inquiry* 54(3): 260–278.

Greil, Arthur L., and David Rudy. 1984. "What Have We Learned from Process Models of Conversion?" *Sociological Focus* 17: 305–323.

Griffith, R. Marie. 2004. *Born Again Bodies: Flesh and Spirit in American Christianity*. Berkeley: University of California Press.

Hamilton, Jean A., and Jana M. Hawley. 1999. "Sacred Dress, Public Worlds: Amish and Mormon Experience and Commitment." In Linda B. Arthur (ed.), *Religion, Dress and the Body*, pp. 31–51. Oxford: Berg.

Hammond, Phillip. 1988. "Religion and the Persistence of Identity." *Journal for the Scientific Study of Religion* 27 (March): 1–11.

Heilman, Samuel C. 1976. *Synagogue Life: A Study in Social Interaction.* Chicago: University of Chicago Press.

Heilman, Samuel C. 1990. "The Jews: Schism or Division." In Thomas Robbins and Dick Anthony (eds.), *In Gods We Trust: New Patterns of Religious Pluralism in America*, pp. 185–198. New Brunswick, N.J.: Transaction.

Heilman, Samuel C. 1992. *Defenders of the Faith: Inside Ultra-Orthodox Jewry.* Berkeley: University of California Press.

Heilman, Samuel C. 2006. *Sliding to the Right: The Contest for the Future of American Jewish Orthodoxy.* Berkeley: University of California Press.

Hinchman, Lewis P., and Sandra K. Hinchman. 1997. *Memory, Identity, Community: The Idea of Narrative in the Human Sciences.* Albany: State University of New York Press.

Hochschild, Arlie. 1989. *The Second Shift: Working Families and the Revolution at Home.* New York: Penguin Books.

Hollinger, David. 1995. *Postethnic America: Beyond Multiculturalism.* New York: Houghton and Mifflin.

Holstein, James A., and Jaber F. Gubrim. 2000. *The Self We Live By: Narrative Identity in a Postmodern World.* New York: Oxford University Press.

Howson, Alexandra. 2004. *The Body in Society: An Introduction.* Cambridge: Polity.

Jacobs, Janet Liebman. 1989. *Divine Disenchantment: Deconverting from New Religions.* Bloomington: Indiana University Press.

Johnston, Eric F. 2013. "I Was Always This Way: Rhetorics of Continuity in Narratives of Conversion." *Sociological Forum* 28(3): 549–573.

Josselson, Ruthellen, and Amia Lieblich. 1999. *Making Meaning of Narratives.* London: Sage.

Josselson, Ruthellen, Amia Lieblich, and Dan P. McAdams. 2002. *Up Close and Personal: The Teaching and Learning of Narrative Research.* Washington, D.C.: American Psychological Association.

Kahn, Moshe. 1989. "Jewish Education for Women." *Ten Da'at* 3(3): 9–11.

Kanter, Rosabeth Moss. 1972. *Commitment and Community: Communes and Utopias in Sociological Perspective*. Cambridge, Mass.: Harvard University Press.

Kaufman, Gershon, and Lev Raphael. 1996. *Coming Out of Shame: Transforming Gay and Lesbian Lives*. New York: Doubleday.

Kazyak, Emily. 2011. "Disrupting Cultural Selves: Constructing Gay and Lesbian Identities in Rural Locales." *Qualitative Research* 34: 561–581.

Kramer, Peter D. 1993. *Listening to Prozac*. New York: Viking Press.

Laderman, Carol. 1994. "The Embodiment of Symbols and the Acculturation of the Anthropologist." In Thomas J. Csordas (ed.), *Embodiment and Experience: The Existential Ground of Culture and Self*, pp. 183–197. Cambridge: Cambridge University Press.

Lane, Jeremy F. 2000. *Pierre Bourdieu: A Critical Introduction*. London: Pluto Press.

Leibman, Charles, and Steven M. Cohen. 1998. *The Two Worlds of Judaism: The Israeli and American Experiences*. New Haven, Conn.: Yale University Press.

Lieberman, Charles S. 1990. "Ritual, Ceremony and the Reconstruction of Judaism in the United States." In Ezra Mendelson (ed.) *Studies in Contemporary* Jewry, vol. 6. New York: Oxford University Press.

Lieberman, Samuel, and M. Weinfeld. 1978. "Demographic Trends and Jewish Survival." *Midstream* (October): 9–19.

Lieblich, Amia, Rivka Tuval-Mashiach, and Tamar Zilber. 1998. "A New Model for Classification of Approaches to Reading, Analysis, and Interpretation." In *Narrative Research: Reading, Analysis, and Interpretation*, pp. 1–20. Thousand Oaks, Calif.: Sage.

Lorber, Judith, and Lisa Jean Moore. 2011. *Gendered Bodies: Feminist Perspectives*. New York: Oxford University Press.

Madsen, Richard. 2009. "The Archipelago of Faith: Religious Individualism and Faith Community in America Today." *American Journal of Sociology* 114(5): 1263–1301.

Mahmood, Saba. 2005. *Politics of Piety: The Islamic Revival and the Feminist Subject*. Princeton, N.J.: Princeton University Press.

Markowitz, Fran. 2006. "Blood, Soul, Race, and Suffering: Full-Bodied Ethnography and Expressions of Jewish Belonging." *Anthropology and Humanism* 31(1): 41–56.

Mauss, Marcel. 2005. "Techniques of the Body." In Mariam Fraser and Monica Greco (eds.), *The Body: A Reader*, pp. 73–77. London: Routledge.

Maynes, Mary Jo, Jennifer L. Pierce, and Barbara Laslett. 2008. *Telling Stories: The Use of Personal Narratives in the Social Sciences and History*. Ithaca, N.Y.: Cornell University Press.

McAdams, Dan P., Ruthellen Josselson, and Amia Lieblich. 2006. *Identity and Story: Creating Self in Narrative*. Washington, D.C.: American Psychological Association.

McGuire, Meredith B. 1990. "Religion and the Body: Rematerializing the Human Body in the Social Sciences of Religion." *Journal for the Scientific Study of Religion* 29(3): 283–296.

McGuire, Meredith B. 2003. "Why Bodies Matter: A Sociological Reflection on Spirituality and Materiality." *Spiritus: A Journal of Christian Spirituality* 3(1): 1–18.

McGuire, Meredith B. 2008. *Lived Religion: Faith and Practice in Everyday Life*. Oxford: Oxford University Press.

Mellor, Philip A., and Chris Shilling. 2010. "Body Pedagogics and the Religious Habitus: A New Direction for the Sociological Study of Religion." *Religion* 27–38.

Monaghan, Lee F. 2006. "Corporeal Indeterminacy: The Value of Embodied, Interpretive, Sociology." In Dennis Waskul and Phillip Vannini (eds.), *Body/Embodiment: Symbolic Interaction and the Sociology of the Body*, pp. 125–140. Hampshire: Ashgate.

Neitz, Mary Jo. 1987. *Charisma and Community: A Study of Religious Commitment within the Charismatic Renewal*. New Brunswick, N.J.: Transaction Books.

Nisbet, Robert. 1966. *The Sociological Tradition*. New York: Basic Books.

Olyan, Saul. 1998. "What Do Shaving Rites Accomplish and What Do They Signal in Biblical Ritual Contexts?" *Journal of Biblical Literature* 117: 611–622.

Orsi, Robert A. 1996. *Thank You, St. Jude: Women's Devotion to the Patron Saint of Hopeless Causes*. New Haven, Conn.: Yale University Press.

Otterman, Sharon and Ray Rivera. 2012. "Ultra-Orthodox Shun Their Own for Reporting Child Sexual Abuse." *New York Times*, May 9.

Pezalla, Anne E., Jonathan Pettigrew, and Michelle Miller-Day. 2012. "Researching the Researcher-as-Instrument: An Exercise in Interviewer Self-Reflexivity." *Qualitative Research* 12(2): 165–185.

Plante, Rebecca F., and Lis M. Maurer. 2010. *Doing Gender Diversity: Readings in Theory and Real World Experience*. Boulder, Colo.: Westview Press.

Polkinghorne, Donald E. 1998. *Narrative Knowing and the Human Sciences*. Albany: State University of New York Press.

Price, Janet, and Margrit Shildrick. 2010. *Feminist Theory and the Body: A Reader*. New York: Routledge.

Ricouer, Paul, and Robert Czerny. 1981. *The Rule of Metaphor: Multidisciplinary Studies of the Creation of Meaning in Language*. Toronto: University of Toronto Press.

Rieff, Philip. 1966. *The Triumph of the Therapeutic: Uses of Faith after Freud*. Chicago: University of Chicago Press.

Riessman, Catherine K. 1993. *Narrative Analysis*. Newbury Park, Calif.: Sage.

Roof, Wade Clark. With the assistance of Bruce Greer et al. 1993. *Generation of Seekers: The Spiritual Journeys of the Baby Boom Generation*. San Francisco: Harper San Francisco.

Roof, Wade Clark. 1999. *Spiritual Marketplace: Baby Boomers and the Remaking of American Religion*. Princeton, N.J.: Princeton University Press.

Rosenwald, George C., and Richard L. Ochberg. 1992. *Storied Lives: The Cultural Politics of Self-Understanding*. New Haven, Conn.: Yale University Press.

Rothbaum, S. 1988. "Between Two Worlds: Issues of Separation and Identity after Leaving a Religious Community." In David G. Bromley (ed.), *Falling from the Faith*, pp. 205–228. Newbury Park, Calif.: Sage.

Saldana, Johnny. 2009. *The Coding Manual for Qualitative Researchers*. London: Sage.

Sanders, Clinton R. 2006. "Viewing the Body: An Overview, Exploration and Extension." In Dennis Waskul and Phillip Vannini (eds.), *Body/Embodiment: Symbolic Interaction and the Sociology of the Body*, pp. 279–294. Hampshire: Ashgate.

Scheff, Thomas J. 2006. *Goffman Unbound! A New Paradigm for Social Science*. Boulder, Colo.: Paradigm.

Schilling, Chris. 2012. *The Body and Social Theory*. London: Sage.

Schrock, Douglas, and Emily M. Boyd. 2005. "Transsexuals' Embodiment of Womanhood." *Gender and Society* 19(3): 317–335.

Schrock, Douglas, and Emily M. Boyd. 2006. "Reflexive Transembodiment." In Dennis Waskul and Phillip Vannini (eds.), *Body/Embodiment: Symbolic Interaction and the Sociology of the Body*, pp. 51–66. Hampshire: Ashgate.

Seidman, Steven. 1985. "Modernity and the Problem of Meaning: The Durkheimian Tradition." *Sociological Analysis* 46(2): 109–130.

Seidman, Steven. 2002. *Beyond the Closet: The Transformation of Gay and Lesbian Life.* New York: Routledge.

Shaffir, William. 1997. "Disaffiliation: The Experiences of Haredi Jews." In Mordechai Bar-Lev and William Shaffir (eds.), *Leaving Religion and Religious Life; Religion and the Social Order* 7: 205–228. Greenwich, Conn.: JAI Press.

Smith, Christian. 1998. *American Evangelicalism: Embattled and Thriving.* Chicago: University of Chicago Press.

Somers, Margaret R. 1994. "The Narrative Constitution of Identity: A Relational and Network Approach." *Theory and Society* 23: 605–649.

Stadler, Nurit. 2009. *Yeshiva Fundamentalism: Piety, Gender, and Resistance in the Ultra-Orthodox World.* New York: New York University Press.

Straus, Roger. 1976. "Changing Oneself: Seekers and the Creative Transformation of Life Experience." In John Lofland (ed.), *Doing Social Life: The Qualitative Study of Human Interaction in Natural Settings*, pp. 252–272. New York: Wiley.

Swidler, Ann. 1986. "Culture in Action: Symbols and Strategies." *American Sociological Review* 51(April): 273–286.

Swidler. Ann. 2001. *Talk of Love: How Culture Matters.* Chicago: University of Chicago Press.

Tavory, Iddo. 2010. "Of Yarmulkes and Categories: Delegating Boundaries and the Phenomenology of Interactional Expectation." *Theory and Society* 39: 49–68

Turner, Bryan S. 1984. *The Body and Society: Explorations in Social Theory.* London: Sage.

Turner, Bryan. 1992. *Regulating Bodies.* New York: Routledge.

Wacquant, Loïc. 2004. *Body and Soul: Notebooks of an Apprentice Boxer.* New York: Oxford University Press.

Walker-Moffat, Wendy. 1995. *The Other Side of the Asian American Success Story.* San Francisco: Jossey-Bass.

Walter, Tony, and Grace Davie. 1998. "The Religiosity of Women in the Modern West." *British Journal of Sociology* 49(4): 640–660.

Warham, Kate. "Engaging with Young People through Narrative Co-Construction: Beyond Categorisation." *Educational & Child Psychology* 29(2): 77–86.

Warner, R. Stephen. 1988. *New Wines in Old Wineskins: Evangelicals and Liberals in a Small-Town Church.* Berkeley: University of California Press.

Warner, R. Stephen. 1993. "Work in Progress toward a New Paradigm for the Sociological Study of Religion in the United States." *American Journal of Sociology* 98(5): 1044–1093.

Warner, R. Stephen. 1997. "Religion, Boundaries, and Bridges." *Sociology of Religion* 58(3): 217–238.

Waskul, Dennis D., and Phillip Vannini. 2006. "Introduction: The Body in Symbolic Interaction." In Dennis Waskul and Phillip Vannini (eds.), *Body/Embodiment: Symbolic Interaction and the Sociology of the Body,* pp. 1–18. Hampshire: Ashgate.

Waxman, Chaim I. 1983. *America's Jews in Transition.* Philadelphia: Temple University Press.

Weaver, La Vita M. 2004. *Fit for God: The 8-Week Plan That Kicks the Devil OUT and Invites Health and Healing IN.* New York: Doubleday.

Wertheimer, Jack. 1989. "Recent Trends in American Judaism." In David Singer (ed.), *American Jewish Yearbook 1989,* pp. 63–162. New York: American Jewish Committee and Jewish Publication Society.

Whisman, Vera. 1996. *Queer by Choice: Lesbians, Gay Men and the Politics of Identity.* New York: Routledge.

Williams, Simon J., and Gillian Bendelow. 1998. "Bodily 'Control': Body Techniques, Intercorporeality and the Embodiment of Social Action." In Simon J. Williams and Gillian Bendelow (eds.), *The Lived Body: Sociological Themes, Embodied Issues,* pp. 49–66. London: Routledge.

Williams, Simon J., and Gillian Bendelow. 1998. "The Emotionally 'Expressive' Body." In Simon J. Williams and Gillian Bendelow (eds.), *The Lived Body: Sociological Themes, Embodied Issues,* pp. 131–154. London: Routledge.

Williams, Simon J., and Gillian Bendelow. 1998. "Pain and the 'Dys-appearing' Body." In Simon J. Williams and Gillian Bendelow (eds.), *The Lived Body: Sociological Themes, Embodied Issues,* pp. 155–170. London: Routledge.

Williams, Simon J., and Gillian Bendelow. 1998. "'Uncontainable' Bodies? Feminisms, Boundaries and Reconfigured Identities." In Simon J. Williams and Gillian Bendelow (eds.), *The Lived Body: Sociological Themes, Embodied Issues,* pp. 113–130. London: Routledge.

Winston, Hella. 2005. *Unchosen: The Hidden Lives of Hasidic Rebels.* Boston: Beacon Press.

Wuthnow, Robert. 1988. *The Restructuring of American Religion: Society and Faith since World War II*. Princeton, N.J.: Princeton University Press.

Wuthnow, Robert. 1994. *Sharing the Journey: Support Groups and America's New Quest for Community*. New York: Free Press.

Wuthnow, Robert. 1998. *After Heaven: Spirituality in America since the 1950s*. Berkeley: University of California Press.

Wuthnow, Robert. 2011. "Taking Talk Seriously: Religious Discourse as Social Practice." *Journal for the Scientific Study of Religion* 50(1): 1–21.

Yafeh, Orit. 2007. "The Time in the Body: Cultural Construction of Femininity in Ultraorthodox Kindergartens for Girls." *ETHOS* 35(4): 516–553.

Yamane, David. 2000. "Narrative and Religious Experience." *Journal for the Scientific Study of Religion* 61: 171–189.

Yang, Fenggang, and Helen Rose Ebaugh. 2001. "Religion and Ethnicity among New Immigrants: The Impact of Majority/Minority Status in Home and Host Countries." *Journal for the Scientific Study of Religion* 40(3): 367–378.

Zakutinsky, Rivka, and Yaffa Leba Gottlieb. 2001. *Around Sarah's Table: Ten Hasidic Women Share Their Stories of Life, Faith, and Tradition*. New York: Free Press.

INDEX

Abby
  abusive family life, 52–54
  first transgressions, 68–71, 92, 96
  lack of secular knowledge, 37–38
  passing, 117–124, 127
  remnants of the past, 195
"The Abominations of Leviticus"
    (Douglas), 78
Abusive families, 49–57, 70, 92, 125, 227n3
Adam, 154–157
Adina, 49–52, 57–58, 71–75
Agnosticism, 83
Aharon, 185, 189–190, 192
Aliza, 90–92, 94, 124–128, 186–187
Ambivalence, 132–135, 159, 186
Amish, 31
Anger
  at children, 54, 56
  at community's strict control, 87
  hiding, 74
  over gender bias, 57, 63, 72, 106
  over mistreatment, 92–94
  at parents, 4, 58, 118
  turned inward, 60
Anomie, 18, 20, 209
Anonymity of web communication, 120
Anorexia, 47
Anti-Semitism, 136
Anxiety and fear
  dissociation and, 18
  first transgression and, 47, 91
  loss of security and, 23

passing and, 105–106, 122
remnants of the past and, 186
stepping out and, 20, 141, 160,
    168, 178
unsettled feeling and, 209. See also
    Unsettled feelings
Appearance. See Dress code of Hasidim;
    Hair styles; Women's dress
Arranged marriages, 14, 117–118
Aryeh, 132–135, 186

Baal Shem Tov, 10–11
Backstage behavior. See Private deviations
    as start of defection process
Bar Ilan University (Israel), 125
Barnard College, 6, 31, 182
Beards, 11, 12, 86, 98, 114–115, 148
Becoming an Ex (Ebaugh), 197
Beis Din (Rabbinical Court), 44
Beis Yaakov (Haredi girls' school), 129
Berger, Peter, 29, 197, 225n2
Binyamin
  first transgressions, 80–83, 102
  passing, 108–115, 117, 127, 139, 140
  remnants of the past within, 183, 191
  stepping out, 163–167
Biographical disruptions, 15–16, 44, 47, 51,
    75, 171, 196, 206, 208–209, 225n3
Birth control, prohibition on, 15, 168, 170
Blessings, daily recitation by Hasidim,
    12–13
Bobover Hasidic sect, 22

Bodily parts, knowledge of, 13, 50, 52,
    73, 188
Bodily practices. *See also* Dress code of
    Hasidim; Hair styles; Kosher dietary
    laws; Women's dress
  centrality of rituals to Hasidic identity,
    11, 12–13, 20, 143, 206, 210–211
  "coming out" and, 25
  conforming with cultural norms,
    25, 196
  defectors and. *See* Disinscribing of bodily
    routines
  dress. *See* Dress code of Hasidim;
    Women's dress
  first transgression involving, 65, 85–102,
    130. *See also* First transgressions
  of heteronormativity, 27
  indicating separation from larger society,
    11, 205
  of larger society, 17, 18, 24, 143
  meaningful within community
    framework, xii, 198, 200, 203–206
  private deviations as start of defection
    process, 18–19, 22, 66–67, 72, 83, 90,
    101, 133
  rejection of. *See* Defectors; Passing;
    Stepping out
  "return of the repressed," 25. *See also*
    Remnants of the past
  sense of self and, 25. *See also* Sense of self
  in Torah's commandments, 11. *See also*
    Punishment for transgressions
Born Again Bodies (Griffith), 197
Brainwashing, 39, 42–43, 85, 130
Bratslaver sect, 11
Brooklyn, New York, 151, 152
  Lubavitch *yeshiva*, 110
Buchwald, Rabbi, 66
Butler, Judith, 204, 212–213

Censorship, 37, 84–85
Charismatic Christian worship, 211–212
Child abuse, 49–57, 70, 92, 125, 227*n*3

Children
  childhood experiences leading to doubt
    and questioning, 29–31. *See also*
    Biographical disruptions
  expectation of living at home until
    married, 177, 181
  family life of, 15–16. *See also* Abusive
    families; Family life
  removing children from unsuitable
    homes, 44
  unhappiness of mother affecting care of,
    168, 170
Christianity
  bodily rituals in, 210
  charismatic Christian worship, 211–212
  child abuse in fundamentalist Christian
    community, 227*n*3
  fitness and diet culture in, 197
  statement of faith in, 200
Church, as moral community of unified
    system of beliefs and practices, 19
Circumcision, 76
Collective effervescence, 164
"Coming out," 25–27, 63, 192
Confusion
  child sexual abuse victim, 52
  defectors in secular world, 36, 110
  passing in multiple worlds and, 127
Conservative Judaism, 8–9
Contempt, 40, 54, 55
Control of own life, realizations about,
    122–123, 172
Courage of defectors, 24, 102, 141,
    160–161, 180
Crown Heights Lubavitcher community, 164
Cultural context. *See also* Socialization
  bodily practices and comportment related
    to, 25, 196
  food practices and, 191
  heteronormativity and, 25–27
  learning new routines of, 17, 18, 24, 149,
    153, 161, 173–174, 198
  passing and, 158

Dancing and dance clubs, 67, 75–79, 119, 124

Danger
  deep questioning as, 44
  as element of transgressions, 96
  of leaving community, 160
  of punishment for leaving community. See Punishment for transgressions
  in secular society, 105, 106, 109

Datiya. Female Modern Orthodox (Centrist)

Davening (praying), 59

Davidman family, 3–7
  death of author's mother, 3–4, 6, 7, 31, 181
  Kosher dietary laws, first violation by author, 22
  Modern Orthodox practice of, 8, 181–183, 188, 207

de Beauvoir, Simone, 169

Defectors
  anxiety of. See Anxiety and fear
  appearance changes of, 17. See also Bodily practices
  biographical disruption situations of, 15–16, 44, 47, 51, 75, 171, 196, 206, 208–209, 225*n*3
  choice of term, 225*n*1, 226*n*10
  confusion of, 36, 110, 127
  developing a new identity. See Identity; Sense of self
  courage and self-confidence of, 24, 54, 57, 102, 141, 160–161, 180
  defiance of, 24, 74, 89, 94, 133, 177
  desire to learn about larger world, 32, 36, 119–120, 124, 148–149, 152, 173
  enjoying forbidden activities, 22–23
  gradual doubts and changes, 18, 21–22, 29–31, 199
  interviews with, 7–8, 16–28, 215–219
  learning bodily practices of larger society, 17, 18, 24, 149, 153, 161, 173–174, 198

moving back and forth between two worlds, 23, 34, 97–98, 103–140, 158. See also Passing
  predisposing factors for, 21, 29–30, 110, 163–180
  private deviations as start of defection process, 18–19, 22, 66–67, 72, 83, 90, 101, 133
  "return of the repressed," 25. See also Remnants of the past
  school aimed at turning rebellious youth back to compliance, 133–134
  stepping out, 141–180. See also Stepping out support as empowering, 150, 154–157, 179–180
  terminology used by. See Language choice of defectors

Depression
  after precipitating event, 47
  exiting and, 147–148, 149, 167, 170
  family mistreatment as cause of, 49, 57
  mother's depression affecting children, 59–60
  passing and, 110, 114, 119, 122, 127, 132
  postpartum, 168
  remnants of the past and, 188

Deuteronomy 30:16, 21

Disinscribing of bodily routines, 213–214
  choice of term "disinscribe," 226*n*11
  conscious choice of, 24, 102
  difficulty of, 20, 153, 187, 195
  first transgressions, 85–102. See also First transgressions
  private first transgressions, 18. See also Private deviations as start of defection process
  sense of self and, 86, 143
  stories of, 123, 157, 162–163, 198

Disowning/disinheriting by family, 6–7, 142

The Divine, 10, 13, 165, 226*n*8. See also God, conception of

A Doll's House (Ibsen), 79, 84–85

Douglas, Mary, 78

Dress code of Hasidim, 11–13. *See also*
Peyos; Yarmulke
defectors and, 16, 17. *See also*
Disinscribing of bodily routines
deviation by community members
from, 53
men's dress, 11–12, 68, 85–86, 140,
148, 161
women's dress. *See* Women's dress
Dual identity. *See* Passing
Durkheim, Emile, 19–20, 31, 113, 164

Eastern Europe, 10, 77
Ebaugh, Helen Rose, 197–198
Education
boarding schools, 129–130, 154
defector's enthusiasm for learning,
80–81
inequality of gender, 32, 57, 62–63, 137
transition between secular high school
and Talmudic studies, 115–117
transition between secular university and
yeshiva, 158
to turn rebellious youth back to
compliance, 133–134
types of *yeshivas*, 138–139
Ehud
exposure to secular world, 32–34
first transgressions, 96–100, 102
passing, 108, 115–117
remnants of the past, 193
stepping out, 145–150, 161
Elisheva, 128–132
Embodiment. *See* Bodily practices
English language mastery, 115, 138,
184–185
Esther, 92–94, 141, 187
Excommunication, 45–46, 167, 171.
See also Shunning
Exiting from community. *See* Defectors;
Stepping out
Exodus 20:2, 66
Exposure to secular world, 29, 31–38.
See also Outside world

Fabrengens (gatherings of Lubavitcher men
led by their rebbe), 110, 164
Facial hair. *See* Beards; *Peyos* (male sidelocks)
Family life, 14–16
abusive families, 49–57, 70, 92, 125
father-less families, 43–49, 75
ideal vs. real family life, 43, 46, 74
non-normative families, effect on
children, 30, 40–49, 80
removing children from unsuitable
homes, 44
Father-less families, 43–49, 75
Fear. *See* Anxiety and fear
Feminist critique, 57–64. *See also* Gender
segregation; Women
First transgressions, 65–102
dancing as, 75–79
defying several rules at once, 95–99
disinscribing of bodily routines,
85–102, 132
of gender roles, 67–75
hierarchy of, 70. *See also* Hierarchy of
transgressions
of knowledge, 80–85
kosher dietary laws, violations of, 22,
88, 98
lack of punishment from God for, 65, 67,
86–87, 101, 103
pleasure in, 96
private nature of. *See* Private deviations
as start of defection process
public transgressions, 94. *See also*
Frontstage behavior
woman's dress as rebellion, 86, 89–90,
91–94
Flatbush, 92–93, 227n2
Friedan, Betty, 59
Friedman, Manis, 99
Frontstage behavior, 19, 67, 113, 120, 129
Fundamentalists, 31, 196–197, 227n3

Gaster, Theodore, 66
Gender
heterosexuality vs. homosexuality, 25–27

religious community setting norms
for, 204. *See also* Gender segregation;
Women; Women's dress
social construction of, 197
terminology, 226*n*14
Gender segregation
among Haredim, 9, 13–14, 68–69, 72–75,
78, 153, 155–156. *See also* Women
dancing, 77–78
defectors and, 16–17
female-male interactions, 68–69, 72–75,
153, 155–156
first transgressions involving ignoring of
norms, 67–75, 86–87
inequality of, 30–31, 58–59
Orthodox maintenance of, 9
Giddens, Anthony, 17, 18, 144
God, conception of, 70–71, 82, 100, 112,
141. *See also* The Divine
Goffman, Erving, 17, 19, 66
Goyim non-Jews or secular Jews. *See*
Outside world
Griffith, Marie, 197
Guilt. *See* Shame and guilt

Hadas, 54–57
Hair styles, 11–12, 13, 86, 88–89, 98,
122–123, 133, 156, 227*n*2 (Ch. 4).
See also Beards; *Peyos*
Hand washing upon arising, 12, 34
Haredi Jews
compared to Modern Orthodox. *See*
Modern Orthodox (Centrist)
deviations from Orthodox practice not
tolerated, 15–16
divisions of, 10
dress of. *See* Beards; Dress code of
Hasidim; Hair styles; Women's dress
recitation of blessings during day, 12–13
stricter prohibitions than in Scriptures,
86, 126
"Ultra-Orthodox," 228*n*1
women's conduct. *See* Gender
segregation; Women; Women's dress

Hasidim
boundaries with other Jews and
non-Jews, 15. *See also* Outside world
defectors. *See* Defectors; Passing
dress and hair of, 11–12, 13. *See also*
Dress code of Hasidim; Hair styles;
Women's dress
family life of, 14–16
history of, 10–11
recitation of blessings during day,
12–13
Head coverings, 11, 12, 16–17, 120, 188
Hebrew, female's limited knowledge of,
137, 168
Heteronormativity, 25
Hierarchy of authority, 15, 41
Hierarchy of transgressions, 34, 70, 88,
112, 122–123
Holocaust, 32, 137
Husband-wife relationship. *See* Marriage
Hypocrisy, 5–6, 49, 51, 52, 74, 81, 160

Ibsen, Henrik, 79, 84–85
Identity
bodily practices and, 204. *See also* Bodily
practices; Disinscribing of bodily
routines
defector taking on new identity, 17–18
narrative as way to construct, 206–209
passing and, 108, 134
remnants of the past and, 190
socialization and, 16, 195–196
stepping out and, 163, 172
Identity crisis, 97
Immigrants, 27–28, 174–175, 200
Immorality, 60, 63
Individualism. *See also* Identity
first transgressions and, 87, 94, 102
Haredi culture rejection of, 16, 24
stepping out and, 24, 144, 162, 172
Inequality. *See* Gender segregation;
Women
Intellectual curiosity, 34, 36, 37, 96–97,
117, 140, 144–145

Interconnectedness of culture, socialization, and physical practices, 19, 65, 78, 126, 142, 199
Internet use, 119–122
Israel
    defector moving to, 160, 161–162
    Orthodox Rabbinate's control in, 162
    study in, 53, 125, 133–134

Judaism. *See also* Haredi Jews; Hasidim; Modern Orthodox (Centrist); Orthodox Judaism
    nineteenth-century development of, 8–9

Kaddish (prayer for the dead), 47, 48
Kant, Immanuel, 81–82, 108
Karo, Yosef, 82, 226n7
Kashrut. See Kosher dietary laws
Kipa (skullcap), 87, 88, 90, 104, 190
Kiryas Yoel (Satmar Hasidic community), 10, 91, 154, 155
    first transgressions involving, 80–85
    forbidden, 121
    of other religions and cultures, 120
    of secular world, 145, 152, 161
Kosher dietary laws
    defectors and, 16, 17, 133, 149
    first transgressions involving, 22, 88, 99–102
    Modern Orthodox approach to, 125–126
    Orthodox maintenance of, 9, 12
    as part of larger life system, 126.
        See also Interconnectedness of culture, socialization, and physical practices
    remnants of the past, 190–191

Language choice of defectors. *See also* English language mastery
    "butch mannish" behavior, 174
    "closeted," 64, 192
    "coming out," 25–27, 64, 192
    "discovery" of outside world, 120–121
    "exposure" and "nakedness," 90
    "first time," 98–100
    "*goyim*," 185
    "lost," 179, 181
    "rebirth," 175
    "regular people," 127, 152
    remnants of the past within, 184–186
    "sinful," 60–61, 184
Leah
    exposure to secular world, 39–40
    feminist critique, 60–64
    first transgressions, 79, 83–85, 94–96
    non-normative family life, 41–43
    passing, 104–108
    remnants of past practices, 186
    stepping out, 150–153, 157–158, 161
Lesbian, gay, bisexual, transsexual/transgendered, and queer/questioning (LGBTQ) community, 25–27, 64, 123, 200, 226n15
Lesbian Haredim, 49–54
Libraries, 36–38, 79, 81, 84–85, 95–96, 112, 124
Litvak (used for Yeshivish), 225n5
Loss, sense of, 159–160, 179, 192–196
Love, lack of, 54–57, 118
Loyola, 158
Lubavitcher sect, 11, 66, 80–82, 108–111, 113, 163–166
Lying, 23, 117, 122. *See also* Passing

Macarena dance, 77–78
Mahmood, Saba, 212
Marriage
    arranged marriage, 14, 117–118
    arranged meetings/dates prior to, 156
    birth order governing marriage order among siblings, 155
    defector hurting prospects of siblings for, 142
    doubter finding marriage partner who equally desired to exit, 150, 154–157
    as exit strategy to leave parents' house, 117–118, 150–151
    Haredi view of, 13–14

sexual discomfort in, 119
wedding night, preparation for, 13
Marxism, 33, 96
McGuire, Meredith, 211
Meditation, 211, 229n4
Men. *See also* Patriarchy
  avoiding temptations when walking
    outside, 79
  depression of, 60, 110, 114, 147–148
  dress and conduct regulations for, 11–12,
    68, 85–86, 140, 148, 161
  male privilege, 151
  Orthodox role of, 15
  religion as province of, 61
  Talmud study. *See* Talmudic scholarship
  Torah study of. *See* Torah study
Menstrual cycle, 13, 37–38, 50, 73, 169–170
Messianic fervor, 164–166
Metanarrative
  of converts to new religion, 213
  first transgressions and, 65
  fluidity of, 136
  harmony with person's life story, 203
  ideological encapsulation reinforcing, 205
  of Marxism, 33
  of Orthodox Jews' worldview, xiv, 9, 30,
    199, 211
  passing and, 158
  rejection/weakening of, 21, 45, 76, 81,
    83, 205
  self-transformation losing connection to,
    24, 25
Mikveh (women's ritual bath), 169, 227n2,
  228n3
Mishnah ancient sacred text, 168, 169
Modern Orthodox (Centrist)
  author's family and, 8, 181–183, 188, 207
  compared to Haredi Jews, 9–10, 68, 93,
    225n4, 228n2
  dress code of, 188–189
  parent changing to, effect on defector,
    124, 128–132
  passing and, 124–128

Modesty *(tzniyus)*, 13, 68, 71, 94, 96,
  186, 187
Monroe, New York, 12, 75, 117,
  122, 155
Monsey, 155
Morristown, New Jersey, Lubavitch
  yeshiva, 80
Mother-daughter relations, 37–38, 49, 55,
  62, 93–94
Motherloss (Davidman), 7
Museums, 110, 111
Muslims, 210, 211, 212
Mutual support for married defectors, 150,
  154–157

Nagel vasser (water for rinsing hands
  upon arising), 12
Name changes, 162
Narrative as way to construct identity, 7–8,
  206–209. *See also* Metanarrative
Newspapers, 36. *See also* Secular media and
  literature
New York Times on sexual abuse in Hasidic
  community, 49
Non-normative families, 30, 40–49, 80
Norms. *See also* Cultural context;
  Socialization
  deviation from Haredi norms, effect on
    children, 30
  questioning of, 30–31, 110
  religious community setting gender
    norms, 204
  sense of belonging and, 31. *See also* Sense
    of belonging
  sexual norms of culture, 25

Ontological security, 17, 144
Orthodox Judaism. *See also* Haredi
  Jews; Hasidim; Modern Orthodox
  (Centrist)
  compared to Christianity, 14
  egalitarian synagogue, 194–195
  overview of, 9–14

Outside world. *See also* Secular media; Secular relatives and friends
desire to learn about, 32, 36, 119–120, 124, 148–149, 152, 173
Internet use and chat rooms, 119–120
non-Orthodox Jews, view of, 185
sheltered existence from, 38
taking on new life in. *See* Stepping out
warnings of dangers of, 24, 31, 38, 105. *See also* Punishment for transgressions
women's adjustment to, 152–153

Passing, 103–140
abrupt change of roles, 116–117
blended family and multiple worlds, 128–132
choice of exit routes and, 123–124
control of own life, realizations about, 122–123
difficult stage of, 23, 105, 111–115, 140
ease with dual roles, 115–117
of married women, 117–124, 140
of men vs. women, 140
Modern Orthodox chosen over strict Haredi approach, 124–128
public performance of piety, 34, 111
rebellious youth and ambivalence, 88, 132–135, 159
speed of, compared among interviewees, 139
Patriarchy, 6, 15, 60, 85, 107, 123, 137, 153, 167, 170, 227n4 (Ch. 4)
Peyos (male sidelocks), 11, 12, 22, 67, 75–76, 86, 104, 156
Physical routines. *See* Bodily practices
Premarital sex. *See* Sexual activity, premarital or outside of marriage
Private deviations as start of defection process, 18–19, 22, 66–67, 72, 83, 90, 101, 133
Psychotherapist consultation and hospitalization, 170, 172, 177–178
Public behavior. *See* Frontstage behavior

Public libraries, 36–37, 79, 84–85, 95–96
Punishment for transgressions, 39–40, 65, 67, 86–87, 103, 109, 126, 132, 141–142, 192–193

Rachel, 100–102
Rebbe's role, 3–4, 11, 15, 82
Reform Judaism, 8–9
Relativism, 29, 32, 108, 117, 153
Religious myths, 20
Religious practices, 82–83, 190–192. *See also* Bodily practices
Remnants of the past, 183–196
dress and bodily comportment, 186–190
ongoing feelings of loss, 192–196
religious practices, 190–192
Ricouer, Paul, 208
Rieff, Philip, 207
Riessman, Catherine Kohler, 208
Rituals, 11, 19–20. *See also* Dress code of Hasidim; Kosher dietary laws; *other specific practices*
Rochel, 191
Role models, 81, 160, 180
Russell, Bertrand, 139
Rutie, 40, 58–60, 176–180

Sacred canopy metaphor, 6, 19, 29, 65, 75, 96, 109, 145, 181, 199, 205, 225n2
Sam, 35–37, 135–140, 158–163
Same-sex relationships. *See* Lesbian, gay, bisexual, transsexual/transgendered, and queer/questioning (LGBTQ) community
Sarah, 43–47, 167–175, 186, 192
Satmar community, 10, 22, 44–47, 48, 52, 58, 71, 74–76, 79, 91, 117, 123, 127, 154
Schneerson, Menachem Mendel, 164–165
Secular media and literature
first exposure to outside world, 29
Internet use, 119–122
movies, 35, 95, 109, 117, 192

public or university library's role, 31–37,
81–82. *See also* Libraries
reading while at *yeshiva*, 139, 144–145
television. *See* Television
Secular relatives and friends, 29, 31, 39–42,
96–98
Security of knowing self-identity. *See* Sense
of self
Self-confidence, 54, 57. *See also* Courage of
defectors
Self-identity. *See* Identity; Sense of self
Sense of belonging
loss of, for defectors, 107, 127
norms and, 31
in school for rebellious youth, 134
Sense of loss, 159–160, 179, 192–196
Sense of self. *See also* Identity
child abuse and, 51, 54
culture and, 16, 196
defectors and, 24
disinscribing bodily rituals and, 86, 143
non-normative family and, 46, 48
"Settled" vs. "unsettled" lives. *See* Unsettled
feelings
Sexual abuse, 49, 50–52
Sexual activity, premarital or outside of
marriage, 69, 73, 78, 99, 117, 119, 156
Sexual activity, within marriage, 170
Sexuality, 13, 50, 52, 73
Sexual knowledge, 13, 50, 52. *See also*
Menstrual cycle
Shabbes/Shabbat (Sabbath)
carrying money on, 98, 105
celebration of, 42–43
claustrophobic nature of, 95
dance clubbing on, 79
dining out on, 98
engaging in forbidden activities on, 67,
70, 83, 87–89, 94, 95, 124
failure to observe, 70, 76
in hierarchy of violations. *See* Hierarchy
of transgressions
no school on, 62

remnant of past life, 195
seriousness of violations of, 70, 88, 123
turning on light on, 89, 100
women's role on, 30, 62
Shakers, 211–212
Shame and guilt
exiting and, 149, 178–179
first transgressions and, 90, 92
gay-shaming, 26
passing and, 109, 119, 133
remnants of past life and, 25, 192
upon realization of difference between
socialization in outside and Haredi
worlds, 174
victims of child abuse, 51
Shlomo, 22, 47–49, 75–79, 86, 94, 119,
121, 127
Shulamit, 184–185
Shulchan Aruch (Jewish legal code), 82,
168, 225n7
Shunning, 30, 39, 45–46, 55, 160
Sima, 89–90, 186, 187
Singing, 57–58, 110, 164, 194
Smoking, 88, 95, 132, 133, 152
Socialization
in Haredi community, 16, 42, 69, 141
language chioce and, 61
passing and, 105, 106, 117
physical markers of religion as part of,
205, 209, 211
remnants of past life and, 25
resocialization of defector, 98
in Satmar community, 76
sin and, 191
women's, 69, 150, 153, 173–174
Society as human product, 197
Spinoza, 81–82
State of collective effervescence, 113
Stepping out, 141–180
distance and moving away from
community, 157–163
father-son relationship, 146–147
gendered exit strategies, 144–157

Stepping out (*continued*)
learning new routines of outside
world, 149, 153, 161. *See also* Outside
world
marriage as exit strategy, 150–151
meeting new people, 148, 149, 152
name change and, 162
precipitating events, 163–180
Suicide attempts, 171, 175
Swidler, Ann, 107, 198, 226n12
Synagogue
girls as children accompanying their
fathers to, 30, 58, 61
women's section, 58–59, 194–195

Talmudic scholarship
exclusion of females from, 63, 168
greatest joy of parents in sons excelling
in, 32, 137
jealousy among men over, 44
rejection of studying, 87
transition between secular high school
and, 115–117
Tefillin (leather prayer boxes), 90, 97,
145–146, 157
Television, 35–36, 95, 121
Ten Commandments, 66
Therapists and therapy, 54, 71, 170, 172,
176–177
Torah's 613 commandments. *See also*
Punishment for transgressions
defectors questioning of, 21
duty to follow, 11
interconnectedness of, 78, 126, 142, 199
male written and enforced, 168
results of following, 20–21, 126
Torah study, 4, 9
Tractatus Theologico-Politicus, 81–82
Tradition in a Rootless World (Davidman),
7, 17, 66, 99, 229n3
Treyf (non-kosher food), 22. *See also*
Kosher dietary laws

Triumph of the Therapeutic (Rieff), 207
Trust issues, 30, 96
Turner, Bryan, 17, 144
Tzniyus (modesty), 13, 68, 71, 94, 96,
186, 187

Unsettled feelings, 107, 113, 127, 134, 158,
198–199, 204, 209

Vulnerability, 90, 144

Wigs. *See* Head coverings
Women. *See also* Gender segregation;
Women's dress
conduct of, 13, 45, 57–58, 95, 104–105
depression of. *See* Depression
drinking in bar, 95, 104–105
education of. *See* Education
English language education of Haredi
girls, 138
exclusion from Talmudic study,
63, 168
family role of, 15, 41–42, 70, 150, 176
inequality of, 9, 13–14, 30–31, 32, 57–64,
78, 125, 168, 204
intelligence of, 168, 227n4 (Ch. 4)
marriage as exit strategy for. *See*
Marriage
Orthodox Judaism's role of, 9
otherness of, 169
passivity of, 45
questioning community's norms,
30–31, 176
shaving head, 11, 17, 122, 123, 227n2
(Ch. 4)
singing not allowed by, 57–58
Women's dress
of defectors, 17
head coverings, 11, 12, 16–17,
120, 188
pants, 86, 89–90, 91–92, 130, 187
for passing in multiple worlds, 129

remnants of former life and, 186–187

rules governing, 11, 12, 13, 86, 89–90, 91–92

socks, 92–94, 125–126, 131

tzniyus (modesty) of, 13, 68, 71, 94, 96, 186, 187

women's liberation movement, 84–85

Yarmulke (skullcap), 87, 88, 104, 190

Yeshiva Torah Va'daas, 138

Yeshivish, 10, 225n5

Yiddish language, 115, 138, 185

Yossi, 86–89, 94

Zalman, Schneur, 11

Davidman, Lynn,
1955-

Becoming un-
orthodox.

DATE			